ALL ABOUT
DERIVATIVES

OTHER TITLES IN THE "ALL ABOUT" SERIES

ALL ABOUT DERIVATIVES

The Easy Way to Get Started

MICHAEL DURBIN

McGraw-Hill

New York   Chicago   San Francisco   Lisbon   London   Madrid   Mexico City
Milan   New Delhi   San Juan   Seoul   Singapore   Sydney   Toronto

6 7 8 9 0   FGR/FGR   0 9 8

ISBN 0-07-145147-1

McGraw-Hill books are available at special discounts to use as premiums and sales
promotions, or for use in corporate training programs. For more information, please
write to the Director of Special Sales, McGraw-Hill, Two Penn Plaza, New York,
NY 10121-2298. Or contact your local bookstore.

This publication is designed to provide accurate and authoritative information in
regard to the subject matter covered. It is sold with the understanding that the
publisher is not engaged in rendering legal, accounting or other professional
service. If legal advice or other expert assistance is required, the services of a
competent professional person should be sought.
—*From a Declaration of Principles Jointly Adopted by a Committee of the American Bar
Association and a Committee of Publishers and Associations.*

To the splendor of Mom and the memory of Dad

CONTENT SUMMARY

ACKNOWLEDGMENTS

Until you've written a book yourself, you might not realize the honesty behind the gratitude expressed in an author's acknowledgments. I sure hadn't.

My deepest appreciation goes to the kind souls who willingly suffered the first draft of a first-time author's manuscript: Lei Fang, Eric Hiller, Xuong and Melissa Nguyen, James Tweedie, Barbara and Greg Vaughan, and Marie Wallden (who also found James, who found a bunch of math booboos before you did). Together their comments were a torchlight for things I could not have seen on my own.

I most heartily acknowledge and thank Stephen Isaacs of McGraw-Hill. Beginning with his first phone call and continuing with months of guidance, he is most responsible for ushering this book out of my briefcase and into the real world. I must also thank here the authors of the books and other publications listed in the bibliography, to which I referred to one degree or another in the preparation of this book, and Professor Ming Huang for getting this University of Chicago B-school B-student so jazzed on derivatives in the first place.

My ultimate thanks, for the time to write this book and for reminding me of what really matters in this world, goes to my wife, Joan Monnig, my amazing son, Marlow, and equally amazing daughter, Greta. They are the best.

CONVENTIONS

Examples in this book tend to be denominated in U.S. dollars. The greenback, of course, has no monopoly on derivatives, as they are a global tool for finance if ever there was one. Forwards, futures, swaps, and options are also denominated in euros, yen, pesos, and about a zillion other currencies. Nonetheless, the word "dollar" and the dollar sign in this book refer to U.S. dollars unless noted otherwise because that's the currency that tends to pop into the author's head from his home base in Chicago.

Terms in *italics* are those you should get to know if you really want to understand derivatives. They are generally defined when italicized. Terms in quotation marks are "looser" terms, or lingo or jargon, or whatever you call those things. They also are worth learning, but we can't guarantee everyone will define them exactly as we do here.

If you are new to the world of financial derivatives, it might seem a vast and beastly place, fraught with disaster and maddening in complexity. And I must inform you now, before you turn even one page more, that it is, indeed, all of those nasty things. But don't run off just yet, for I can also tell you this: At the center of this world lies a stable and accessible core of ideas. Rest assured, there is a relatively undisputed foundation of facts and formulas upon which everything else is built around here, a body of knowledge that fits easily between the covers of a cheap paperback. Like this one.

This slender tome explains the wily financial instruments known as *derivatives*. We've tried to make it the book anyone would want when first learning about any new subject—complete, readable, and all about fundamentals. So while it does not explain all the fancy stuff, it does explain the basic contracts—forwards, futures, swaps, and options—from which nearly every derivative is derived. And it certainly doesn't explain every way one can use derivatives, but it does provide numerous examples in simple language of how derivatives are used every day by scads of individuals and organizations around the globe. And our modest book doesn't waste ink on things like "technical trading" strategies (they're mostly bunk anyway) and other surefire miracles for making money, but it does explain things like what it means to be "long a put" or "short a call." And it explains a raft of terms like *volatility, arbitrage, forward rate,* and *delta.* And how to price the darn things. And where they are traded and by whom. And—well, that's about it.

Is this book for you? Want to learn the basics in a hurry without suffering too much math? Then it's for you. Of course there is math, but we've done our best to tuck it away such that you needn't bother with it if you don't want to. Students will certainly want to know all this stuff, math and all. But our book can be handy too if you don't really work with derivatives but occasionally need to understand them. We're thinking about accountants, lawyers, nonfinancial managers, human resource professionals, software developers, government workers, bus drivers (you never know), and folks like that. And if you do work with derivatives but come across some tidbit in your work you don't recognize, and would prefer not to reveal your ignorance by asking, then just flip to one of these pages and nobody will know.

Is this book for the individual investor? Sure it is. Just don't make *any* investment based on what you read in this book. Ever. Want to get some idea of how derivatives fit into the larger world of investments? Then read and learn. Want ideas for where to invest your money? Go somewhere else my friend, anywhere but here. While the things in here apply to your world in concept, they don't always apply in practice. Bottom line, what's between the covers of this measly book is not investment advice, so please do us all a favor and don't get any ideas.

So back to the math. Is there a lot of it required in learning about derivatives? Only if you need to delve into the details of how they are valued. You can understand more than you might think about derivatives with no more math than what you learned in high school. We'll barely talk about math until the second half of the book, and then we'll explain all the math before we use it. Or direct you to an appendix. All you really need to absorb this book is a healthy curiosity and modicum of patience.

It's easier than you might think to "get" what derivatives are all about. And once you do, you'll be well equipped to venture further into this vast and beastly world. Or decide not to.

ALL ABOUT
DERIVATIVES

Derivatives in a Nutshell

FOUR BASIC DERIVATIVES

When you first learned about trees as a child, someone no doubt pointed to one and said "Tree!" and not "Norway Maple!" and certainly not "Acer platanoides!" Only later did you learn there are many types of trees, alike in some ways and different in others. This method of learning employs the concept of abstraction, and our brains are rather wired for it. We can learn about derivatives the same way. What then is a derivative in the abstract? A derivative is a price guarantee.

Nearly every derivative out there is just an agreement between a future buyer and future seller. Every derivative specifies a future price at which some item can or must be sold. This item, known as the *underlier*, might be some physical commodity such as corn or natural gas, or some financial security such as stock or a government bond, or something more abstract like a price index (we'll explain those in just a bit). Every derivative also specifies a future date on or before which the transaction must occur. These are the common elements of all derivatives: buyer and seller, underlier, future price, and future date.

Just like a shrub is much like a tree but not exactly like a tree, some derivatives guarantee something other than a price. Chief among these are credit derivatives. These are performance guarantees, not price guarantees, and we'll cover those in their own chapter. And weather derivatives guarantee things like temperature or rainfall. Still, the vast vast majority of derivatives are price guarantees, so it's plenty safe thinking of them like that for now.

As do trees, derivatives come in various shapes and sizes (but not nearly as many!). Some derivatives are so simple they are known as "vanillas" and are employed nowadays with no more fanfare than when a plumber uses a wrench. Other derivatives are known as "exotics" and are so complex that the counterparties themselves may not truly understand them (this can lead to quite a bit of trouble). It turns out all derivatives, no matter how exotic, are variations or combinations of just four basic types:

- A *forward contract* is an agreement to buy something at a specified price on a specified future date.
- A *futures contract* is a standardized forward contract executed at an exchange, a forum that brings buyers and sellers together.
- A *swap contract* is an agreement to exchange future cash flows. Typically, one cash flow is based on a variable or floating price and the other on a fixed one.
- An *option contract* grants its holder the right, but not the obligation, to buy or sell something at a specified price, on or before a specified future date. Most are executed at an exchange.

The chapters that follow delve into the fundamental characteristics of, and differences among, these four related contracts. We'll see, for example, that a forward contract is like a highly customizable futures contract. And a swap is essentially a bundle of related forwards. Forwards, futures, and swaps commit their parties to a future transaction, whereas the option conveys no such commitment to its buyer. The option, however, is the only one of the four with any inherent value upon inception. And because they are exchange-traded, futures and options tend to be more liquid (there are more of them traded on a given day) and fungible (one is as good as another) than are forwards and swaps.

Despite such differences, the forward, futures, swap, and option are all just variations of a price guarantee. And they are the pulleys and pistons from which virtually all derivative contraptions are built.

WHY ARE THEY CALLED DERIVATIVES?

A derivative is often defined as "a financial instrument whose value derives from that of something else." It's a fair definition but slim. Let's dissect and expand it a bit to see what this "deriving" is all about. Oh, and remember the derivatives you learned about in calculus? If you ever took calculus? Homonyms. These aren't them.

A *financial instrument* is just a standard type of agreement, or contract if you will, that bestows certain financial rights and responsibilities to its parties. A mortgage is a type of financial instrument whereby in return for making monthly payments (your responsibility) you get to keep your house (your right). Stock is a common instrument that grants a right to some portion of a company's equity, or worth. Currency notes are instruments (Japanese yen, U.S. dollars, etc.) that grant a right to purchase. Term life insurance is another common instrument that pays out some cash if you expire before it does. And so on.

Quite importantly, instances of financial instruments have *value*. Shares of Microsoft may be selling (in finance we like to say "trading" because we think it will impress people) on the New York Stock Exchange for $24.98 each, whereas shares of IBM may go for $74.21. Those are their values, or, loosely speaking, their *prices*. One British pound may trade for 0.65 U.S. dollars and a 10-year U.S. Treasury bond may trade for $95,000. Now each of these is a nonderivative instrument because its value does not depend directly on the value of another instrument or commodity. Stock prices are determined by earnings expectations, supply and demand, and who knows what. Currency prices are determined by interest rates, confidence in the issuer's economic health, and so on.

Derivative financial instruments also have value. But unlike nonderivative instruments, their value is tightly linked to the current market price of their underliers. Consider a tortilla maker who 6 months ago contracted with a farmer to buy 1000 bushels of corn today for $25 per bushel (an example of a forward contract, by the way.) Say the market price of a bushel of corn, known as its *spot price* (the price you can buy it "right here on the spot" for immediate delivery) is now $28. What is the value of the tortilla maker's contract today? For each bushel of corn, they pay 3 dollars less than they would have to pay on the spot market; so the contract must be worth 1000 times 3 dollars or $3000. Were the spot price of corn not $28 but $30, the contract would be worth $5000 using the same math. As you can see, the value of this contract depends quite a lot on the spot price of corn. Now there are other factors in the valuation of a forward contract, but the value of this and any derivative is principally derived (hence the name "derivative") from the spot price of its underlier.

Intuitively we might think of "value" as something positive. But with derivatives (and many nonderivative instruments), a value can just as easily be negative. It all depends on one's perspective. In the previous example, we examined the value of the forward contract to the tortilla maker. What is the value of that same contract to the farmer? With a spot price of $28 and contract price of $25, the farmer must sell those bushels to the tortilla maker for 3 dollars less than they could in the spot market. So to them the contract must be worth 1000 times −3 or a negative $3000. Whether a derivative's value is negative or positive depends chiefly on which side of the deal you are on. In this sense many types of derivative are known as *zero-sum games*, as for every "winner" with a positive gain there is a corresponding "loser" with an offsetting loss.

HOW DERIVATIVES ARE USED

You might think there are a zillion different reasons for using derivatives, but it turns out they are mostly used for just one of two basic functions: *hedging* and *speculation*. Hedgers use derivatives to manage uncertainty, and speculators use derivatives to wager on it.

Hedgers use derivatives to reduce financial risk, or the prospect that the price of things might "move against them." Consider our tortilla manufacturer who knew 6 months ago they would need to buy corn today. They faced the prospect of corn prices rising excessively in the meantime and used a forward contract to mitigate that risk. They might also have used a futures contract, or even an option. The key observation here—somewhat surprisingly—is that financial risk occurs naturally in a world without derivatives, and derivatives can be applied to reduce, or hedge, that risk. Chapter 7, "Using Derivatives to Manage Financial Risk" is all about hedging.

Speculators use derivatives not to reduce financial risk but to potentially profit from it. Doing so is known euphemistically as "taking a view" of future prices, because "taking a view" sounds more legitimate than "gambling." But speculating really is little more than gambling on an uncertain outcome. If one has a view that IBM's stock price will be higher in 6 months than it is today, he or she can buy options to buy IBM stock in 6 months at today's price.[1] If their prediction comes true they can profit handsomely. If not, they lose whatever they have paid for the option—or 100 percent of their investment. That's speculating.

It's worth noting that hedgers can hedge and speculators can speculate without derivatives. Many hedges and views can be executed by trading just the underlier. Then why use derivatives? Because derivatives use a powerful financial force known as *leverage*. Technically, it refers to doing something with borrowed money. And just as a nutcracker exploits leverage in the physical world, focusing mechanical energy so even a child can crack the hard shell of a nut, derivatives focus "financial energy" so hedgers and speculators can get more work done with less effort. Consider our IBM speculator. Instead of buying options, they could have simply bought up a bunch of stock and held it for 6 months, making the same basic "upside" when (and if) their prediction came true. By using options they make the same basic play but lay out much less cash up front, as stock options are much less costly than the stock itself. But leverage does not come for free—and to the speculator its price is increased "downside" risk. When the IBM speculator using options was wrong, they lost 100 percent of their investment. Had they purchased stock, they would have lost only some fraction of their investment. And they would still have that stock, which could yet appreciate in the future.

Two other users of derivatives are *market-makers* and *arbitrageurs*. Market-makers are the merchants of derivatives. Not unlike fishmongers and fish, they buy at one price and sell at a higher price, pocketing the difference as their profit. They might also eat one now and again (not always by choice), but mostly they act as sellers to want-to-be buyers and buyers to want-to-be sellers,

---

[1] Such a speculator is known to be "bullish" on IBM. A "bearish" view is one that the stock will decline.

and they like to do so by taking on as little risk as possible. (We'll see how in a later chapter.)

Arbitrageurs also avoid taking risks. They search for pricing "mistakes" or "inefficiencies" in the capital markets and attempt to profit from them—taking on no risk whatsoever if they do it right. If an arbitrageur sees the exact same option trading in one market for $5 and in another for $5.10, and can simultaneously buy at $5 and sell at $5.10, they make a dime with virtually no risk. While "arbing" is harder and harder to do as markets become more efficient, the very fact they exist is a powerful driver of how all derivatives are valued. We'll see how later on. There are others with an interest in derivatives—regulators, accountants, systems developers, etc.—but hedgers, speculators, market-makers, and arbitrageurs account for most of them.

And where do investors fit into the world of derivatives? Most investors, certainly most small investors, do not trade derivatives. They simply aren't necessary to achieve their investment objectives. Some investors do use derivatives, however, as hedgers or speculators. Later on we'll learn about "protective puts" one can apply to stock positions to reduce the risk of loss in the event of a market downturn. And as we saw above, the IBM investor used options to speculate on the future price of IBM stock.

DERIVATIVE MARKETS

So where do derivatives happen? They happen in *markets* where they are traded. Now "trading a derivative" just refers to a buyer and seller coming together and committing themselves to one of these price guarantees. A *trade*, then, is one of these transactions. These parties to a trade are known formally as *counterparties*. And just as there are markets for buying and selling nonderivative instruments such as stock (think New York Stock Exchange) and mortgages (think your bank), there are well-established markets for trading derivatives. And as with nonderivatives, there are two basic types of derivative markets: over-the-counter markets and exchange markets.

The *over-the-counter* or "OTC" market is where two parties find each other then work directly with each other—and nobody else—to formulate, execute, and enforce a derivative transaction.

If I am an oil driller and you are a refinery, we might execute a forward contract for the sale of X barrels of crude oil at a price of Y to be delivered Z days from today. We can set X, Y and Z however we like, as this a completely private affair. This ability to tailor a contract to the exact needs of the counterparties is among the chief benefits of OTC derivatives. Forward contracts are by definition OTC instruments, and most swaps are traded OTC as well.

The *exchange* market (sometimes known as the *listed* market) is where a prospective buyer and seller can do a deal and not worry about finding each other. The exchange provides *market-makers* who act as sellers for those who wish to buy and buyers for those who wish to sell. It provides this feature, known as *liquidity*, by establishing and enforcing strict definitions for derivatives tradable on the exchange. So a buyer or seller gives up the ability to customize a deal, but in return need not worry about finding a counterparty. Futures contracts are by definition exchange-traded instruments and most options (not all) are traded on an exchange as well.

Another crucial distinction between OTC and exchange markets relates to guarantee of performance. With an OTC trade, the two parties have no fundamental assurance that the other side will hold up their end of the deal. When it comes time to execute a transaction, the seller may decide not to sell or the buyer may decide not to buy. With an exchange trade, the exchange itself (actually a clearing organization associated with the exchange) guarantees that all counterparties will fulfill their responsibilities. It provides this assurance with margin accounts and daily marking to market, two mechanisms we will examine later on.

Beyond the exchange and OTC markets there are also derivatives "markets" where the "traders" don't even know they are trading derivatives. Consider the typical mortgage that allows the borrower to pay off the balance early without penalty. The borrower has essentially executed an *embedded option* giving them the right, but not the obligation, to terminate the agreement. Another example is the *convertible bond* issued by many corporations, which gives the bond-holder an option to convert their position into company stock. (Arbitrageurs have a field day when the implied price of these embedded options diverge from the price of actual options.) We won't delve into these "stealth" markets in this book, but rest assured that the fundamentals of derivatives apply to those markets just as they do to the traditional exchange and OTC markets.

PRICING DERIVATIVES

A considerable amount of fuss and bother is spent on calculating the price, or value, of a derivative. And don't worry too much about the distinction between the terms "price" and "value." For most purposes you can think of them as interchangeable terms for answering the question, "What is one of these darn things worth?" Technically, *price* refers to an amount of money someone pays or receives, or is willing to pay or receive, in a transaction. A price typically includes some margin of profit or "edge" for one party or the other. *Value* is a price at which neither party would make any profit and for this reason is known more formally as a *fair market value*. Despite the technical difference, when you hear the term "pricing," it usually refers to calculating a value. Go figure! It's just one of those things to get used to around here, and we'll go with the crowd and generally use the term "pricing" in this book to refer to valuation.

It's worth knowing, by the way, that derivative prices are often expressed in the form of a *quote*. A quote is just a price at which someone is willing to buy or sell. A price at which one will buy is a *bid*. A price at which one will sell is an *ask*, or *offer*. You'll often hear of a *bid-ask spread* for a given contract, which is just the difference between bid and ask. (A *quote with size* includes not just a bid or offer price, but also the number of contracts the quoter is willing to buy or sell at that price.) So at any moment during a trading day, when markets are behaving normally, a contract might have three basic monetary amounts associated with it: a bid price, a value greater than the bid price, and an offer price greater than value. These are illustrated in Figure 1-1.

Are bid prices always less than value? Are offers always greater? Theoretically they should be but in reality they sometimes are not. Because derivative markets are so fast, vast, and complex, it does indeed happen that someone will bid above value or offer below it. But not for long. There's no shortage of arbitrageurs ready to "pick off" such bargains just as fast as they appear.

FIGURE 1-1

Typical Quote with Size

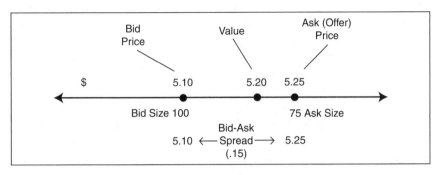

DERIVATIVE MATHEMATICS

You might have the notion that pricing a derivative requires a Nobel Prize in your back pocket, or at least an advanced degree in math. And it is indeed true that Wall Street hires a remarkable number of people with impressive sheepskins as *quantitative analysts* or "quants" as they are kindly known.[2] But fear not, many derivatives can be priced with little more than moderately advanced arithmetic.

Pricing a forward, futures, or swap is mathematically rather simple. The main task here is the adjustment of values for time by calculating present values and future values. The formulas for present valuation and future valuation are rather intuitive, and we'll explain them fully before we actually use them, at the beginning of the chapter on forward and future pricing. For understanding the math behind swap pricing, it helps to also understand the distinction between a *spot rate* and a *forward rate* and what a *yield curve* is all about. We'll explain all of that in the "All About Interest" appendix. The hard part in forward, futures, and swap pricing is not the math itself but in more practical challenges such as which interest rate to use, or which price to plug in for the underlier.

---

[2]Interestingly enough, you'll often find more physicists than mathematicians at a typical derivatives shop. It turns out physicists have lots of practice with partial differential equations, which are used for option pricing.

Understanding the intuition behind option valuation is easier than you might think. The basic idea is to construct an imaginary portfolio of nonoption instruments—whose prices are comparatively easy to obtain—such that the portfolio payoff mimics or "replicates" that of the option. The price of such a portfolio gives you the price of the option due to the "law of no-arbitrage," which says two things with the same payoff must cost the same to prevent arbitrage. The one-step binomial tree, at the top of the chapter on options pricing, illustrates this idea using very little math.

Understanding some of the mechanics behind option pricing can be challenging, as it involves nontrivial statistics and calculus. Actually pricing an option, thankfully, does not require much understanding of the math any more than operating a car requires you to understand the physics of internal combustion. For the mathematically curious, adventurous, or rusty, however, we will explain a ton of the math behind option pricing. It's pretty cool stuff. The mathematically bashful can safely skip those sections of the book.

Another challenge when pricing derivatives is the sheer speed at which it must be performed. Some underlier spot prices change almost continuously. This means a derivative value calculated a moment ago can be dangerously obsolete. For example, when the price of an underlier changes, market-makers often have only a few milliseconds to recalculate the price of an option and respond accordingly.[3] If not they can get "picked off" and lose a pile of money. It's no wonder that firms in the derivatives business, especially market-makers and arbitrageurs, spend vast sums of money on ever-faster computer systems for pricing and trading derivatives.

Mathematics comes into play not just in the pricing of derivatives but also in the area of financial risk-management. This is especially true when hedging a derivatives position, when you need to know how the value of an existing derivatives position changes in response to changes in valuation factors—underlier price, time to expiration, interest rates, etc. If you recall anything

---

[3]A millisecond is one-thousandth of a second. In the land of derivatives, an entire second is a near eternity.

from calculus, you'll recall that calculus is particularly suited for quantifying how things change, so you won't be surprised there's a fair amount of calculus in this corner of the derivatives world.

COMMON UNDERLIERS

As noted before, a derivative's underlier is the thing that can or must be sold on or before some future date, at a predetermined (guaranteed) price. It is the thing bought and sold in a spot market whose value, which changes continuously and unpredictably, principally determines the value of a derivative. A "simple" underlier (we'll also talk about "index" and "derivative" underliers later on) can be a physical commodity such as a barrel of corn, or a financial security such as a share of stock. Now there are at least a zillion (perhaps two) types of things bought and sold in open markets, from rubber bands to skyscrapers. Which of these are underliers to derivatives?

Theoretically, any traded item can be an underlier to a derivative. But things that become good derivative underliers tend to be both fungible and liquid. *Fungible* just means one is as good as another, as with barrels of oil and dollar bills, and *liquid* in this sense means there are large numbers of active buyers and sellers at any given time. It turns out there are a couple hundred or so types of things on this planet that meet these criteria. The vast majority of these fall into one of four categories: commodities, foreign exchange, interest rates, and equities.

Commodities These are physical goods, grown or manufactured and processed and shipped. They include grains such as corn and wheat, foods such as coffee and sugar, and meats such as live hogs and pork bellies (dead hogs). Commodities also include metals such as gold and copper, and energy goods such as crude oil and natural gas. Commodities tend to be wholesale goods intended for manufacturers and service providers rather than consumers like you and me. Most commodity derivatives are exchange-traded at places like the Chicago Board of Trade and the New York Mercantile Exchange, or NYMEX.

Foreign Exchange Currency meets the criteria for a good underlier. The market for currency, also known as the *foreign exchange* or "FX" market, is in fact the world's largest spot market of any kind.

On any given day more than a trillion units of currency are bought and sold, with the price of each note changing almost continuously. Currency is a popular underlier for all sorts of derivatives, both OTC and exchange-traded.

Interest Rates Money is itself "bought and sold" (or "rented") when it is borrowed or lent in the form of loans, or bonds. When a government or corporation issues a bond, it is simply borrowing money. The price of money to an issuer is, of course, interest, which it pays to the bond holders (lenders) according to the terms of the bond. The market for this is known anachronistically as the *fixed income* market from the days when all bonds paid a fixed rate of interest to its holders. There is a massive market for interest rate derivatives, the most common being interest rate swaps in the OTC market and a variety of futures in the exchange world.

Equities An extremely popular derivative underlier is corporate equity, or stock. A share of stock represents a sliver of ownership in the company who issues it, and the stock market is, of course, a massive one. Options on stock trade heavily in both the OTC and exchange markets, at places like the International Securities Exchange and Chicago Board Options Exchange, and equity futures trade on numerous exchanges around the globe.

INDICES AND CASH SETTLEMENT

Many derivatives have as their underlier not some simple item such as a share of stock or type of oil, but rather an *index*, or average price, of a broad group of related items. One of the most well-known indices of all is the Dow Jones Industrial Average in the United States. The "Dow" is a weighted average of a dozen or so individual stock prices. It may not seem like an average stock price, being in the thousands of dollars when most stocks trade for under a hundred. But it's only so large because it is adjusted to account for corporate actions such as stock splits, where one share of stock is divided into two or more shares. Despite the mathematical legerdemain, the Dow is just an average stock price.

Now you generally can't buy or sell on a spot market the "average" stock represented by an equity index. That's just a numerical abstraction. You can only buy or sell actual stock whose price is probably not exactly the average.[4] And if a derivative is just a price guarantee for some future transaction, this begs an interesting question: How on earth can you have, say, a futures contract on something you cannot actually buy or sell spot? How can you commit to buy something tomorrow you can't buy today? We deal with this conundrum using *cash settlement*. This just means when the time comes for the underlier to be sold (or even before), the parties don't actually buy and sell the underlier. Instead, they figure out the cash value of the derivative position and exchange the cash. Say as a result of a forward agreement I am obligated today to buy from you something for $3 that is currently selling for $2 on the spot market. If I were to actually buy that thing, you are $1 ahead. I can settle that obligation by simply giving you $1. Cash settlement, by the way, can be employed for just about any derivative; it must be employed for index derivatives.

And that's about enough for the nutshell.

---

[4] In some markets you can trade a "tracking stock" or *exchange-traded fund* such as "spiders" (SPYDR) and "the Qs" (QQQQ). These pseudoequities look like stock but take their value from an index. You can also trade options on ETFs.

CHAPTER 2

The Forward Contract

A forward contract is an agreement to buy something on a future date at a specified price. If you've ever purchased a car and agreed to buy it before the date you actually took delivery (while the dealer installed your accessories or whatever), you've already been "long a forward contract." Here's another quick example involving a future purchase of foreign currency:

> The U.S.-based Gizmo Company agrees to purchase 100,000 circuit boards from a South Korean manufacturer in one year, at a price of 24 won (the currency of South Korea) each. At the time, the won-dollar exchange rate is 1200, that is, one U.S. dollar will buy 1200 won. The total delivery price of 2,400,000 won, then, will be $2000 at the current exchange rate. Should the won-dollar rate decrease over the next year, the dollar price of the purchase will increase.
>
> To fix the future price of the circuit boards in U.S. dollars, Gizmo executes a forward contract with a bank to purchase 2,400,000 won for $2000 in one year's time. After one year, the dollar-won exchange rate has decreased to 1000 won per U.S. dollar. Thus, 240,000 won would cost $2400 on the spot market. Gizmo, however, executes their forward contract and spends only $2000 for 2,400,000 won, which they use to pay for the circuit boards.

A SALES AGREEMENT IN ADVANCE

The forward contract is the simplest of all derivatives. This OTC derivative obligates one party to buy the underlying commodity or security and the other party to sell it, for a set price on some certain date in the future. The party with an obligation to buy is known as the *long party*, as they hold the *long position*. The party with an obligation to sell is the *short party*, as they hold the *short position*. The guaranteed price is the *delivery price* or *contract price*, and the date on which the sale will transpire is the *delivery date*.

The key benefit of a forward is the mitigation of uncertainty; both buyer and seller lock in a price that does not change. On the flip-side of this benefit, in nearly every case, is a virtual guarantee of loss by one party or the other come delivery; unless the spot price equals contract price, either the long party will pay more than spot, or the short party will receive less than spot. Consider again the forward purchase of a car. Say the day after you sign your purchase agreement, some celebrity talks up the car on their TV show and it becomes wildly popular, driving up the price consumers are willing to pay. You still pay the contract price. Not only did you "trade a derivative," but you also pulled off a very effective hedge. (Much to the chagrin of the dealer, who is stuck selling at the contract price.)

We tackle forwards first because they provide a nice starting point for learning derivatives. Other derivatives behave much the way forwards do with some variations. A futures is just a forward traded on an exchange, and a swap is just a portfolio of forwards. Even an option is very much like a forward in some cases, when it is "deep in the money." So in this chapter we'll spend a bit of extra time on concepts we'll return to again and again.

COMMON FORWARDS

Among the most common forwards are those on currency. Foreign exchange forwards or *FX forwards* mitigate uncertainty around exchange rates. As we saw in the Gizmo example, a *foreign exchange rate* gives the price of one unit of some currency (USD) in units of another (KRW). So an exchange rate is really just a price. Corporations regularly commit to advance sales or purchases in a currency different from their own, and FX forwards let them lock in the prices of those purchases in their own currency.

Forwards are also common in the energy commodity markets, where drillers, refineries, industrial consumers, and other participants often commit to large sales and purchases months or years in advance for things like oil and natural gas. The spot price of these commodities can fluctuate wildly over the course of time, so commodity forwards allow them to plan transactions at a guaranteed price.

Another common underlier is money itself. Borrowing money costs money, and interest rates change all the time. If a firm knows they will need to borrow money in the future they can lock in the interest rate with a *forward rate agreement* or *FRA* (rhymes with "ahh"). Here the underlier is some fixed amount of money (say $1 million), the delivery price is an interest rate (say 3.5 percent), and the delivery date is some time in the future (say 6 months). Using a FRA, the firm can be certain of their ability to borrow a million bucks in 6 months at 3.5 percent no matter what the prevailing interest rate turns out to be. We'll get back to FRAs when we turn to swaps; a swap, it so happens, is just like a portfolio of FRAs.

FORWARDS AND OBLIGATION

A distinguishing characteristic of the forward is its bestowal of obligation. No matter what the spot price of the underlier come delivery date, the long party must buy and the short party must sell. Even if it hurts. If you are long at $30 and the market price on the delivery date is $25, you must buy at $30. Having to buy something for $5 more than its worth, you lose $5. Conversely, if the market price on the delivery date is $35, then the short party is the loser.

Now the losing party in a forward deal can also default. Should the market "move against them," a long party might simply refuse to buy or a short party refuse to sell. As an OTC instrument, this possibility of default, an example of *credit risk*, is another distinguishing characteristic of a forward. In practice, forward counterparties can post collateral with each other in the form of cash or marketable securities, which the gaining party can keep should the losing party walk away. (If you want to avoid the default risk inherent to a forward, you may be able to use a futures contract instead, but you will have to give up some flexibility and choose from a standard set of predefined contracts. Or you can use an option, but you'll need to pay a premium up front whether you exercise or not. More on these later!)

PAYOFF

A very handy device for understanding any derivative is its *payoff* as illustrated by a *payoff diagram*. Think of a payoff diagram as a snapshot of possible contract values come delivery date. And what is payoff? It's essentially the value of the contract on its delivery date. And we know already that payoff (value) can be either negative or positive depending on whether one is long or short. Recall how we valued the tortilla maker's forward contract on the date of delivery in the previous chapter, by taking the difference between the delivery price and spot price. That's just what a payoff diagram illustrates, only it does so for a whole range of spot prices all at once.

The payoff diagram is a visual representation of the not-so-visual *payoff function*. In mathematics (don't worry; this will be brief and worthwhile) a function is just a formula into which you plug inputs to get some output. There are two payoff functions for any derivative, one for the long party and one for the short party. Remember why? One party's gain is equal and opposite to the other's pain. Here are the payoff functions for a forward:

$$P_{FWD,LONG} = S - K \qquad (2.1)$$
$$P_{FWD,SHORT} = K - S \qquad (2.2)$$

Formulas 2.1 and 2.2 say the payoff for the long party ($P_{FWD,LONG}$) is spot (S) minus delivery price (K). For the short party, payoff ($P_{FWD,SHORT}$) is delivery price (K) minus spot (S).

To get a feel for these things let's imagine a forward contract on gold with a delivery price of $400 (per ounce). Now consider five possible spot prices come delivery date: $600, $500, $400, $300, and $200. Let's plug these into the payoff function (for the long party) and chart the results in Table 2-1.

The payoff table clearly illustrates why some payoffs are positive and some are negative. The long party is, of course, obligated to buy at the delivery price K. If on the delivery date the spot price S is greater than the delivery price, they will buy something for less than market price and therefore make a gain, or positive payoff.

TABLE 2-1

Long Forward Payoff Table

S	K	$P_{FWD,LONG} = (S - K)$
600	400	200
500	400	100
400	400	0
300	400	−100
200	400	−200

If spot is below delivery price, they will buy something for more than market price and therefore have a loss, or negative payoff. So the long party payoff is just spot minus delivery price in all cases. If the difference is positive, they have a gain, if negative a loss.

And notice for any value of S there is only one possible value for P. This makes drawing a payoff diagram quite easy. The format for a payoff diagram (for any derivative) is shown in Figure 2-1.

The vertical axis represents all possible payoffs. (For our gold forward example, think of the numbers on both axes as multiples of $100.) Note that the payoff stretches endlessly up and down with

FIGURE 2-1

Payoff Diagram Format

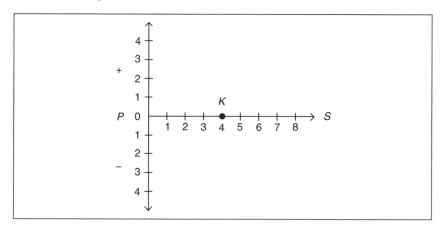

positive payoffs (gains) represented above the 0 point, and negative payoffs (losses) represented below.

The horizontal axis represents all possible spot prices on delivery date. It stretches endlessly in a positive direction only, as underlier prices can go no lower than zero. (Remember we're talking here about spot prices being lower-bound by zero, not derivative payoffs or values, which of course can be either positive or negative.)

To illustrate the long party payoff for our gold forward, we simply plot the payoffs from the payoff table at the various intersections of S and P. (Remember K is just a fixed point on the horizontal axis, that is, one possible spot price.) Choose any S value and use the payoff table or payoff function to determine the corresponding P value. If P is positive, place a point P units above the line at point S. If negative, place it P units below the line at point S. Now do this for a few more values of S to get something like Figure 2-2.

Now connect the points and you are done, as we see in Figure 2-3.

Notice that payoff is a straight line, so you really need only two points to make a complete payoff line. And now notice that the

FIGURE 2-2

Sample Payoff Points

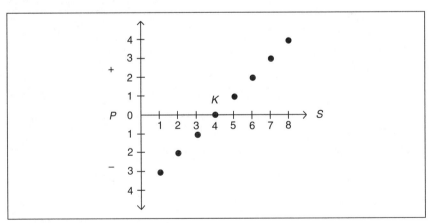

FIGURE 2-3

Long Forward Payoff Diagram

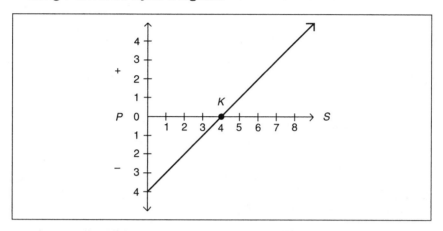

payoff line is at 45 degrees to the X axis. This is true of all forward payoffs expressed on a payoff diagram and means you only need one point, and a line drawn at 45 degrees through that point.[1] And one point is always just K, so you need not calculate any payoffs really. Just draw a line intersecting the X axis at K with an angle of 45 degrees.

And what of the short party? We know already their payoff is just the opposite of that of the long party. Table 2-2 shows the payoff for both parties.

To draw the short party payoff, you again choose values for S and plot payoff points and connect the lines. Or, knowing the short payoff is just the opposite of the long payoff, you can just draw a second line intersecting the X axis at point K going 45 degrees in the other way. Either way, you will end up with a short party payoff diagram as shown in Figure 2-4.

So payoffs illustrated on a payoff diagram are always straight lines, they always intersect the X axis at K at 45 degrees, and the long payoff is always the opposite of the short payoff. What

---

[1]This is just an application of the $y = mx + b$ thing you might recall from algebra.

TABLE 2-2

Long and Short Forward Payoff Table

S	K	$P_{FWD,LONG} = (S - K)$	$P_{FWD,SHORT} = (K - S)$
600	400	200	−200
500	400	100	−100
400	400	0	0
300	400	−100	100
200	400	−200	200

FIGURE 2-4

Short Forward Payoff Diagram

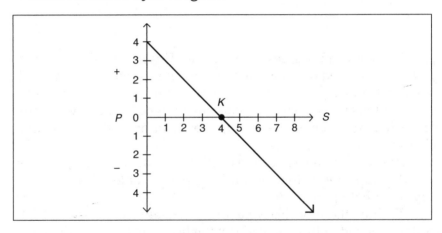

happens if we add these payoffs to determine the net payoff of a forward deal? On a payoff diagram showing both long and short payoffs, this is trivial. Choose a few values for S and find the vertical midpoint between the short and long payoff at S. Plot a few of those points, then connect them with a line, as shown in Figure 2-5.

The result, of course, is zero, because of the zero-sum game thing: one party's gains are perfectly offset by the other party's equal and opposite losses.

FIGURE 2-5

Net Forward Payoff Diagram

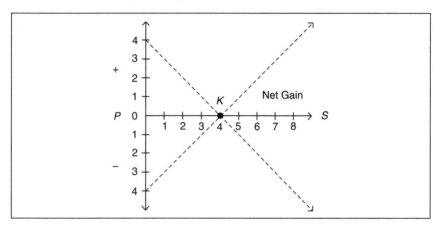

We'll see plenty more payoff diagrams in the chapters that follow. Although not terribly intuitive at first blush, once you get a feel for these things you'll find them quite handy.

CHAPTER 3

The Futures Contract

A *futures contract* is a highly standardized forward contract executed at an exchange. Here's a quick example:

> The Royal Mill buys wheat to make flour. Lots of it. In 6 months Royal plans to buy 50,000 bushels of wheat, and they want to lock in a price now.
>
> Royal executes 10 wheat futures contracts at the Minneapolis Grain Exchange with a delivery price of $3.00. Each contract guarantees the delivery of 5000 bushels of wheat in 6 months for $3.00 per bushel. Royal can now expect to pay a net total price of $150,000 for their wheat.
>
> In 6 months, the going price of wheat has risen by 50 cents to $3.50. The total value of Royal's futures position on 50,000 bushels, with an original delivery price of $3.00, has thus risen by $25,000.
>
> Royal buys 50,000 bushels from their regular supplier at $3.50, or $175,000 altogether. The net price of Royal's wheat purchase is $175,000 less the $25,000 futures gain, or $150,000 as desired.

AN EXCHANGE-TRADED FORWARD

A futures contract or "futures" is very much like a forward: A party agrees to either buy or sell an underlying commodity or security at a specified price on a specified date in the future. As with a forward, agreeing to buy is to assume a "long position" and agreeing to sell is to assume a "short position." The specified price in a futures contract is the *delivery price*. In later chapters we'll see that a futures price is calculated in nearly the same way as a forward price—bonus! But unlike the over-the-counter forward contract, a futures contract is traded on an *exchange*, a meeting place for buyers and sellers. As a result, a futures differs from a forward contract in three important ways:

Anonymous Counterparties

Unlike parties to a forward, the buyer and seller of a futures contract don't know each other. The exchange takes care of matching up buyers and sellers, helping to provide an important market quality known as *liquidity*. (A "liquid" market is one where trading is more-or-less continuous, or "flowing" like a liquid.) This can be a great advantage over the OTC forward in which prospective counterparties must find each other.

Standard Contracts

Exchanges also provide liquidity by strictly defining the terms of every contract executed. The type, quantity, and grade of underlier; its delivery price and date; even the delivery location are spelled out in great detail. A prospective buyer or seller must choose from one of these predefined contracts. Parties to a forward, by contrast, are free to define the terms of their contract however they mutually agree to.

Daily Settlement

This is the biggie. Parties to a forward realize their payoff on delivery, or on some earlier date if they agree to cancel or unwind a contract. Parties to a futures contract, however, realize a payoff at the end of every trading day. This helps to substantially reduce the risk of a party failing to meet its obligations—an inherent risk of an OTC contract like a forward. It also affects the value of a future as compared with an otherwise identical forward.

Bottom line, futures are generally more liquid than forwards and carry a smaller degree of default risk. Not all futures contracts are liquid, mind you, as exchanges from time-to-time offer contracts that just sit there barely traded at all. But the more popular futures trade hundreds of thousands of contracts in a single day. (The term of art for number of contracts traded is *volume*.) And while an exchange guarantees the performance of contract counterparties—technically speaking, its clearing corporation provides the guarantee—it is possible that highly unusual market conditions could lead to widespread defaults on futures contract obligations—possible, but far less likely than forward contract default.

And here's an interesting thing about futures: 99 percent of all futures contracts are effectively cancelled before any delivery actually occurs! Why? As we saw in the example above, the real reason Royal Mill contracted to purchase wheat on the exchange was not to actually secure the physical wheat, but to offer them protection against rising wheat prices. That is, to guarantee a price. Even though most commodities bought and sold on an exchange are never delivered, the fact they *can* be delivered—and *must* be delivered if the long party chooses—is one of the things that keeps a futures price fair.

COMMON FUTURES

There are hundreds of types of futures contracts regularly traded on exchanges around the globe. Like forwards, their underliers fall into two groups: *Commodity underliers* are physical goods that can be (but need not be) physically delivered; *financial underliers* are securities such as a government bond or currency, or an index as discussed in Chapter 1. When futures were invented more than 100 years ago, (did you imagine derivatives have been around so long?) all underliers were commodities. Financial futures did not come into prominence until about the 1970s, and today something like 80 percent of all futures are financials.

There are a dozen or so exchanges around the world where futures contracts are traded. Each is not unlike a produce market where producers and consumers meet up to do business.

Some contracts are traded exclusively on one exchange and others are traded on multiple exchanges. Here are just a few:

New York Mercantile Exchange (NYMEX)

Contract:	Light, Sweet Crude Oil Futures
Underlier:	*1000 barrels (42,000 U.S. gallons) of crude oil delivered at Cushing, Oklahoma*

Chicago Board of Trade (CBOT)

Contract:	30 Year US Treasury Bond Futures
Underlier:	*One 30-year U.S. Treasury Bond with face value at maturity of USD$100,000*

Minneapolis Grain Exchange (MGX)

Contract:	Hard Red Spring Wheat Futures
Underlier:	*5000 bushels of No. 2 or better Northern Spring Wheat with at least 13.5 percent protein*

Hong Kong Futures Exchange (HKFE)

Contract:	Hang Seng Index Futures
Underlier:	*Weighted average stock price of 33 stocks traded on the Stock Exchange of Hong Kong*

As with any securities exchange, you don't just call a futures exchange directly and place an order. Rather, an exchange has clearing members entitled to actually execute trades, who can take orders from brokers who take orders from commercial and retail folk like you and me.

DAILY SETTLEMENT

At the end of every trading day all outstanding futures positions are valued or *marked to market* by the exchange. "Marking to market" is just another way of saying "calculating current value" based on a new futures price, how many contracts are in the position, and whether they are long or short. These "MTMs" determine each parties payoff. Parties with a positive payoff (gain) get some money that same day. Those with a negative payoff (loss) get a bill. Losing parties don't always have to pay their entire bill. Instead, based on creditworthiness and other factors, they may be entitled to pay only some percentage of their obligation into a *margin* account. If their obligation should exceed a certain threshold, they receive a *margin call*. (The margining mechanism is not unique to futures; it is used for options and other exchange-traded securities as well.) A margin deposit for an exchange-traded contract is analogous to collateral that OTC counterparties typically demand of each other.

In a way, futures positions are terminated at the end of every day and replaced automatically with new ones having identical terms. This means that at the start of a trading day the value of every futures position is zero! Those values change throughout the day, of course, due to changes in futures prices based on spot price changes and other factors. At day's end those value changes result in new MTMs, contract holders realize a gain or loss, and the whole thing starts over again the next day. This really simplifies the valuation of a futures contract, as we'll see later on.

This daily marking to market is also the key to mitigating credit risk. Because everyone "settles up" daily, realizing any profit or loss before they go home, no party's obligation is permitted to grow unbridled for more than one day. With a forward, one's exposure is allowed to grow for the entire term of the contract, resulting potentially in a staggering debt for the losing party. Not so with a futures, which are nearly devoid of the extreme credit risk inherent to forwards.

Daily settlement also has a subtle effect on futures prices as compared with otherwise identical forward prices, and a dramatic affect on their comparative valuation. As mentioned earlier, a futures price—the guaranteed price at which the long party must buy and short party must sell—is intuitively the same as an otherwise identical forward price when a contract is executed. Income, storage, interest, and anything else reflected by a forward price are similarly reflected by a futures price. But because futures are settled daily, you need to consider the daily cash flow requirements and the present value of those settlements. We won't delve further on this, and there is little practical effect of the difference anyway. However, the value of a futures contract *after* execution is different from the value of an otherwise identical forward in a big way. Why? Because the daily settlement is essentially the realization of any profit or loss. So at the start of any trading day, a futures contract has a zero value. The value at any time during the day is simply the value change since the opening bell. The value of a forward, in contrast, is the value change since its execution. In the chapter on pricing forwards and futures, we'll see an example that makes this (hopefully) clear.

LIQUIDITY RISK

While an exchange provides liquidity by always having buyers for prospective sellers and vice versa, some contracts are more liquid than others. And the liquidity for a given contract can change over time. This leads to *liquidity risk*, which is simply the chance that you may not find a trading opportunity at a desirable price when you are ready to get out of a position. For example, when demand for long contracts is comparatively high, trading activity tends to increase and so does the price as buyers "bid it up." Or, when both supply and demand are comparatively low, trading activity decreases and *bids* (the price at which you can sell) will tend to be low and *offers* (the price at which you can buy, also known as an ask) will tend to be high. This difference between the bid and ask at a given point in time is known as the "bid-ask spread." The point is, to get out of a position you may have to buy at a price higher than you would like or sell for a price lower than you'd like. That's liquidity risk, and it's just part of trading futures.

CHAPTER 4

The Swap Contract

A swap contract is an agreement to exchange future cash flows. Swaps are used to exchange cash flows based on all sorts of things—stock returns, the price of electricity, etcetera—but typically we're talking about cash flows stemming from interest payments. In most interest rate swaps, one cash flow is based on a variable or *floating rate* of interest and the other on a *fixed rate*. Here's a quick example:

> The Gondor Corporation has borrowed $10 million dollars from a commercial bank. Under the terms of the loan, every 3 months for the next 2 years they will make an interest-only payment based on a floating rate of interest according to the Libor rate index. Thus, they do not know today how much interest they will pay for this loan.
>
> To reduce their exposure to changing interest rates, Gondor enters into a fixed-floating swap agreement with Marlow Securities. Under the terms of the swap, every 3 months Gondor will make an interest-only payment on $10 million to Marlow based on a fixed rate of 3.75 percent. In return, they will receive from Marlow an interest-payment based on Libor with which to make their payment to their bank. Using the swap, Gondor has effectively converted their floating rate obligation to a fixed rate and mitigated their exposure to unpredictable interest rates.

AN EXCHANGE OF CASH FLOWS

The grandpappy of all swaps, and the one we'll focus on, is the *fixed-floating interest rate swap*. Owing to its ubiquity, this OTC instrument is often known as a "plain vanilla swap," and once you understand this one you'll basically understand them all. The plain vanilla is the most common of a whole breed of instruments known as *interest rate derivatives* or *fixed income derivatives* (from the olden days when most bonds paid fixed rates of interest). Interest rate derivatives are derivatives whose underlier is money. The price of borrowing money is, of course, more money, or interest, hence the name.

We defined a swap as an exchange of cash flows. What is a "cash flow" and what does it have to do with buying and selling? How is this a price guarantee? Recall first that when we borrow money we typically pay interest at regular intervals over the life of the loan—once a month for your mortgage, perhaps quarterly for a commercial loan, and so on. Each of these interest rate payments is a cash flow. The cash "flows," of course, from the borrower to the lender. (The term "cash flow" is misleading with its conjuring of a liquid substance moving continuously, not sporadically as it does really with a number of discrete payments over time. "Cash squirt" would be more descriptive, but who could keep a straight face?) So cash flows are just payments, and payments involve a price. When that price (interest rate) is specified and guaranteed up front, the loan is known as a *fixed-rate* loan, or debt, or obligation. When that price is not specified up front, and subject to change for reasons we'll get to later on, the loan is known as a *floating-rate* loan. A fixed-floating swap is an agreement to exchange cash flows based on a fixed rate of interest with cash flows based on a floating rate of interest. Plain vanillas are most often used to effectively convert a fixed-rate loan to a floating-rate loan or vice versa.

In the Gondor-Marlow swap example above, one of the parties (Marlow Securities) is a "swaps dealer" or financial institution that makes a market in swaps, that is, provides them to parties who need them. This is true of most swaps, and a swaps dealer is, of course, just as likely to pay fixed as receive it. In this example, as the "seller of money" at a fixed price of 3.75 percent, Marlow has the short position. Gondor likewise has the long position, as they are buying at that rate. It's not always easy to tell who is long and who is short in a swap. Just think of it in terms of the fixed rate: the fixed payer is the long party; the fixed receiver is the short party.

The traditional method of teaching swaps involves two parties where neither is a dealer. Each has a preexisting liability—one a fixed-rate loan and the other a floating-rate loan—and each desires the other's liability. The party with the fixed obligation would prefer floating, and the party with the floating obligation would prefer fixed.

To illustrate, imagine that entrepreneurs Boris and Chloe have each taken out separate, million dollar loans on which they will make yearly interest payments for 10 years to their respective lenders, Aaron and Dimsdale. Say Boris has a floating rate loan; he pays a variable rate of interest based on Libor. And say Chloe has a fixed-rate loan; she makes regular, 6 percent interest rate payments, as in Figure 4-1.

Imagine Boris would prefer a fixed rate and Chloe would prefer a floater. Say Boris promises to Chloe, "Every 12 months for the next 10 years I will pay you 6 percent of a million bucks." That cash flow—$60,000 "flowing" once a year for 10 years—constitutes the fixed part of the swap, known as the *fixed leg*. And Chloe says back to Boris, "Every 12 months for 10 years I will pay you the current Libor rate of interest on a million bucks." That's the floating part, or *floating leg*. Boris and Chloe have now executed a swap, the proceeds from which they will use to pay their respective loans, effectively converting those loans between fixed and floating. It's like Boris agrees to make Chloe's loan payments and Chloe agrees to make his, as in Figure 4-2.

FIGURE 4-1

Floating-Rate and Fixed-Rate Borrowers

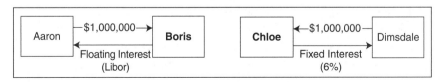

FIGURE 4-2

Floating-Rate and Fixed-Rate Borrowers with a Swap

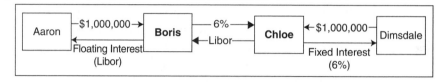

That million dollars on which Boris and Chloe base their swap is known as the *notional* amount of the swap, and in most swaps it never actually exists—that is, there is no million dollars in some account or a million dollars being wire-transferred from one party to another. (We're not talking about the original loans here, just the swap). The notional is simply a number used when it comes time to calculate payments. It's worth understanding this distinction because when you hear about a "hundred million dollar swap," it's not at all the same thing as, say, a hundred million dollar loan. About the only time a swap notional is realized is in the case of a cross-currency swap, a swap in which one leg is in one currency and the other leg is in another, and we do exchange notional amounts to remove the effect of foreign exchange rate changes on the swap.

Do Boris or Chloe "pay" anything for this swap? Does one pay the other a fee of some kind? Generally, no. The basic theoretical swap is defined such that neither party pays anything to the other party at the outset of the deal. (The trick here is setting a fixed rate such that the fixed side of the swap has exactly the same value as the floating side—more on that when we get into valuation.) Payments are made only on the payment dates prescribed by the swap, in this case every 12 months for 10 years. And notice too that both parties have agreed to pay each other some money every 12 months. Of course this isn't literally necessary. If I owe you 12 dollars and you owe me 10, I can simply give you 2 and you keep your 10. Same with swap payments. If on some payment date Boris owes Chloe $60,000 and Chloe owes Boris $48,000, then Boris simply pays Chloe $12,000 or the difference between the two. This practice is a form of *netting* and comes up all the time in finance.

In our example, payments occur once a year. This is known as the swap's *tenor* or *coupon frequency*, and in practice these tenors are often something less than a year. A common tenor is three months. So instead of swapping cash flows once a year the parties do so four times per year, or quarterly. Other common tenors are 6 months and 1 month. And, the two legs of a swap need not have the same tenor. One common configuration is the "semiquarterly" swap, with a 6-month fixed leg and 3-month floating leg.

By entering into the swap with Chloe, Boris can count on receiving each period funds with which to pay his debt to Aaron. And he knows exactly what he must pay to Chloe in return— 6 percent of a million bucks, or \$60.000. No longer is Boris at the mercy of the floating Libor. No matter where Libor "sets" each year, he knows he'll get just the right amount from Chloe for paying off Aaron. And his obligation to pay at 6 percent is fixed—so no more uncertainty. He is not free of all risk, however, as he still faces the possibility, say, that Chloe defaults on her end of the bargain and doesn't make her payments. This is an example of *credit risk* (more on this when we get to credit derivatives). But he is generally free of the market risk he would otherwise face were it not for the swap.

SWAPS IN PRACTICE

Now in practice swaps get more complicated than this example. First, one party is nearly always a big bank or derivatives dealer of some kind and not another debtor with an actual obligation. And often the principal changes or *amortizes* over the life of the contract, the interest payments might *compound* or be based on an average rate, we may handle holidays this way or that—blah, blah, blah— we explain all of these in the appendix. It might seem a painfully tedious job to specify dozens of variables when constructing a swap. Fortunately, before working out a particular trade, swap counterparties typically have already executed something called a *master agreement*. It's basically an agreement to terms that can apply to any trade the two parties might execute. Further, the master agreement itself almost always refers to a set of *ISDA* definitions, or "izduhs" as they're known, to really be sure both sides know what they're agreeing to. These are named for the International Swap and Derivatives Association, which so kindly takes care of this tedious aspect of the swaps business. ISDAs spell out in exacting detail, using orders of magnitude more words than we do here, what precisely is meant by terms such as "modified following" and "actual/360." And without ISDAs, I can assure you, the swaps business would be nothing but a headache. ISDAs are like the dictionary Scrabble players agree to consult before starting a game, just in case there's a debate over whether or not words like "qat" and "hmph" can be played.[1]

But behind all the bells and whistles are those swapped cash flows, each sometimes known as a "coupon," another term borrowed from the old days of fixed income. And each coupon period, it turns out, is really just a forward contract in disguise. It's a forward with an underlier of money, with an interest rate for a delivery price, whose spot rate is given by an index. We can also view a swap as two bonds, one with a fixed coupon and the other floating, with the bond cash flows exchanged. This is in fact the simpler way to view a swap and one we'll use ourselves when we price a swap.

OTHER INTEREST RATE DERIVATIVES

As with ice cream, not all interest rate derivatives are plain vanilla. There are variations, not as prevalent as the fixed-floating swap but certainly worth knowing about.

Basis Swap

The first of these is the *basis swap*, which is like a plain vanilla but with two floating legs and no fixed leg. So instead of swapping a fixed-rate payment for a floating-rate payment, we swap a payment based on one rate index for that on another index. Say we borrow money from Citibank at their prime rate but would prefer to pay at Libor. We can execute a pay-Libor, receive-Prime swap with the same notional and payment schedule as our loan. Then every period we effectively pay Libor on the swap and use the proceeds from the swap to pay our loan. The term "basis" comes

---

[1]According to my dictionary, they most certainly can.

from the idea of basis risk. Basis risk here refers to the idea that two price streams, think two rate indices, say Prime and Libor, may or may not move in unison. A basis swap can mitigate such uncertainty.

Currency Swap

So far we have only considered swaps where both legs are denominated in the same currency. A *cross-currency interest rate swap* or "currency swap" is one in which the legs are denominated in different currencies. Say we borrow Australian Dollars at a floating rate and really wish to pay a fixed rate in U.S. dollars. An ASD-USD fixed-floating swap is all we need. Basis swaps can similarly have legs in different currencies.

The key practical difference between a currency swap and a noncurrency swap has to do with the notional. As noted before, in a single-currency swap the notional amount, or principal, need not change hands. It's just a computational convenience, really, because there is nothing to be gained by two parties exchanging the exact same thing. But in a currency swap we need to think about foreign exchange rates. Consider a currency swap with one leg denominated in Australian dollars and the other in U.S. dollars. If the ASD-USD exchange rate should fluctuate over the life of the swap, one party or the other is going to pay a price, as this changes the value of a payment in terms of the other currency. By exchanging notionals at both ends of the trade, we mitigate that risk. We won't go into the details to see how this is so, but imagine I give you $1 million Australian and you give me $1 million U.S., then five years later you give me back my $1 million Australian and I give you back your $1 million U.S. No matter what happens to the exchange rate in the meantime, we both end up with what we started with in terms of our local currency. So we exchange notionals to remove *exchange rate* uncertainty from the picture, because recall that the purpose of an interest rate swap is to remove *interest rate* uncertainty. Now to deal with exchange rate uncertainty there are all sorts of foreign exchange or "FX" derivatives we can turn to—forwards, futures, options—but here we're only talking about interest rate derivatives. It's a subtle distinction but an important one.

Interest Rate Options

The family of basic interest rate derivative also includes the cap, floor, collar, and swaption. A *cap* is a guarantee that an interest rate will not rise above a certain level, a *floor* similarly guarantees a lower bound, and a *collar* identifies a range in which rates are guaranteed to fall. A *swaption* grants the right, but not the obligation, to enter into a swap in the future. We'll see an example of using a cap in the chapter on Using Derivatives to Manage Risk. There are plenty of other variations as well, and all are types of options with an underlier of money. And speaking of options ...

CHAPTER 5

The Option Contract

An *option* grants its holder the right, but not the obligation, to buy or sell something at a specified price, on or before a specified date. Here's a quick example:

> Greta is a small investor who likes to trade stocks and options in her spare time. She believes the stock of the ZED corporation, currently trading at $60, is undervalued and will increase over the next several months.
>
> Rather than buy the shares and hold them, Greta buys 6-month call options on ZED with a strike price of $60. The options give her the right, but not the obligation, to buy ZED for $60 at any time over the next 6 months.
>
> In 6 months, ZED is trading for $62. Greta exercises her option and buys ZED for $60, realizing a gross profit of $2 per share.

A CONDITIONAL SALES AGREEMENT

An option is a price guarantee that may or may not result in a future sale. The parties to an option are its seller or short party or *writer*, and buyer or long party or *holder*. Upon execution, the writer receives from the holder a *premium* based on the option's value. In return for the premium, the option holder obtains the right *but not the obligation* to buy the underlier from the writer if it's a *call option*, or sell the underlier if it's a *put option*, on or before some specified date. Note how the value-based premium makes an option radically different from a forward, future, or swap, all of which have no theoretical value upon execution.

It's easy to get tangled up in the buying and selling of the option versus the buying and selling of the underlier. See Figure 5-1. It's a diagram that shows what changes hands and when.

When you buy a *call* option you buy the right to *buy* the underlier (or "call it in" from the writer). When you buy a *put* option you buy the right to *sell* the underlier (or "put it back" to the writer). In both cases you are buying the option. But later on, you might be buying or selling the underlier depending on what kind of option you bought.

The price at which a call holder may buy (or a put holder may sell) is known as the *strike price* or *exercise price*. Electing to

FIGURE 5-1

Buying and Selling of Options versus Underliers

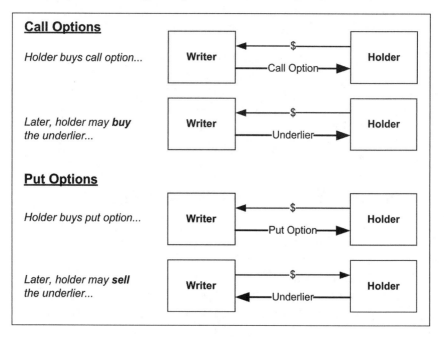

buy or sell the underlier is known as *exercising* the option. With exchange-traded options the flipside of exercise—the effect of exercise on the writer—is known as *assignment*.[1] All options specify an *expiration date*. The holder of an *American* option may exercise on or before expiration. The holder of a *European* option may exercise *only* on expiration. We'll say more about the American-European thing in just a bit.

Consider another simple example. Say you buy an American call option on some company's stock. It expires in 6 months and has a strike price of 20. Imagine in 6 months the stock is trading (has a spot value) of 25. You can buy for 20 what others must pay 25. So you exercise the option and buy the stock for 20. Nice. Now turn back the clock and imagine the same scenario, except you already own the stock and bought a put instead of a call. At expiration, you can exercise your option and sell the stock for 20—or sell it on the spot market for 25. Clearly you are better off selling spot than exercising your option, so you let the option expire, worthless. Oh well.

A financial instrument closely related to the option is the *warrant*. A warrant for all intents and purposes is just like the options we'll discuss in this book except the writer of the contract and the underlying stock issuer are the same party. If IBM, say, writes a call option on its own stock, then it's really written a warrant. There are subtle pricing differences between warrants and call options, which we won't get into, because when a warrant is exercised, for example, the company issues new stock to the holder, which itself has an effect on the value of the stock.

Price Paths and Moniness

A *price path* is the course of an asset's actual price as it changes over time. Imagine that the price path in Figure 5-2 depicts the daily "closing prices," or the last price at which it trades each day, of the imaginary stock ZED over the course of several months. In a minute we'll make it an option underlier. For now just notice that

---

[1]Most options are exchange-traded so counterparties are not literally matched up with each other. When a holder exercises, however, the exchange must choose some writer to sell (or buy) the underlier. Choosing that writer is known as "assigning" the exercise.

CHAPTER 5

FIGURE 5-2

Stock Price Path

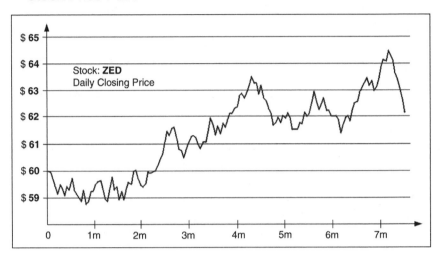

at time zero ZED trades at 60, after which it meanders randomly up and down over time. At the 3-month mark it trades around 61, climbs past 63, then drops back to around 62 at 5 months, and so on. The price follows no predictable pattern whatsoever. In financial parlance a price path like this is known as a *random walk*. In fact, one of the basic tenets in the lands of derivatives is that *all* price paths are random walks.

Imagine we are at time zero. Of course we cannot know the future price path of ZED because it's unpredictable. Now imagine three different European call options on ZED all expiring in 6 months with three different strike prices: 60, 62, and 64. Call them cZED60, cZED62, and cZED64. The lowercase "c" indicates these are European call options; later we'll use uppercase to indicate American. Figure 5-3 shows how the option strikes appear superimposed atop the price path.

Notice ZED is trading at 62 upon expiration (or "expiry" as it is sometimes know). Take a look at the options and consider their payoff, or value at expiration. Remember they are call options granting the right to buy ZED at the strike price. Now cZED60 lets

FIGURE 5-3

European Call Option Strike Points

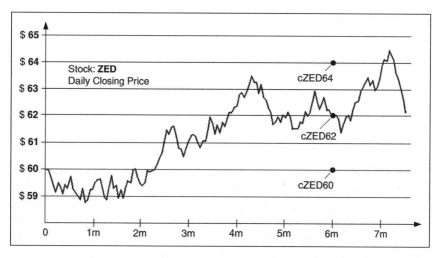

the holder buy for 60 what otherwise would cost 62—so it must be worth 2 dollars. An option that pays off upon exercise like this is said to be *in the money* or ITM. Our cZED64, on the other hand, lets the holder by for 64 what otherwise cost 62. It is, of course, worthless. An option that does not pay off upon exercise is said to be *out of the money* or OTM. And what of cZED62? It lets the holder buy for 62 what otherwise cost 62 so it, too, is worthless. An option like this, with a strike price equal to the underlier spot price, is said to be *at the money* or ATM. The so-called "moniness" of an option gives an intuitive sense of an option's value. Question for extra credit: What if these were puts instead of calls? Does it change their moniness?[2] Answer in the footnote.

And here's a bit that might come in handy for you some day. An option whose strike price is way off spot is known as "deep in the money" (e.g., a put with a strike of 60 when the stock is trading

---

[2]It changes the moniness of the 60-strike and 64-strike options. A 60-strike put expires out of the money when the underlier trades at 62, as it does no good to sell for 60 what you can otherwise sell for 62. The 64-strike expires in the money. The 62-strike remains at the money whether a call or a put.

at 15) or "deep out of the money" (e.g., a call with a strike of 60 when the stock is trading at 15). A position in a deep option is nearly identical to a position in a forward. The idea here is that the deeper the option, the more likely it is to expire in the money. So holding a really deep ITM call is like holding a long forward position in the stock—you can pretty much count on owning the underlier, especially if expiration is approaching. Holding a really deep ITM put is like holding a short forward position—the underlier is good as sold.

Americans versus Europeans

Now let's turn back to the whole European versus American thing. *European-style options* may be exercised only on their expiration date. *American-style options* may be exercised at any time up to and including their expiration date. These labels, by the way, have nothing to do with geography; European options trade all the time in the states and Americans trade all the time in the old country. Let's turn our cZED62 into an American option and rename it slightly to CZED62. The uppercase "C" indicates American-style. Figure 5-4 shows how we might represent this option on the price path.

FIGURE 5-4

American Call Option Strike Line

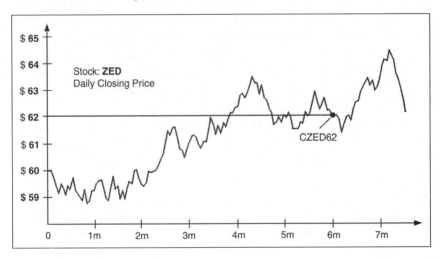

This illustration shows the strike price and stock price at the end of each day until expiration. Unlike the European version, this American option can be exercised at any time up to and including the expiration date. And while it still expires at the money, ergo worthless, it goes in and out of the money a number of times between execution and expiration. Its holder could theoretically exercise at one of the times it is in the money and therefore make some money. This illustrates how American-style options are always more valuable than otherwise identical European-style options. With Europeans you can only exercise on expiration, so it doesn't matter whether or not the option goes in the money before then. (Incidentally, this convention of using lowercase letters to signify Europeans and uppercase to signify Americans reinforces this idea that American options are more valuable than European options. Lowercase equals less valuable; uppercase equals more valuable.)

It's easy to spot the moniness of an option on a price path illustration with a superimposed strike line. A call is in-the-money when the stock price is above the strike line. It's out-of-the-money when stock price is below strike, and at-the-money whenever the stock price crosses the strike line. (A put is just the reverse; ITM when stock price is below strike, and OTM when above.) Figure 5-5 depicts the changing moniness of CZED62 against our imaginary price path.

OPTION UNDERLIER TYPES

Like most derivatives, and a great many other things come to think of it, there are different ways to answer the seemingly simple question, "What kind of options *are* there?" The difficulty derives from the fact there are different ways to slice and dice the universe of options, that is, organize it. There are at least three reasonable ways. First is by structure, and here we think of calls versus puts, Americans versus European, as covered above. Think of these as the terms of the deal, or the rights and obligations of each counterparty. Second is by market, or the places where options happen. There are basically two: exchange markets and over-the-counter (OTC) markets. Options are traded on both.

FIGURE 5-5

Call Option Moniness

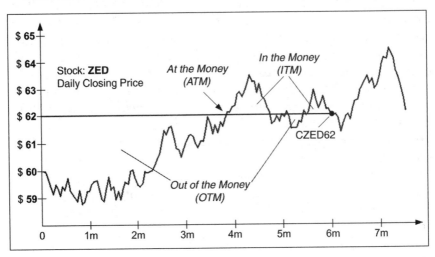

A third way we can organize the universe of options is by underlier; along this dimension the universe is vast. There are all sorts of things on which you can buy or sell options. Now the range of possible "things" we covered in the first chapter—commodities, securities, and so on—and this is no different really from derivatives in general. But when it comes to option underliers, we can also organize them structurally. And thankfully, almost any option underlier can be plunked into one of three buckets, which we will label "simple," "index," and "derivative."

Simple Underliers

These are some individual commodity or financial security. Options on simple underliers grant the holder the right to buy or sell some "thing." If the thing is a commodity, it might be bushels of corn, barrels of crude oil, megawatts of electricity, or some other physical good. If the thing is a security, it might be a stock, a currency, a government bond, or something else along those lines. These options can either be physical-settled or cash-settled.

An example of a simple underlier option is the Microsoft stock option contract traded on the International Securities Exchange (ISE) and elsewhere. One contract allows the holder to buy or sell 100 shares of Microsoft on or before the third Saturday of the expiration month, at one of several different strike prices. If you are new to options, most options you've probably encountered have had simple underliers.

Index Underliers

These underliers are price indices. Options on these underliers grant the holder the right, but not the obligation, to buy or sell some units of an index. Recall that an index is just an average like the Dow Jones Industrial Average. In finance an index is often thought of as a "basket" of a variety of goods, like a sampler basket from an apple grower—you got a Macintosh in there, a Golden Delicious, Granny Smith, and maybe some others. Index options are virtually always cash-settled. You cannot easily buy or sell the index per se, but you can use index derivatives to make or lose money as if you could.

An example here is the SPX option contract. The underlier of the SPX is 100 times the Standard & Poor's 500 Stock Price Index, which is an average price from 500 sample stocks. We'll see an example of using the SPX in Chapter 7.

Derivative Underliers

These underliers are themselves derivatives. That sounds remarkably weird until you notice we've been talking about "buying and selling" forwards and futures and swaps and whatnot all along. And as we noted before, if you can buy or sell it, and it's fungible and liquid, you can probably use it as a derivative underlier.

The most common derivative underlier for options are futures: futures on a simple underlier or futures on an index. For example, at the Chicago Mercantile Exchange one can trade the S&P 500 Futures Option contract, an option whose underlier is one S&P 500 Futures contract (whose own underlier is $250 times the Standard & Poor's 500 Stock Price Index).

FIGURE 5-6

Option Underlier Types

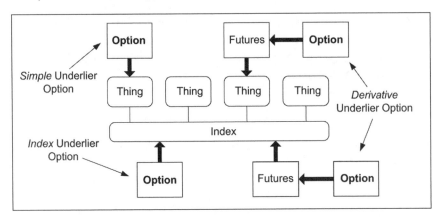

It all might seem rather confusing ... and here's a diagram to prove it! Figure 5-6 uses just one technical term—"thing"—to represent any commodity or security traded on a spot market, be it stock, barrels of oil, currency, whatever.

OPTION PAYOFF

Hockey Sticks

The payoff diagram is a very handy tool for understanding options. For a forward, you'll recall, a payoff diagram gives a snapshot of possible contract values upon delivery. It's just a visual representation of the payoff function with a zero payoff indicated by delivery price. Figure 5-7 shows the long forward payoff from before.

Payoff diagrams work the same way with options with just slightly different terms: they give a snapshot of possible contract values upon exercise, with a zero payoff indicated by strike price. Formula 5.1 shows the payoff function for a long call, and Figure 5-8 shows a corresponding diagram (for the smarties: we're ignoring for now the effect of premium):

$$P_{CALL,LONG} = MAX\,(0, S - K) \qquad (5.1)$$

FIGURE 5-7

Long Forward Payoff Function and Diagram

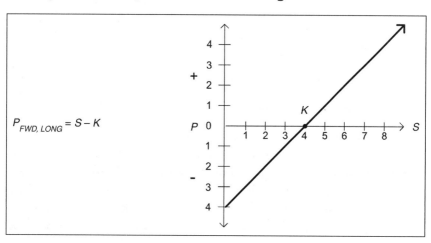

$$P_{FWD,\ LONG} = S - K$$

FIGURE 5-8

Long Call Option Payoff Diagram

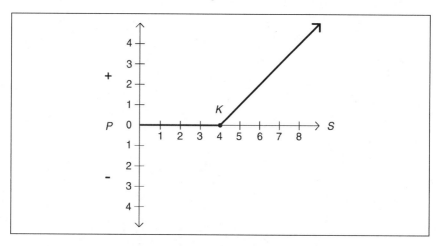

You can see right away the big difference between a forward and option payoff. The long forward payoff can go negative, but the long call option payoff cannot. And this makes sense, right? A call option holder has the right but not the obligation to buy; they will not buy at the strike price if they can buy at a better price on

TABLE 5-1

Long Call Option Payoff Table

S	K	$P_{CALL,LONG} = MAX(0, S-K)$
30	40	0
50	40	10
60	40	20

the spot market. (If you have a coupon to buy milk at $2 per gallon, and milk is selling for $1.80 at the market, will you use the coupon?) This fact is illustrated in the payoff function by the "$MAX(...)$" thing. It's a function that returns the greater of its arguments, which in this case are zero and $S-K$. So the long call option payoff is just the greater of zero and the difference between strike price and spot price.

Say we have a call option with a strike price of 40. Now consider three possible spot prices on exercise: 30, 50, and 60. Table 5-1 has the payoffs under each of the three scenarios:

And Figure 5-9 depicts the three scenarios on the payoff diagram. Notice how each is just one point on the payoff line?

FIGURE 5-9

Long Call Option Payoff Diagram with Payoff Points

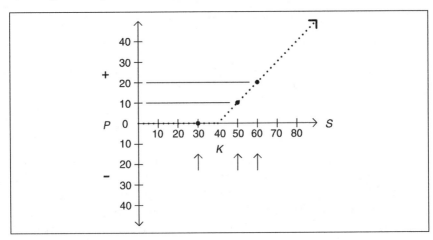

TABLE 5-2

Short Call Option Payoff Table

S	K	$P_{CALL,SHORT} = MIN(0, K - S)$
30	40	0
50	40	−10
60	40	−20

And what of the writer, or short party to a call option? What is their payoff? It's just the opposite of the long party's payoff. Formula 5.2 gives the payoff function for the short call.

$$P_{CALL,SHORT} = MIN(0, K - S) \qquad (5.2)$$

If the long party gains $10 the short party must lose $10. Their payoffs are shown in Table 5-2 and Figure 5-10.

Because the short payoff is the exact opposite of that of the long, the sum of both payoffs is always zero. It's a zero-sum game, remember? We can combine the diagrams and see a nice illustration of this idea, as in Figure 5-11.

FIGURE 5-10

Short Call Option Payoff Diagram with Payoff Points

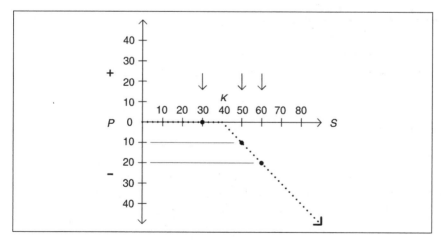

FIGURE 5-11

Net Call Option Payoff Diagram

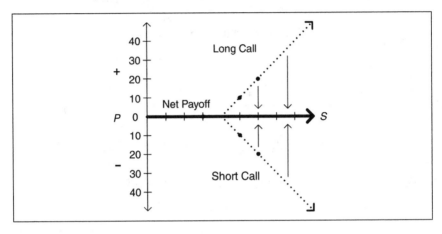

TABLE 5-3

Long Put Option Payoff Table

S	K	$P_{PUT,LONG} = MAX\,(0, K - S)$
30	40	10
50	40	0
60	40	0

TABLE 5-4

Short Put Option Payoff Table

S	K	$P_{PUT,SHORT} = MIN\,(0, S - K)$
30	40	−10
50	40	0
60	40	0

Put options payoffs are just the reverse of call option payoffs. With calls, there is no payoff for either party when spot is below strike. With puts, there is a payoff *only* when spot is below strike. Take a look at Tables 5-3 and 5-4, and Figures 5-12 and 5-13.

FIGURE 5-12

Long Put Option Payoff Diagram with Payoff Points

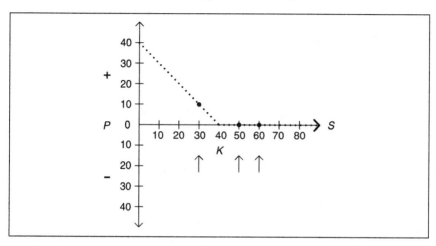

FIGURE 5-13

Short Put Option Payoff Diagram with Payoff Points

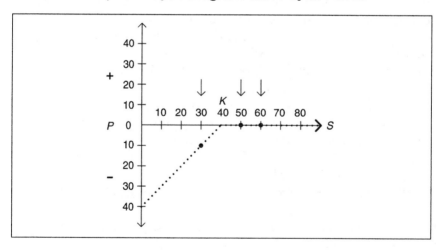

And while we're here, let's step off the bus for just a minute. What happens if we plot the combined payoff of the long call position and short put position on the same diagram? We get the net payoff shown in Figure 5-14.

FIGURE 5-14

Forward Payoff Synthesized with Options

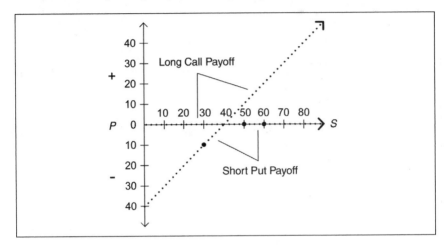

Does the diagonal line look like something we've seen before? Yes! It's just the payoff of a long *forward* contract. This illustrates how the payoff of a long forward position is the same as the combined payoff of a long call and short put position. It's a great illustration of *replication*. We can replicate, or synthesize, one position by constructing a position using different instruments which, when combined, give the same payoff. And by the law of no-arbitrage, two positions with the same payoff must have the same value. This powerful notion of position replication is everywhere in the world of derivative pricing and is indeed like glue that holds it all together. We'll get back to this when we arrive at option pricing, so keep it in mind. Now back on the bus.

Figure 5-15 illustrates the four basic option positions and their respective payoffs. If you plan to work with options, it's worth learning these so-called "hockey stick" patterns till they pop into your head without too much thought.

Effect of Premium on Option Payoff

So far we've ignored the effect of an option's premium on its payoff. The premium is money paid up front by the long party to the short party, so naturally it affects the net payoff of both parties.

FIGURE 5-15

Option Payoff Patterns

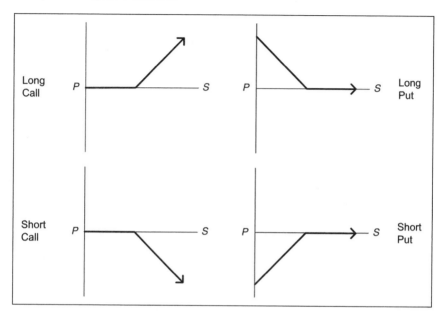

To the long party it decreases the payoff and to the short party it increases it. This is indicated on the payoff diagram by a slight shift down, in the amount of the premium, for the long payoff and up for the short payoff. Imagine the options from before each with a strike price of 40 and 5 dollar premium. Their true payoffs, net of premium, are shown in Figure 5-16.

The long party payoff can actually go negative by the amount of the premium. In other words, they are out the premium whether they exercise or not. And if they do exercise, their payoff is decreased by the amount of the premium. To the short party, the premium is money they get to keep no matter what. They still can lose money, of course, as soon as the spot price increases sufficiently over strike. But the money they lose is offset by the premium.

OPTION STRATEGIES

Before we put away the hockey sticks, let's use them to illustrate common positions involving multiple instruments, often known as option *strategies*. The instruments in a strategy might be two or

Option Payoff Diagrams Net of Premium

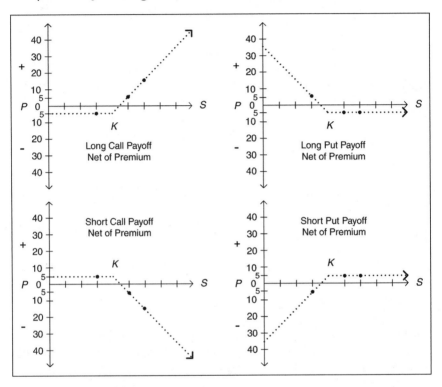

more of the same calls or puts at different strike prices or expiration dates, or an option plus a stock or bond position, or calls and puts together. To get a feel for these, first consider the speculator who is convinced a stock price will increase. This trader can buy a simple call option and sit back and wait (perhaps nervously, depending on how many they bought). Figure 5-17 shows the payoff of a call with strike price K, an instrument we'll refer to as $c(K)$.

Now consider the speculator with a view that a stock price will change in one direction or the other but isn't sure which. This trader can buy both a call and a put, both with the same strike price and expiration and different premiums, resulting in a net payoff that looks roughly like Figure 5-18.

FIGURE 5-17

Long Call Option Payoff Diagram Net of Premium

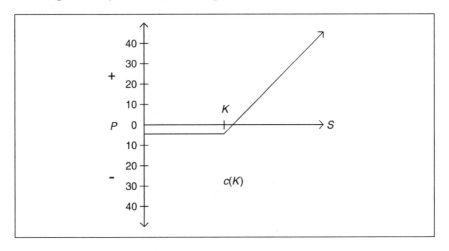

FIGURE 5-18

Long Straddle Payoff

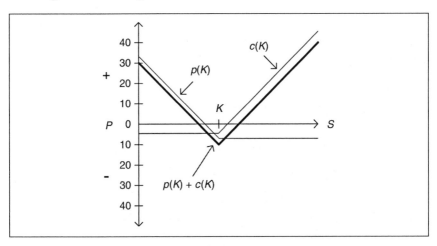

This simple strategy is known as a *straddle*. The long party here will profit whether the underlier price goes up or down, as long as it goes up or down by more than an amount to recoup their combined premiums. If it stays in that range, they lose some or all of their premium. The short party to a straddle, by the way, has the same but opposite payoff. It looks like an inverted "V."

A variation of the straddle is the *strangle*. A long strangle is made of a long put and long call at different strike prices, K_1 and K_2, and its payoff looks roughly like Figure 5-19.

A *covered call* position consists of a written call $c(K)$—in the diagram we attach a negative sign to denote it is a short position—and long stock S purchased for S_0. As the option writer you're protected should the stock price skyrocket and the call go deep into the money. You just hand over the stock you already own, covering your, um—downside on the option contract. Its payoff is shown in Figure 5-20.

The idea of a covered put is the same but in reverse. When you write a put you face a substantial loss should the option expire deep in the money, that is, when the stock price declines far below the strike price. So you cover it with a short position in the stock, whose value will increase with the falling stock price, compensating you for your loss on the put. A written option without a cover is known as a "naked option." Writing naked options is rarely a good idea.

FIGURE 5-19

Long Strangle Payoff

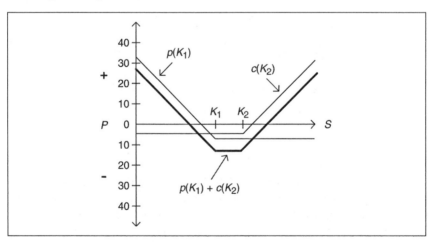

FIGURE 5-20

Covered Call Payoff

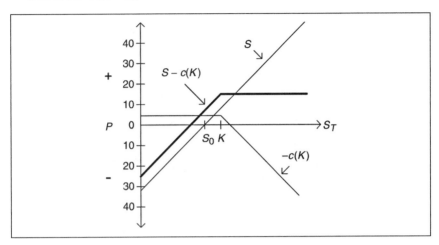

Those strategies are just some examples to give you the basic idea. The number of option strategies one can cook up is limited only by one's imagination and tolerance for risk. Other common strategies include "bear spreads," "buggy whips," "bull combos," and "butterflies." (Okay, I made one of those up. Guess which one?)[3] Each combines two or more instruments to cook up some particular payoff to suit one's needs.

It's tempting to think one can cook up some brand new strategy to crank out money like a machine no matter where prices go, but all strategies are bound by the laws of arbitrage, so the prospect of creating a money machine becomes more remote each day. There are beaucoup well-healed traders out there, with plenty of money to spend on impressive computer systems, allowing them to respond to opportunities at nearly the speed of light. And you have the nagging fact that arbitrage opportunities are by nature self-destructive upon discovery. Oh well.

---

[3]Buggy whips.

CHAPTER 6

Credit Contracts

The derivatives we have covered thus far deal with the *market risk* associated with the price of some underlying security or commodity. Credit derivatives deal with the *credit risk* associated with the performance of a party in fulfilling a financial obligation. Here's a quick example of the most common credit derivative of them all, the *credit default swap*:

> An investor buys 10 million dollar's worth of 5-year corporate bonds issued by a large manufacturer, in essence lending the manufacturer $10 million in exchange for periodic interest payments and return of their principal in 5 years. Over the life of the bond, changes in the creditworthiness of the issuer affect the value of the bond. For example, should the manufacturer declare bankruptcy, casting doubt on their ability to fulfill their payment obligations, the value of the bonds may drop to something well below $10 million.
>
> To protect against the possibility of such a drop in bond value, the investor enters into a credit default swap with an insurance company. Under the terms of the swap, the investor pays an annual premium of 150 basis points on $10 million, or $150,000 per year for 5 years. Should the manufacturer declare bankruptcy over the course of that time, the insurance company agrees to buy the bonds from the investor for $10 million—no matter what their value. The investor house has thus rid themselves of the credit risk of owning these bonds.

PERFORMANCE GUARANTEES

Just as we viewed forwards, futures, swaps, and options as variations on a price guarantee, you can think of credit derivatives as variations on a *performance* guarantee. These instruments deal with the possibility of some party not fulfilling their financial obligation. Like other derivatives, they have counterparties and underliers. And their value derives in part from the value of the underlier—but only as that value is affected by a so-called "credit event" such as bankruptcy. In the example above, were the value of the bonds to decline due to changes in market interest rates (the chief factor in bond valuation changes), the credit default swap would not compensate the investor. Only if the bond value declines as a result of bankruptcy, in this case, does the credit default swap payoff for the investor. And this illustrates one of the prime attractions of credit derivatives: they enable the decomposition or "unbundling" of overall risk into different types of risk, each of which can be dealt with on its own. For example, a lender can use a fixed-floating swap to hedge away their exposure to changes in interest rates on a fixed-rate loan they write, so they need not lose sleep should market rates go through the roof. But that swap won't help them if the debtor defaults. So they add a credit default swap to the mix and sleep even better.

Credit risk exists with all sorts of financial instruments, but most credit derivatives are concerned with debt securities, for example, bonds issued by corporations or sovereign states. Now lenders for years have used a variety of mechanisms for mitigating default risk. They use loan syndication to spread risk across multiple lenders, borrower diversification (lending to multiple borrowers across multiple economic sectors so as not to keep all eggs in one basket), third-party loan guarantees, letters of credit, and other such devices. Then what's so special about credit derivatives? They make possible a *market* in credit risk.

While credit derivatives certainly cater to the inherent needs of lenders, they also afford participation in the credit market by parties with no preexisting exposure to a credit default. This makes them much more than "just" default protection. Credit derivatives are available to speculators, arbitrageurs, and market-makers just as they are to lenders with a direct exposure to a borrower skipping town. A speculator who is confident a bond issuer will not default, for example, can sell a credit default swap just to collect the premium.[1] A sharp arbitrageur or market-maker can earn the spread between the market price of a credit derivative and a price at which they can confidently synthesize it—just like the options arbitrageur or market-maker.

What is the ultimate value of such marketization of credit risk? It's hard to say for certain, but a few things come to mind. In theory, anything that makes credit protection more accessible should encourage more lending by reducing a lender's exposure to default risk—although it's difficult to say whether the data supports such an assertion. It should also facilitate the fair pricing of credit protection because arbitrageurs stand by to snatch up profits from any "bad" pricing of credit. And if nothing else, a liquid market in credit protection certainly makes credit protection more accessible. And this is a very liquid and sizeable market, with several trillion dollars worth of protection sold each year. So these instruments must be valuable to someone.

Three of the most common credit derivatives are the *credit default swap, total return swap*, and *credit linked note*. There are other types, but these are some of the biggies. Most other credit derivatives are variations or extensions of one of these, and we'll touch on some of them later on.

Credit derivatives are generally traded on the OTC market in a market structure not unlike that of interest rate swaps and FX forwards. Market-makers publish so-called "indicative prices" on some electronic forum or another, helping the prospective protection buyer or seller find a counterparty. But indicative prices are inherently nonbinding, and a firm trade price is set only after the two interested parties find each other. The exact price and other terms of the trade are typically documented in a master agreement or confirmation letter following guidelines published by ISDA.[2]

---

[1]This begs the question, of course, of how a protection buyer can be assured the protection seller won't default. It's a fine question, a serious question, but one we simply shan't get to. Sorry!

[2]International Swap and Derivatives Association.

THE CREDIT DEFAULT SWAP

The *credit default swap*, or *credit swap*, is the plain vanilla of credit derivatives. There are two primary parties to a CDS: the *protection buyer* and *protection seller*. The protection buyer pays a *premium* or *CDS spread* to the protection seller. The premium is typically expressed in some number of basis points[3] payable annually. There is a third party, the reference entity, which issues some debt security (i.e., borrows some money). The reference entity's creditworthiness determines the value and payoff of the CDS, however they are not a direct party to the CDS. Should the reference entity experience one or more credit events over the term of the swap, the protection seller agrees to compensate the protection buyer for any loss incurred as a result of the credit event, for example, by purchasing the bond at face value, after which the buyer no longer pays the premium. Incidentally, this type of CDS is known as a *single-name CDS*, as it relates to a debt security issued by a single reference entity. The entity is typically a large corporate entity, but can also be a sovereign state that issues government debt. There are also *portfolio CDS* instruments whose payoff can be triggered by a credit event by more than one reference entity (more on these below). As you might imagine, the primary buyers of single-name credit default swaps are commercial lenders and corporate bondholders. The primary sellers tend to be insurance companies and large financial institutions. The fundamental structure of a CDS is shown in Figure 6-1.

Now, calling these things "swaps" may seem a bit of a stretch. The swapping is not as obvious as with an interest rate swap, but you might view the premium payments as a stream of "fixed" payments and the potential payment of loss compensation as a single "floating" payment. Whatever. Credit default swaps are much more like a traditional insurance policy—replace "credit event" with "a tornado wrecks your house" and these things are mostly indistinguishable from a homeowner's policy. If it helps, just think of one of these instruments as a tradable insurance policy called a CDS.

---

[3]One basis point is one one-hundredth of a percent. 150 basis points, for example, is the same as 1.5 percent.

FIGURE 6-1

Credit Default Swap

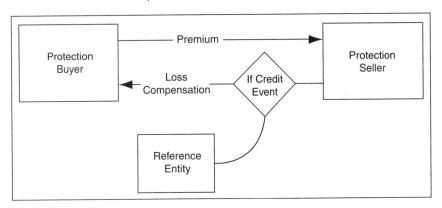

Credit swaps can be *cash-settled* or *physically settled.* This basically determines how loss compensation works. In the case of
cash-settlement the protection seller pays the net loss incurred by
the protection buyer as a result of a credit event. If the buyer's
$10 million bond portfolio devalues to $2 million, they receive
a check for $8 million. Physical settlement can apply when the
subject of the swap is a publicly traded corporate security such as a
bond. If the terms of a swap call for physical settlement and the
buyer's $10 million bond portfolio devalues as a result of a credit
event, the buyer transfers ownership of the portfolio to the seller
and receives a check for $10 million in return. Same net effect.

The credit event that triggers settlement can be anything the
two parties agree to but is typically one or more of five credit
events defined by ISDA: bankruptcy, failure to pay, obligation
default, obligation acceleration, or restructuring. *Bankruptcy* involves
seeking court protection against creditors when a company can't
pay its bills, *failure to pay* is essentially like missing a payment on a
car loan, *obligation default* is when the lender declares the borrower
in violation of payment terms and demands return of the principal,
obligation acceleration is when the terms of a debt call for immediate
payment of some or all of a debt "ahead of schedule" as a result of
some issue, and *restructuring* is a broad event that includes things
like debt consolidation.

The CDS premium is often known as a *CDS spread*, although there is no explicit "spread" per se. The term is borrowed from the portion of a corporate bond yield attributable to the credit risk, a portion known as a *credit spread*. If you subtract from a corporate bond yield the risk-free rate, you are left with the compensation that investors receive for taking on the risk of the bond issuer defaulting. This "spread over treasuries," as it is sometimes known, is often used as a measure of the probability of default by the issuer. (Treasury securities are generally considered free of default risk.) And in theory a reference entity's CDS spread should be equivalent to the credit spread on its debt securities trading at *par*, or time-adjusted face value. In practice that's not always the case for all sorts of reasons. Bottom line, the CDS premium is known as a spread for its close relationship to a corporate bond's credit spread.

And speaking of premium, it's a fine term for what the protection buyer pays for a credit default swap because it really is an option premium. A put option premium in fact. How so? Just think of the CDS notional (face value) as the strike price on a company's bond, and the market value of the bond is it's spot price. Should a credit event occur, the CDS-as-put-option goes "in the money" by an amount given by strike minus spot—just like any put option. When it comes to calculating payoff, a CDS is very much like a put option. It is quite different, however, when it comes to whether or not the payoff occurs. With a real put option, the holder is entitled to a payoff simply if the strike price is above spot price on or before some expiration date. With a CDS-as-put-option, the spot price can be far below the strike, but the holder gets no payoff. For example, when the spot price is below strike due to changing interest rates. The CDS goes in the money, remember, only if a credit event occurs. But otherwise it's just a put. Remember how very early on we said nearly any derivative can be seen as a variation on one of the four basic types? Primo example right here, folks.

THE TOTAL RETURN SWAP

A total return swap, also known as a *total rate of return swap*, is a credit derivative and more. Here the protection seller makes a stream of regular payments, say Libor plus 30bp, to the protection

FIGURE 6-2

Total Return Swap

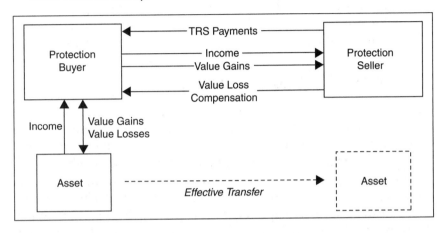

buyer. Now this might seem backwards at first—with the protection "seller" making payments, but stay with me. In exchange for those payments, the protection buyer transfers to the seller all income (think coupon payments) and capital changes (think changes in market valuation) with respect to a reference asset—i.e., the "total" return—but continues to own it for accounting purposes. The bidirectional payments are generally lined up to occur at the same time, so this really is a "swap" in the terms of a promised exchange of future cash flows. The TRS thus allows the seller to enjoy (or suffer) the economic consequences of owning an asset without actually owning it. In accounting terminology the asset remains "off their balance sheet" as they essentially "rent" another's balance sheet for the duration of the agreement.[4] The TRS is illustrated in Figure 6-2.

And where does credit risk protection fit into this picture? If the asset is a debt security, and its value decreases due to the creditworthiness of the issuer, the protection seller compensates the buyer—much as they do in a credit swap. Unlike a credit swap,

---

[4]The idea of off-balance-sheet accounting is not universally accepted as a good idea.
A discussion of the pros and cons is, alas, beyond the scope of our slender text.

however, the seller compensates the buyer for value loss due to any reason and not just credit events. And the asset of a TRS need not be a debt security at all. It can just as well be an equity, a stock index, or pretty much anything else on a balance sheet. As such, the TRS is indeed much more than just a credit derivative.

THE CREDIT LINKED NOTE

A credit linked note is a vehicle for raising capital in which invested funds are held in reserve in case they are needed to compensate a protection buyer in the event of a credit loss. The overall structure, in fact, is very similar to a credit default swap: a protection buyer pays a premium in return for compensation should a credit event occur with respect to a reference entity. The protection seller, however, raises capital for the express purpose of credit protection by issuing CLNs to investors. Should a credit event occur, the capital is used to compensate the protection buyer for their loss. Otherwise the capital is returned to the investor at the maturity of the note. In return for this possible loss of some (or all) of their investment, the investor is compensated with receipt of the protection buyer premium, less a spread to compensate the protection seller, as well as interest on their capital. The structure of the CLN is illustrated in Figure 6-3.

FIGURE 6-3

Credit Linked Note

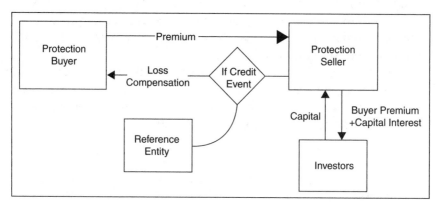

The protection seller in a credit linked note may be some arm of an existing financial institution, or it might be a specially created entity known as a *special purpose vehicle* or "SPV." These are more-or-less independent legal entities created expressly for a purpose such as this with credit reputations impeccable by design; that is, they generally have the highest credit rankings possible. They also tend to be isolated from the credit woes of any other entity. Among other things, the use of an SPV here helps mitigate any credit risk from the CLN issuer itself.

Plenty of variations on the basic theme of a CLN are possible. For example, the once-mighty Enron issued a series of *credit sensitive notes* in 1998 that offered a coupon rate inversely tied to Enron's credit rating. As their Moodys or Standard & Poors ratings decreased, the promised coupon rate increased. That coupon rate presumably skyrocketed as Enron self-destructed some years later. It would be interesting to know, however, if the investors actually received the coupon payments given Enron's disappearing act.

OTHER CREDIT CONTRACTS

There is a nontrivial number of variations and close relations on these things that fill out the credit derivative market. Here are a few and what they're all about in a nutshell.

Portfolio CDS	A credit default swap with more than one reference entity, or "multiname" CDS. Has a higher premium than a single-name CDS due to the increased level of protection.
Basket Default Swap	A form of portfolio CDS also known as a *first-to-default* CDS, this credit default swap pays the protection buyer upon a credit default by any one of multiple reference entities, after which the agreement ceases to exist.
Binary CDS	A credit default swap where the protection buyer receives a fixed payment amount, rather than the difference between notional and market value, should a credit event occur. Also known as a *digital CDS*.
Forward CDS	A forward contract to buy or sell a CDS on a particular reference entity at a specified date in the future. As you would expect, the CDS spread for a forward CDS is the one that makes the value of the forward equal to zero.
CDS Option	An option, typically European style, that grants a right but not the obligation to buy or sell a CDS on some particular reference entity on some future date. A CDS option generally ceases to exist should a credit event occur prior to option expiration.

PRICING CREDIT DERIVATIVES

As we'll see when we get to the pricing chapters, there is a solid body of knowledge on how one can determine the fair market value of forwards, futures, swaps, and options, and little disagreement among market participants on how one should price these price guarantees. This is not yet the case for our performance guarantees or credit derivatives. Even though the market for credit contracts is impressive and growing every day, compared to the market for forwards, futures, swaps, and options, it is still rather small. This means, among other things, there is still a comparatively healthy debate on just how one should go about pricing these things, as there are limited markets for so-called price discovery.

One approach for pricing credit derivatives is the same one we'll use for pricing other derivatives in later chapters. In essence, this approach gets the value of a credit derivative by discounting the expected risk-neutral payoff of the derivative using the risk-free rate of interest. We'll explain the risk-neutrality and risk-free rate things in those later chapters. And we've not yet explained discounting, but this just involves determining the value today of some future cash flow. The future cash flow in the case of a credit default swap, for example, is the payment from the protection seller to the protection buyer in the event of default by the reference entity, that is the contract payoff.

Say you are a seller of a CDS where the reference entity is the corporate issuer of a bond with a face value of $10 million. To simplify things, let's say under the terms of the CDS you will write a check to the protection buyer in 1 year's time for $10 million if the reference entity defaults over the course of the year. There is some probability of the default occurring, so there is some probability of your writing that check. To price this contract—that is, determine how much premium you should charge the buyer—you want to know the *expected value* of that payment. Expected values are calculated all the time in finance by multiplying some future cash flow by the probability of it occurring. Say there is a 1 percent chance of the reference entity defaulting and your writing a check for $10 million. The expected value of that payment is simply 1 percent of $10 million, or $100 thousand. You might set the premium, then, to at least $100,000.

There are at least a couple of complicating factors when doing this for real. In our example, we presumed the payout would total $10 million, or 100 percent of the face value of the guaranteed bond. In reality, when companies default, some amount of their debt is "recovered," leading to the idea of a *recovery rate*. In the example above, perhaps the terms of the CDS are such that the protection seller would only have to pay, say, 60 percent of the $10 million because that's the extent of the loss. The recovery rate, as you can sense, has a huge impact on the expected payoff of the derivative. And it's hugely difficult to predict.

Another not-so-easy feat is calculating a probability of default. In the example, we took a wild guess at 1 percent. In practice there are a couple of ways one can obtain a probability of default. One is the credit spread between the yield of the reference entity's bond and an otherwise equivalent government bond—say U.S. Treasuries. If the yield on a Treasury is 4 percent, and the yield on the corporate bond is 4.25 percent, you can say the extra .25 percent compensates the bond-holder for the risk of default. And from that credit spread, using a bit of algebra you can back out a probability.

CHAPTER 7

Using Derivatives to Manage Risk

Risk, it is said, simply means more things can happen than will happen. Financial risk is when things can happen to cause you a financial loss. *Financial risk management* is the term of art for what you do to reduce the probability or degree of financial loss in the face of uncertainty. Derivatives are an excellent tool for a particular type of risk management known as *hedging*. Indeed, it's why they were invented in the first place. Generally speaking, hedging involves recognizing and measuring the financial risk of an existing position, then taking on some new position with opposite exposure characteristics such that the gains and losses of the positions cancel each other out. In essence, you no longer care if the original position loses money because the hedge position will make money to compensate. And if the hedge position loses money, no worries, the original position makes money to compensate—provided it's a good hedge, of course.

Imagine how you might manage an exposure to a nonfinancial risk: weather. Say you take an afternoon off work for a nice walk in the park. In investment terms you are taking a position in a walk. There's only a slight chance of rain, but you bring along your umbrella, taking a position in that instrument, just in case you need one. Now if it does not rain you will have lugged an unused umbrella all day, thus "losing" on your umbrella position. But the position in the walk will have paid off nicely. If it does rain, you lose on the walk position but gain handsomely on the umbrella position. It's not a perfect analogy nor a perfect hedge, as the umbrella won't keep every drop of water off you. But at least you can count on a dry head on your walk home no matter whether it rains or not.

Derivatives are a natural financial risk management tool for two key reasons that we've already seen. First, because a derivative's value is determined chiefly by the value of its underlier, offsetting positions in a derivative and its underlier (long the derivative and short the underlier, or vice versa) tend to neutralize changes in the underlier's value. It's the playground seesaw thing: One side goes up; the other side goes down. Which is just what you want. Second, derivatives employ the power of leverage. On the playground, move the center point or fulcrum on the seesaw, and the kid farther from the fulcrum has a much easier time than the other kid. In finance, leverage allows you to replicate a payoff pattern of something you want to hedge at a lower cost than simply trading more of the thing itself. As we saw in the first chapter, for example, you can buy stock options to replicate a stock portfolio's payoff for much less money than buying some desired amount of the stock itself. Hedging with futures also employs leverage, as in most cases you need only put up a margin, or portion of your position's value. For the speculator, leverage raises the stakes and can spell disaster if your bet is bad, or riches if your bet pays off. For the hedger, leverage lets you manage risk at a price far less than you might otherwise need to pay.

In this chapter we'll look at risk management from the perspective of the "classic" derivatives user: someone who uses derivatives to hedge an exposure created by a position in some nonderivative instrument. Those who take positions in derivatives for reasons other than hedging—think market-makers or arbitrageurs—also face financial risk. And the same leverage that makes derivatives such powerful hedging instruments makes them potentially devastating if not properly hedged. Many a career in derivatives have met swift ends when poor souls have forgotten to hedge a trade! The final chapter, Hedging a Derivatives Position, is all about this sort of hedging, which involves carefully quantifying the exposure of a derivatives position and using both derivative and nonderivative instruments to hedge it.

Now we've already seen several examples of hedging with derivatives in the preceding chapters. In the sections that follow, we'll revisit some of these for a second look and consider some alternative hedging strategies.

ALL ABOUT POSITIONS

We talk a lot about positions in this chapter, so it's worth reviewing some position-related concepts. A *position* is just an interest or stake in the financial value of something, some present or future asset or liability to be exact.

Take a look at Table 7-1. With respect to forwards, futures, swaps, and call options, a long position connotes an interest or obligation with respect to buying the underlier. A short position implies an interest or obligation with respect to selling. The long party to a forward, for example, is obligated to buy the underlier while the short party is obligated to sell. The long party to a call option is entitled to buy the underlier if they so choose, in which case the short party is obligated to sell. The positional ramifications of a put option are just reverse that of the call: the long party may have an interest in selling the underlier, in which case the short party is obligated to buy. Such obligations are sometimes known as "contingent liabilities."

When hedging, the general idea is to choose a hedge position with an exposure opposite that of the thing you wish to hedge, that is, in these cases, the underlier. So the decision whether to go long

TABLE 7-1

Derivative Position Obligations and Rights

	Long Position	Short Position
Forward	Obligation to *buy* the underlier	Obligation to *sell* the underlier
Future		
Swap		
Call Option	Right to *buy* the underlier	Obligation to *sell* the underlier
Put Option	Right to *sell* the underlier	Obligation to *buy* the underlier

TABLE 7-2

Underlier Positions

	Long Position	Short Position
Underlier	Present or future *ownership*	Present or future *need*

or short on your hedge position depends on whether you are long or short the underlier in the first place. And how can you tell? One way is by thinking of a long position in the underlier as connoting "ownership" and a short position a "need," as shown in Table 7-2.

Say you own crude oil or will own it in the future. Consider yourself "long oil." As the owner of oil, you are exposed to a decline in the spot price of crude because you won't be able to sell it for as much as you can today. To hedge the market risk of this long position, you might secure a short position in a forward or futures, or a long position in a put option, affording you the right or obligation to sell your oil at a price you like. On the other hand, if you will need oil in the future, consider yourself "short oil." You are likewise exposed to changes in spot prices the other direction. Should the price of oil increase, you will have to buy it for a higher price. So you can hedge this short position with a long position in a forward or futures, or a long position in a call option, affording you the right or obligation to buy at a price you like.

Incidentally, there's a peculiar twist to the idea of a short position when the underlier is equity, or stock. To be "short in stock" means you have borrowed shares, sold them, and taken the cash. This is known as *short selling*. The classic hope if you're a short seller is that the stock price will decrease so when it comes time to return those borrowed shares, you buy them at a lower price than you sold them, pocketing the difference. Again, the idea of being short is analogous to a need. You will need shares in the future to return them to whomever you borrowed them from. To be long stock is just what you would imagine. You own the shares, plain and simple. We'll come across short selling again in the final chapter on hedging a derivatives position.

HEDGING WITH FORWARD CONTRACTS

In Chapter 1, the tortilla maker bought forward contracts to lock in the price of corn for purchase in 6 months. And in Chapter 2, the Gizmo company bought FX forwards denominated in U.S. dollars to lock in the price of a future purchase to be denominated in South Korean won.

In both cases the hedger reduced the uncertainty of future prices. The hedged tortilla maker need not worry about the price of corn rising and cutting into their profits, and Gizmo need not worry about changes in the won-dollar exchange rate. (Recall that an exchange rate simply conveys the price of one currency in units of another currency.) Also, in both cases the hedger assumed long positions in the forward as they intended to buy the underlier to satisfy their future need. And most important, both hedgers assumed an obligation to buy at the forward price whether the underlier price rose or fell in the meantime.

Both of these examples had the hedger assume a long position in the forward contract, but consider the case where a short forward contract is what you need. Say you live in Chicago and purchased some property in Paris some time ago in Euros, at a time when the U.S. dollar was much stronger against the Euro than it is today. Back then you could buy fewer Euros per dollar than you can today. So in dollar terms your property investment has appreciated due to the change in the Euro-USD exchange rate. Say you plan to sell that property in 6 months, receiving Euros. Can you lock in today the dollar-value of those Euros you expect to own in the future? Sure can. Just enter into a short position in a dollar-denominated FX forward contract, to sell Euros in 6 months at today's exchange rate. Future ownership, future sell. But remember two things: This won't protect you should the property decline in Euro terms, in which case you won't own quite so many Euros to convert to dollars. And if the dollar should *continue* to decline, so the dollar value of your investment climbs even more over the next 6 months, you won't realize that appreciation. You're locking in the dollar value today of those future Euros, no matter what happens. Is there any way to avoid that? Sure. Buy FX put options instead, to sell Euros in 6 months at today's rate. Future ownership, future sell. You'll need to shell out a premium, of course, but should the dollar weaken further you can just let those options expire worthless. If the dollar strengthens, lowering the price of Euros in dollar terms, you can exercise the option and realize your gain. Table 7-3 summarizes when you hedge to buy and when you hedge to sell.

A forward hedge is really simple. The preexisting position in Gizmo's case is a future need for South Korean won. The value (if you will) of that position will decrease as the price of won increases. The value of the forward position also changes with the price of won, but in the opposite direction. Compared to other hedges, "settling" a forward hedge is uncomplicated: you simply take delivery of the good and pay or receive the agreed-upon price.

HEDGING WITH FUTURES CONTRACTS

In Chapter 3, Royal Mill used wheat futures to lock in the price of wheat for a purchase in 6 months. This might seem a lot like what the tortilla maker did with forward contracts, but there's one big difference: the Royal Mill had no intention of actually buying wheat at the futures price, even though a futures contracts commits them to buy. When the delivery date came they bought their wheat from their usual supplier—at a price greater than they had wanted to pay—and effectively cancelled their long futures position by taking on a matching short position. They paid more for the wheat than they had wanted to, but made some money off the futures to compensate. So just like the vast majority of all hedgers who use futures contracts, they did not have to deal with delivery of the physical underlier. But they did walk away with a financial gain, or trading profit, which they used to offset the fact that wheat prices had risen while they held their futures contract. Had the spot price of wheat fallen, Royal Mill would have experienced a loss on the contracts. But the price they paid on the spot market would have likewise fallen (i.e., they would have paid a lower

TABLE 7-3

Underlier Positions and Hedge Guidelines

| Long underlier | Present or future *ownership* | hedge to *sell* |
| Short underlier | Present or future *need* | hedge to *buy* |

price to their grain supplier than they were willing to pay), again neutralizing the change in the market price of wheat.

As you'll recall, a futures contract is just a highly standardized form of a forward contract, traded on an exchange where it is marked to market at the end of every trading day. In many ways, then, hedging a future need with futures is like hedging it with a forward: You figure out how much of the underlier you want to buy on some future date and go long the appropriate number of contracts. The big difference, though, is the vast majority of futures contracts do not result in the delivery of the underlier. They are closed out on (or before) the delivery date. It's the pure value-change the hedger cares about and not the literal delivery of the underlier.

Now because futures contracts are so highly standardized, it's often difficult to effect a truly perfect hedge. With respect to price uncertainty, the FX forward hedge above is virtually perfect— Gizmo will get exactly what they need, when they need it, for the price they want to pay. Not so for Royal Mill. For example, the delivery point of the contract wheat may be 1000 miles from where they need it, so shipping costs alter the net hedge. Or the wheat specified in the contract may not be exactly the type of wheat they need. So the spot price of the wheat they need may change in a different way from the price of the contract wheat. Maybe the price of their wheat goes up a lot and the price of the contract wheat only goes up a little, or maybe changes in the opposite direction. In any of these cases they won't realize the offsetting gains and losses they had hoped. This is an example of *basis risk*, which comes into play when you hedge with something whose price doesn't change the same way as the price of the thing you are hedging. In the ideal case the value of your hedge position is "perfectly negatively correlated" as a mathematician would say, meaning it changes in the exact opposite way of your preexisting position. But this is simply not possible all the time. A little basis risk is generally okay, however, and knowing how much is acceptable is what separates effective hedgers from the not-so-effective.

So why do people hedge with a futures instead of a forward contract? Liquidity and credit risk. You simply may not find a counterparty willing to do the forward you need, and if you do, how sure can you be that they'll stick around when it comes time to deliver if the market moves against them? Now for sure, there are many situations in which you can find a creditworthy counter-party willing to write you a forward contract. It happens all the time in the OTC markets where buyers and sellers know how to find each other, and where they typically employ some form of *collateralization* (i.e., one party or the other pledges some cash or marketable securities in the event they can't fulfill their obligation) to mitigate default risk. But when you can't find someone, it sure is nice to have those liquid futures markets.

Not every futures hedge position is a long position. Wheat growers, for example, are exposed to the spot price of wheat but in the opposite way from that of the miller. If the price of wheat decreases, they make *less* profit when it comes time to sell. So they can put on a hedge consisting of short positions, whose value will also change with the spot price of wheat but in the opposite way from that of a long position.

HEDGING WITH SWAPS

In Chapter 4 the Gondor Corporation executed a plain vanilla interest rate swap with Marlow Securities to effectively convert a preexisting floating-rate loan to a fixed rate. Entrepreneurs Boris and Chloe executed a swap with each other, allowing Boris to convert his preexisting floating-rate loan to fixed, and Chloe to convert her fixed-rate loan to floating. The Gondor example, where one party was a swaps dealer, is far more common than the Boris-Chloe example. Swaps certainly can be executed between hedgers, for virtually no cost, as it's in the interest of both parties to set the terms of the swap such that it has no value at the outset.[1] In practice, however, most swaps are actually executed with a swaps dealer who "marks up" the fixed rate (or applies a *spread*, or "margin," to the floating rate) such that the swap has some nonzero present value to the dealer.

Regardless of your counterparty, a swap mitigates uncertainty about the future price of money as conveyed by interest rates. And just like forwards and futures, parties to a swap are obligated to

---

[1]The theory here, and it makes some sense, is that each party is making the best of their "comparative advantage" over the other. The same idea is often applied in international economics in the debate over free trade versus protectionism.

buy or sell at the predetermined rates no matter what happens in the spot markets. And because swaps are generally traded in the over-the-counter market, they are more akin to forwards than futures. As forwards-in-disguise, then, swaps are inherently not as liquid as futures and carry more credit risk. But in practice, the OTC swaps market is so darn vast, it's pretty easy to find a dealer to do a swap, and most swap transactions require one or the other party to post collateral to mitigate the possibility of defaulting on their obligations.

You might have this question in your mind about Gondor, or anyone who uses a swap to convert a floating-rate loan to a fixed rate: Why don't they just borrow at a fixed rate and forget about all this swapping? Excellent question. It turns out that often a fixed-rate loan is more expensive (that is, the present value of the interest charge is greater) than a floater. In these cases it can be less costly in the long run to take out a floating-rate loan and convert it to fixed with a swap. And as you know, credit is a factor when lenders decide whether or not and how they will lend money. A business desiring a loan may simply not have good enough credit for a fixed-rate loan but can secure a floater. Bottom line, floating-rate debt is easier to come by, so there's a lot of it out there.

Alternatives to a Swap

Later on, in the chapter on swaps pricing, we'll demonstrate how a swap is exactly the same as a bundle of forward contracts known as *forward rate agreements* or "FRAs." This means a hedger could in theory use a portfolio of FRAs instead of a swap to convert a fixed-rate obligation into a floater or vice versa. But in practice it's difficult to set up such a portfolio that exactly offsets your preexisting loan, which may include amortization or compounding or other features not commonly found in FRAs. No matter how unusual your situation, you can probably find any number of swaps dealers ready to concoct a hedge that fits like a glove.

And while we're on this vein of alternatives, you could also hedge your loan using the same exact hedging instruments that swaps dealers are likely to use to hedge their exposure: interest rate futures contracts or government bonds or some combination of the two. (We'll see how this is done in the final chapter on hedging a derivatives position.) And you would even save yourself the dealer's fee. But you'll have a *lot* of work to do constructing a hedge of futures and bonds with an acceptable level of basis risk. For example, Eurodollar Futures expire on set, quarterly dates. Those dates might not line up with the dates you need. And EDFs have notionals of $1 million, so if you don't have a loan principal rounded to the millions you won't get a perfect hedge. It comes down to packaging. Swaps dealers don't have as much of a problem here as they hedge hundreds or thousands of swaps all at once as a portfolio of swap obligations, and this *diversification* is itself risk-reducing. (The swaps in the portfolio have a variety of exposure characteristics, and some of them are bound to cancel each other out for a "natural" hedge.) And because of the sheer size of a dealer's operation, they simply have more "wiggle room" when it comes to basis risk than an individual hedger. And maintaining a futures and bond hedge takes nearly constant work. With a swap you let the dealer take care of that and get on with your own business.

When it comes to hedging an exposure to changing interest rates, swaps are the most popular of interest rate derivatives. But there are others. If you don't want to give up both downside (the prospect of loss) and upside (the prospect of gain) by locking in a fixed rate—remember these are forwards—but just want to shed the downside in the event your floating rate goes up, you could use an interest rate cap instead of a swap. You'll pay a premium up front, as a cap is an option, but should rates decline you'll get to enjoy it. For example: Say you take out a floating-rate loan on $1 million. At the outset of this loan you have no idea what rate will be used to calculate your loan payments—6 percent? 7 percent? Say you're comfortable with the prospect of making payments at a rate up to 6.5 percent but no higher, for a maximum payment of $65,000. You of course have to make the payment no matter how high rates go, but what if you could count on someone "paying the difference" between 6.5 percent and wherever rates happen to go? Say rates go to 7.5 percent, which is 1 percent higher than your limit. You could use a cap, with a notional of $1 million and strike price of 6.5 percent, such that you would receive $10,000 (1 percent of a million), or the payoff of the cap. If rates go to 8 percent you receive $15,000. And so on.

HEDGING WITH OPTIONS

In Chapter 5, small investor Greta buys call options on a stock, but not to hedge! She is a speculator with a view that the stock ZED is undervalued and the price will rise. In the example it turns out she is right and makes a nice profit. However, in reality the price of ZED could have fallen, causing her to lose 100 percent of her bet. Options can also, of course, be used for hedging. One common example is the "protective put," to provide "portfolio insurance" against a decline in the value of a stock portfolio. Here's an example:

Boxwood Capital, a small hedge fund,[2] has a diversified portfolio of U.S. stocks whose current value is roughly $120 million. They want to protect the portfolio against a large decline in value, and in particular do not want to it to fall below $110 million. And they're willing to pay a premium for such "insurance." So they buy put options on a market index, struck such that they will be compensated for a market decline taking their portfolio below the $110 million floor.

The instrument Boxwood uses is the SPX index option contract. It's a cash-settled, European style option whose underlier is the S&P 500 index. The value of the index changes all the time, pretty much in step with the overall market, and conveys an average price (adjusted for stock splits and what not) of 500 different stocks. Calls and puts are available at a variety of stock prices above and below the current index value, at a variety of expiration dates.

Now the index is currently at 1200, the current value of Boxwood's stock portfolio is $120 million, and they don't want it to fall below $110 million. So they buy 100,000 puts expiring in 3 months, with a strike price of 1100, for a premium of $6 per contract.[3] Why did they go long puts and not calls? Because they are hedging an ownership.

---

[2]Generally speaking, a *hedge fund* is just a firm that manages investor's money, not entirely unlike a mutual fund. However, they tend to invest money more aggressively than a typical mutual fund, using a combination of speculation, arbitrage, and whatever else they can dream up.

[3]In reality they buy one one-hundredth of this number of contracts at a premium 100 times this amount—but that's just an operational detail we'll leave out for clarity. The math works out the same.

Now fast forward 3 months. The S&P 500 index has fallen steeply to 1050. And because their portfolio is nearly identical in composition to the S&P 500 index portfolio, it's value has likewise fallen to $105 million. Damn. But their put options, struck at 1100, expire in-the-money with a payoff of 50 each. So their 100,000 options together pay off to the tune of $5 million. Add that to the $105 million value of their portfolio and the net value comes to $110 million, just where they wanted to be. Now this insurance didn't come for free, of course, as they paid 6 bucks per contract—more than half a million dollars. Had the index been equal to or greater than the strike price of 1100 on expiration, they would have lost the entire premium. And the "policy" was only for 3 months. If they want to continue this hedge, they'll need to keep buying puts.

The protective put is a common application of options, especially when stocks are trading at record highs. It's not a perfect hedge unless your stock portfolio matches exactly the portfolio of the index, but if set up properly it can at least offer some income in the event of a major "dip," to help offset the loss on your stocks. Also, when considering a protective put it's crucial to consider the option premium. An option is not free, so money you spend on a premium lowers the net return of your portfolio. This insurance ain't cheap. Between the portfolio mismatch and premium cost, deciding on whether or not a protective put makes sense for a particular situation is not a trivial exercise—but hey, what is?

HEDGING WITH CREDIT DERIVATIVES

In Chapter 6, an investor holding $10 million of corporate bonds purchased a credit default swap from an insurance company to protect it in the event the bond issuer declared bankruptcy. As mentioned previously, credit derivatives in this sense provide a "performance guarantee"—i.e., guaranteeing that the bond issuer will perform up to its financial obligations and remain solvent—in contrast to the price guarantee inherently provided by forwards, futures, swaps, and options. The CDS also differs from the other derivatives we've seen with respect to payoff. The payoff of an option, for instance, is proportional to the extent to which it expires in the money. If a 50-strike call option expires when the underlier is trading for 52, the payoff is 2. If the underlier is trading for 56, then the payoff is 6. And so on. Same for forwards, futures, and swaps. A CDS like our example, on the other hand, pays the holder $10 million no matter if the underlier (the bond) is worth $8 million or $2 million. This sort of "binary" or "all or nothing" characteristic can also be employed in exotic versions of just about any derivative, especially options, but it's not an inherent quality of those derivatives as it is with the CDS.

And that's what hedging with derivatives is all about. Now we turn to the valuation, or pricing of derivatives. Assessing the value of a derivative is crucial no matter what you use them for. And by the way, the following chapters on pricing include plenty of additional examples of risk management, so be sure to check those out if we've not quite slaked your thirst with the examples thus far.

CHAPTER 8

Pricing Forwards and Futures

The essence of pricing a forward or futures contract, and for that matter the swap, centers on taking an observed spot price and adjusting it for time. With each of these contracts you are dealing with a future transaction you are certain will occur. (With options you don't have that certainty, so the pricing task is more difficult.) Knowing with certainty that a transaction will occur allows us to price a contract by adjusting the spot price for things like interest, storage costs, and other costs that stem from the deferral of the transaction. We can safely disregard any probability of the underlier increasing or decreasing in value because it just doesn't matter. Provided the contract is not cancelled, the long party will buy and the short party will sell.

Recall the delivery or contract price for a forward or futures contract. It's the fixed price at which the long party commits to buy and the short party commits to sell at some point in the future. The essence of this entire chapter is all about determining a delivery price. And here's the key to that: For a new forward or futures contract, the delivery price is the one—and only one—such that the value of the contract is zero. In a forward or contract where the sole objective of each party is to lock in a price for a future transaction, neither party wants to pay any more than the other. And since a forward is zero-sum game, with one party's gain offset by the other's pain, the only fair price of a forward upon execution must be zero. Any other price gives one party a benefit and the other a cost. Now again we're only talking about the forward upon execution. Once the parties shake hands and time starts ticking, and the underlier price starts changing, the value of a contract is a different story. But at the moment of execution, neither party has an advantage over the other.[1]

The delivery price of a new, zero-value forward contract is known as a *forward price*. Its analog for futures is the *futures price*. Because forward prices and futures prices are calculated intuitively the same way, and to simplify the text, whenever you read "forward price" you can safely assume it applies to a futures price too. (There is, technically, a subtle difference between a forward and futures price due to daily settlement, a difference we won't go into.) We'll spend a fair amount of ink in this chapter on the various formulas for calculating a forward price. These formulas produce a forward price by adjusting a spot price for the costs and benefits of waiting for a delivery date, known collectively as *costs of carry* and encompassing such things as storage cost, interest charges, and the benefit or "convenience" of having a good in your possession.

It's not always easy when learning this stuff to get straight the differences between "delivery price" and "value" and "forward price." Just remember the *delivery price* is the guaranteed price at which the long party will buy and short party will sell, set in stone when the forward is first executed, never to change over the life of the forward. The *value* is a measure of how much better or worse-off the parties are for having entered into the forward agreement. And a *forward price* is the delivery price of a theoretical new contract whose value is zero. (This makes a forward "price" quite a different thing altogether from a stock "price.") If it still seems the

---

[1]Notice I conditioned the zero-value thing by saying it applies when the sole objective of *both* parties is to lock in the price for a future transaction. Oftentimes only one of the parties has a real concern about a future transaction and the other party enters into the forward only as a service to the other. Here we are talking about the "broker/ dealer" who specializes in selling (or buying) forwards. The broker/dealer for OTC forwards typically requires a fee for their service, and therefore adds some booty to the zero value, often by adjusting the delivery price. But theoretically, and certainly for the sake of learning these things, think of a forward value at execution as just a goose egg.

delivery price and forward price are the same thing, just think of it this way: A delivery price is associated with an actual forward contract (Farmer Joe agrees to sell 200 bushels of grapes to winemaker Leo for $5 per bushel next October). A delivery price may also include a fee paid from one party to the other. A forward price is the delivery price of a zero-value, theoretical forward contract that may or may not actually happen. It does not include any fees.

And what is the value of an existing forward or futures contract? As we'll see, for a forward it's the present value of the difference between its delivery price and the current forward price. (If there is no cost of carry, there's a simpler way to look at it.) The value of a futures contract is the difference between the current futures price for that contract and the previous day's closing futures price. Forward contract value and futures contract value differ due to daily settlement, and we'll see further on exactly why.

DISCOUNTING, PRESENT VALUES, AND FUTURE VALUES

If you're comfortable with the concepts and mechanics of discounting and continuous compounding, you can jump right over this section. If not, you will be delighted to know that the vast majority of math required for pricing forwards and futures involves just one mathematical procedure: adjusting monetary values for time. The fundamental concept here is that money invested (or lent) grows with time. Going forward in time, in which we calculate a *future value*, takes a known value today and calculates a value for a future date given some interest rate or other rate that behaves like interest. Adjusting backwards is known as *discounting*, and here we calculate a *present value* given some future value and an interest rate.

Think of time as a line going off endlessly in either direction from a zero point at its center. The zero point represents a time at which you know the value of something. All points to the right represent a later time, and all points to the left an earlier time. Future valuation takes a monetary value known at time zero (typically "now") and asks, what does it grow to as we go forward in time? Present valuation takes a monetary value known at a time zero and asks, what does it shrink to as we go back to some earlier time?

FIGURE 8-1

Future Valuation and Present Valuation

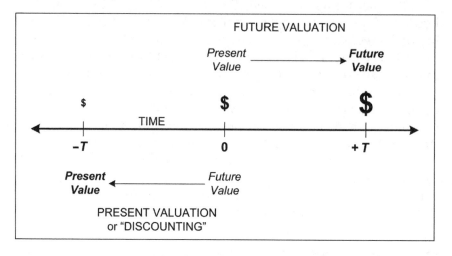

That "earlier time" is typically the present time or "now." Take a look at Figure 8-1.

One of the reasons money can grow with time is, of course, interest. Interest is the price of borrowing money (or payment received for lending it) and is just a growth rate. From our example above, a present value of $100 (think of this as the investment or "principal" amount) in an account that pays 6 percent annually grows to $106 (a future value) in one year. Here's the math:[2]

$$FV = PV * (1 + rt)$$
$$FV = 100 * (1 + [.06 * 1]) = 100 * 1.06$$
$$FV = 106$$

where

$$FV = \text{future value}$$
$$PV = \text{present value}$$
$$r = \text{annual rate of interest}$$
$$t = \text{time in years}$$

---

[2]Notice we indicate multiplication both by the asterisk (*) and by squishing two symbols together (*rt*). We'll do this throughout, choosing whichever seems to express things more clearly.

Now the key to how much money actually grows is not just the interest rate but also the *compounding frequency*. In other words, we need to know the frequency at which earned interest is added to the principal in order for the earned interest itself to earn interest. In the one year example above, we assumed annual compounding so it wasn't an issue. But say interest is compounded every 6 months. After the first 6 months, we have earned \$3 of interest (I), like so:

$$I_{first-six-months} = 100*(.06)(.5) = 100*.03 = 3$$

Notice we used a t factor of .5 for one-half year. This \$3 of interest is added to the principal, giving us 103 on which to calculate interest for the second 6 months. Here then is the total value of this investment after one year:

$$I_{first-six-months} = 100*(.06)(.5) = 100*.03 = 3$$
$$I_{second-six-months} = 103*(.03) = 3.09$$
$$FV = PV + I_{first-six-months} + I_{second-six-months}$$
$$FV = 100 + 3 + 3.09 = 106.09$$

So we earn a tad more interest—\$6.09 instead of \$6 even—by compounding every 6 months instead of annually. And what if we compound every 3 months, or quarterly?

$$I_{q1} = 100*(.015) = 1.5$$
$$I_{q2} = 101.5*(.015) = 1.5225$$
$$I_{q3} = 103.0225*(.015) = 1.5453$$
$$I_{q4} = 104.5678*(.015) = 1.5685$$
$$FV = PV + I_{q1} + I_{q2} + I_{q3} + I_{q4} = 106.14$$

Now we earn even more interest—\$6.14—by compounding quarterly. Clearly, the more frequently we compound, the more interest we earn. So how far does this go? What if we compound daily? Or every minute? Or how about continuously? Is there some limit to how much we can earn? Yes. The *limit* is in fact fundamental to calculus, which gives us a remarkably simple formula for calculating the end value of an investment where interest is compounded continuously. Here it is for our example above:

$$FV = PV*e^{rt}$$
$$FV = 100*e^{.06(1)} = 106.18$$

So the most interest we can earn is 6.18 for a maximum future value of 106.18. But what is this "e" that we raised to the power of our annual interest rate? It's Euler's Number, the base of the natural exponential function e^x, an irrational number that starts out 2.7182 ... Now you can ignore that fact and let your calculator worry about it. Any decent calculator has a button for raising e to some power, or exponent (if you don't have such a calculator, go get one). And don't let this Euler stuff scare you away. It really is the simplest way to deal with interest calculations.

For periods longer than one year, we simply increase the t factor. So for a future value over, say, two years we have:

$$FV = PV * e^{r(2)}$$
$$FV = 100 * 1.1275 = 112.75$$

Now so far we have calculated future values. How do we go backwards in time, to calculate the present value of some known future value and a given interest rate? Just swap the FV and PV and put a negative sign on the interest rate:[3]

$$PV = FV * e^{-rt}$$

Let's give this a test drive by starting with our one year future value of 106.18 and our interest rate of 6 percent. What is the present value, or principal required today to grow to this future value in one year's time? Using the formula above and rounding the result to the nearest penny, we get:

$$PV = 106.18 * e^{-.06(1)}$$
$$PV = 106.18 * .9418 = 100$$

Just as we expect. And what is the present value when the 1-year future value is 100, again using 6 percent?

$$PV = 100 * e^{-.06(1)} = 94.18$$

---

[3] Recall from algebra raising something to a negative power is equivalent to dividing 1 by the same thing raised to a positive, so if you prefer you can think of the present value formula as:

$$PV = FV \times \frac{1}{e^{rt}}$$

FIGURE 8-2

Present Value and Future Value Examples

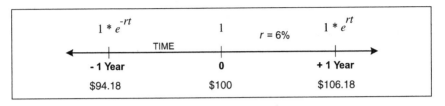

Figure 8-2 shows how it all looks on the timeline. And formulas 8.1 and 8.2 are the future value and present value formulas for calculating changes in value as time glides in either direction, due to interest or any other factor that causes money to grow continuously with time. Notice that the only difference is the sign of the interest rate factor.

$$FV = PV * e^{rt} \qquad (8.1)$$

$$PV = FV * e^{-rt} \qquad (8.2)$$

where

FV = future value
PV = present value
e = Euler's Number = 2.71828183 ...
r = annual rate of interest
t = time in years

COST OF CARRY

Consider the value of a forward upon delivery. That's just the payoff, as illustrated by the payoff diagram, which we know is given by the difference between the spot price and delivery price. Recall the tortilla maker's long forward to buy 1000 bushels of corn at $25. The spot price on the delivery date was $28 for a valuation of ($28 − 25) * 1000 or $3000.

So what then is the value of a forward on some date before delivery? There are two basic components. The first is the spot-delivery difference we just talked about, which naturally changes with time. (The spot price changes over the life of a forward, but the delivery price does not; the difference between them must change as well. Easy.) The second component is known as *cost of carry*. This is the cost of maintaining or "carrying" a forward position over time. Consider storage. Commodity underliers such as corn and oil must be stored, and storage costs money. And who pays this cost? Until delivery day, the goods are held by the short party, so they incur this cost, which will affect the value of a forward. (Think what a merchant might say if you ask to buy something from his inventory but not for 6 months: "You want me to keep this stuff for 6 months and then you buy it from me? Okay but you have to pay me for storage...")

Another cost of carry common to all forwards is interest. Now interest is simply the cost of borrowing money, or put another way, the payment for loaning or investing it. And how is this a cost of carry? Consider that a long party to a forward contract is obligated to buy the underlier—but not, of course, until the delivery date. Were they to buy spot they would be out some cash. But with a forward they get to hang on to that cash and can invest it, earning interest. And the short party, of course, doesn't get that cash until delivery. So they miss the opportunity to invest the proceeds of the sale, thus incurring an *opportunity cost*. (To the short party interest truly is a "cost" of carry; to the long party it's actually a benefit, but we still call it cost of carry.)

Other costs of carry can include income paid to the holder of an underlier, such as dividends for stock underliers (these are periodic payments to the stockholder, i.e., the short party) and something less tangible known as *convenience yield* (this is the benefit of possessing the underlier, such as the ability to survive a shortage). We'll get back all of these a bit later on.

THE IDEA BEHIND A FORWARD PRICE

By piecing together what we've seen so far, the value of a forward at any time is basically the sum of two things: the difference between the ever-changing spot price and never-changing delivery price, and cost of carry (which can be a positive or negative value as we will see in a bit). Here's how it looks as a basic formula for forward value:

$$ForwardValue_{LONG} = (SpotPrice - DeliveryPrice) + Carry$$
$$ForwardValue_{SHORT} = (DeliveryPrice - SpotPrice) + Carry$$

Now think about what you know when setting up a new forward contract. You know the spot price, you know the carry, and you know the value has to be zero. You don't know the delivery price. The delivery price of a new contract—the forward price—is the only unknown factor at the outset of a deal. So to calculate a forward price, we just "back it out" of the basic valuation formula. Consider again the formula for a long contract:

$$ForwardValue_{LONG} = (SpotPrice - DeliveryPrice) + Carry$$

When crafting a forward, the parties have no control over spot price (call it s), nor over cost of carry (C), nor over the value of the forward (v), which must be zero. They can only tweak the delivery price (F, for forward price). Rearranging the basic formula, we get an algebraic expression that looks like this:

$$v = (s + C) - F$$

This equation just says the value of a forward is the result of adding spot price and cost of carry (which remember can be negative) and subtracting the forward price. Recall that this is basically how we calculated the value of the tortilla maker's forward, only we valued as of delivery date, so there was no carry. Now v at inception is zero, so let's plug that in and rearrange:

$$0 = (s + C) - F$$
$$F_{LONG} = s + C$$

So a forward price is just spot plus cost of carry. And by "cost" we mean an actual cost to the short party. If it's a "benefit" to the short party, we subtract it. Let's make our formula clearer by separating C into c (lower case) for cost to the short party and b for benefit to the short party:

$$C = c - b$$

Ergo:

$$F_{LONG} = s + c - b$$

Consider a one-year forward on a barrel of oil whose spot price upon execution is $100. By executing such a forward, the long party is obligated to buy that barrel of oil, but not for 1 year. If they bought today they would be out $100. But they get to keep that $100 for 1 year and put it to work earning interest. Let's say the interest rate is 6 percent with annual compounding and the rate is absolutely guaranteed, or "risk-free." (More on this later.) Upon execution of the forward, and the simultaneous investing of $100, the long party can count on receiving $6 of interest on the same date they will buy the oil. They will also get their $100 back, giving them $106 to buy that barrel of oil. Therefore the correct delivery price for this contract, assuming no other cost of carry, is $106. And what does the short party think of this price? Suits them fine. Because on execution of the forward, they are obligated to sell the oil, but not for 1 year, so they lose the opportunity to invest the $100 and earn that $6. So the extra $6 compensates them for the "opportunity cost" of selling forward versus selling spot. Clearly with respect to interest, the fair delivery price for this deal is spot price adjusted for interest, or $106.

Now oil is a physical good that must be stored, and storage costs money. Now the long party need not pay for storage between now and delivery price (they don't have it yet to store). The short party does. Say the annual storage cost of a barrel of oil is $7. This is another cost (an actual out-of-pocket cost this time, not an opportunity cost) to add to the interest we calculated above. So now the fair price of this forward is $113, or $100 + $6 + $7.

THE RISK-FREE INTEREST RATE

Before we get to the formulas, we need to think about what interest rate we'll use. For virtually all derivative valuations, we use a *risk-free interest rate* for discounting. (For interest rate derivatives, we generally use a different rate for calculating payments.) The risk-free or "reference" rate is essentially a guaranteed rate of return on an investment with no risk of loss. Why use a risk-free rate? Strange as this may seem, it turns out we can safely price derivatives assuming all investors are perfectly "risk neutral" and don't really give a dang whether prices go up or down. This characteristic is known as *risk-neutrality* and we'll explain it later. For now, suffice it so say we can disregard risk preferences when pricing derivatives and can therefore eliminate the "risk premium" component of an interest rate and use what's left over. One risk-free rate commonly used for derivative valuation is known as *Libor*. It is based on the "London Inter Bank Offered Rate" (hence the name) and commonly incorporates rates paid by U.S. Treasury securities as well. There's much more about Libor the appendix, "All About Interest."

The risk-free rate is almost always lower than a rate-of-return that carries risk. Why? It's that risk premium again. Think of interest as a reward for taking risk. The more risk you take, the more you earn. The stock market, for example, generally provides a return greater than U.S. Treasuries over a sufficiently long period of time. But as any stock investor knows, that market can also return quite a bit less than Treasuries, especially over a short period of time. Stocks are riskier than Treasuries over the long haul, so they return more to their investors. And consider the return of "investing" in roulette, blackjack, or a slot machine. You can make quite a handsome return, but only by taking the considerable risk of losing your investment (er, bet) entirely. A U.S. Savings Bond won't make you wealthy, but you can count on Uncle Sam to return your investment and at least a little bit more. Uncle Sammy the blackjack dealer offers no such assurance.

Enough of the background stuff! We're ready now for the formulas for calculating a forward price.

FORWARD PRICE FORMULAS

Basic Forward

The simplest of underlier requires no storage cost and generates no income (e.g., dividends). The only cost of carry is interest. The forward price for such an underlier is just the future value of the underlier given a spot price S, interest rate r, and time period t. It's given by Formula 8.3.

$$F = Se^{rt} \tag{8.3}$$

Example: You agree to buy from your brother 100 shares of stock in MGrove Inc. in 6 months. MGrove pays no dividends and is now trading for 15.50. The risk-free interest rate is 2 percent. What is the fair market forward price? We are given all we need for the right side:

$$S = 15.50 * 100 = 1550$$
$$r = .02$$
$$t = .5$$

The value of e, of course, never changes, and we let a calculator worry about converting it to a number anyway. So putting it all together we have:

$$F = Se^{rt}$$
$$F = 1550 * e^{.02(.5)}$$
$$F = 1550 * 1.01005$$
$$F = 1565.58$$

The fair-market delivery price for this contract is $1565.58, or $15.66 per share.

Forward with Storage

When an underlier incurs a fixed storage cost, the forward price is the future value of the sum of two things: spot S plus the present value of storage U. (By "fixed" we just mean it does not change with the price of the underlier.) It's given by Formula 8.4.

$$F = (S + U)e^{rt} \qquad (8.4)$$

Example: Indostan Energy agrees to buy from the Diablo Drillery 5000 barrels of crude oil one year forward. The oil is selling on the spot market for $32 per barrel. The cost of storing this kind of oil is $1.50 per barrel per quarter, payable at the beginning of each quarter. The risk-free interest rate is 3 percent. What is the correct forward price for this deal?

First let's handle storage. For the formula we need the present value of storage costs, from which we will calculate a future value. (Sounds weird, I know, but just hang in there.) Over the life of this forward there will be four payments for storage made at the start of each quarter in the amount of $7500 (i.e., 5000 barrels at $1.50 each). Think of these as four cash flows. One occurs now (upon execution of the forward), one in 3 months, one in 6 and one in 9. To calculate the present value of all storage, we just calculate the PV of each of the four cash flows and add up the results. Notice the PV of the first cash flow does not including any discounting.

$$PV_{storage} = cf_{0m} + cf_{3m} + cf_{6m} + cf_{9m}$$
$$PV = 7500 + 7500e^{-.03(.25)} + 7500e^{-.03(.5)} + 7500e^{-.03(.75)}$$
$$PV = 7500 + 7443.96 + 7388.34 + 7333.13$$
$$PV = 29{,}665.43$$

Now we have everything in present value terms, so we just plug it into the formula to get the future value of the whole enchilada:

$$S = 32 * 5000 = 160{,}000$$
$$U = 29{,}665.43$$
$$r = .03$$
$$t = 1$$

Putting it all together we have:

$$F = (S + U)e^{rt}$$
$$F = (160{,}000 + 29{,}665.43) * e^{.03(1)}$$
$$F = 195{,}441.60$$

The fair-market delivery price for this contract is $195,441.60, or just about $39 per barrel.

When storage costs change with the spot price of the under-lier, we call those *proportional storage* costs. Such costs are not unlike the cost of interest, which also depends on the price of the under-lier. The forward price of an underlier with proportional storage cost, then, is the future value of the underlier given a spot price S, annual interest rate r, and time period t, with the interest rate "adjusted" by the proportional storage cost u. It's given by Formula 8.5. What's an example of a proportional storage cost? Spoilage. If some portion of a good is expected to spoil, we can think of that as a "storage" cost to the short party.

$$F = Se^{(r+u)t} \tag{8.5}$$

Example: Juice-maker SqueezeMax agrees to buy 1000 bushels of apples from apple grower Joe in 3 months. Joe knows from experience that stored apples lose 2 percent of their value to bugs, mice, and rot. Apples are currently selling wholesale for $6 per bushel. The risk-free interest rate is 4 percent.

There is no precalculation this time, as we already have what we need:

$$S = 1000 * 6 = 6000$$
$$u = .02$$
$$r = .04$$
$$t = .25$$

Putting it all together we have:

$$F = Se^{(r+u)t}$$
$$F = 6000 * e^{(.04+.02)(.25)}$$
$$F = 6000 * e^{.015}$$
$$F = 6090.68$$

The fair-market delivery price for this contract is $6090.68.

Forward with Income

Income, such as dividends on a stock underlier, are like storage costs in reverse. They represent benefits to the short party. Now the forward price is just the future value of spot S less the present value of income I. See Formula 8.6.

$$F = (S - I)e^{rt} \qquad (8.6)$$

Example: You agree to buy from your sister 400 shares of stock in Acme Industries in 1 year. Acme is currently trading for $36.00 per share. Acme pays a quarterly dividend to its shareholders; the expected dividend is $0.25 cents per share. The risk-free interest rate is 2 percent. What is fair market forward price?

As with storage, we need the PV of income. Over the life of this forward, there will be four dividend payments (cash flows) made at the end of each quarter for $100 (i.e., 400 shares at 0.25 each). One occurs in 3 months, the next in 6, then 9, then 12.

To calculate the present value of all storage, we just calculate the PV of each of the four cash flows and add up the results.

$$PV_{income} = div_{3m} + div_{6m} + div_{9m} + div_{12m}$$
$$PV = 100e^{-.02(.25)} + 100e^{-.02(.5)} + 100e^{-.02(.75)} + 100e^{-.02(1)}$$
$$PV = 99.50 + 99.01 + 98.51 + 98.02$$
$$PV = 395.04$$

We are given all we need for the right side of the formula:

$$S = 36 * 400 = 14{,}400$$
$$I = 395.04$$
$$r = .02$$
$$t = 1$$

So putting it all together we have:

$$F = (S - I)e^{rt}$$
$$F = (14{,}400 - 395.04) * e^{.02(1)}$$
$$F = 14{,}287.88$$

The fair-market delivery price for this contract is $14,287.88.

Sometimes underlier income is proportional to its spot price. For example, when the underlier is a stock index with dozens or hundreds of individual stocks, we treat the dividend income from such a "basket" as some percentage of the index spot price. (Much easier than figuring the actual dividend stream of hundreds of stocks!) So as with proportional storage, we adjust the interest rate (r) by the proportional income factor (i) when calculating the future value of the underlier. See Formula 8.7.

$$F = Se^{(r-i)t} \tag{8.7}$$

Example: You agree to buy from your broker 200 shares of the Midland stock index (MLX) in one year. MLX is an index composed of stock from the 50 largest agricultural companies in the Midwestern United States and is currently trading for $54.00 per share.[4] MLX is expected to pay an annual dividend equal to .5 percent (i.e., .005) of its share price. The risk-free interest rate is 3 percent.

---

[4]Don't call your broker. MLX exists only in my head.

This is easier than it might seem. Again, no precalculation of *PV*s this time, as we already have what we need:

$$S = 200 * 54 = 10{,}800$$
$$r = .03$$
$$i = .005$$
$$t = 1$$

Putting it all together we have:

$$F = Se^{(r-i)t}$$
$$F = 10{,}800 * e^{(.03-.005)(1)}$$
$$F = 10{,}800 * e^{.025(1)}$$
$$F = 11{,}073.40$$

The fair-market delivery price for this contract is $11,073.40.

Holding an underlier can have a less tangible benefit than income, known as a *convenience yield*. For example, if there's a shortage on a good, it can be quite nice (convenient) to have it on hand. Dealing with this convenience yield is computationally identical to dealing with proportional income. Just substitute the convenience yield for the income rate, as in Formula 8.8.

$$F = Se^{(r-y)t} \qquad (8.8)$$

Incidentally, convenience yields are often implied from, or "backed out of" observed market prices and not explicitly entered into a formula like the other factors. They are something of a "fudge factor" to make the equality between forward prices and their other input factors hold true.

Forward Price of Currency

When the underlier is a foreign currency, we consider not only the domestic interest rate but also the (risk-free) foreign rate. No need to go into details, but suffice it to say that exchange rates are influenced in part by prevailing interest rates in the respective countries. Bottom line, the foreign interest rate represents income to short party and is just proportional income. See Formula 8.9.

$$F = Se^{(r-rf)t} \qquad (8.9)$$

Example: You agree to buy 5000 Tuluvian Krinkets from a currency dealer in 9 months. Krinkets are currently trading for $0.35 U.S. dollars. (When dealing with foreign currency, just think of each unit of the other currency as a share of stock, which you buy with some amount of local currency.) The risk-free interest rate in Tuluvia is 2 percent. The risk-free interest rate at home is 6 percent. This is exactly like a forward on an underlier with proportional income, replacing i with rf (foreign rate). Here's what we've got:

$$S = 5000 * 0.35 = 1750$$
$$r = .06$$
$$rf = .02$$
$$t = .75$$

Putting it all together we have:

$$F = Se^{(r-rf)t}$$
$$F = 1750 * e^{(.06-.02)(.75)}$$
$$F = 1750 * e^{.03}$$
$$F = 1803.30$$

The fair-market delivery price for this contract is $1803.30.

Forward Price Summary

Here are the forward price formulas in a nutshell. Just remember that U and I are the present values of storage and income, respectively. If they are given as future values, you need to discount them before plugging them into these formulas.

Basic Forward Price	$F = Se^{rt}$	(8.3)
With Fixed Storage	$F = (S + U)e^{rt}$	(8.4)
With Proportional Storage	$F = Se^{(r+u)t}$	(8.5)
With Fixed Income	$F = (S - I)e^{rt}$	(8.6)
With Proportional Income	$F = Se^{(r-i)t}$	(8.7)
With Convenience Yield	$F = Se^{(r-y)t}$	(8.8)
Foreign Currency Forward	$F = Se^{(r-rf)t}$	(8.9)

Putting these all together we get Formula 8.10:

$$ForwardPrice = (S + U - I)e^{(r+u-i-y-rf)t} \qquad (8.10)$$

where

$$S = \text{spot price}$$
$$U = \text{fixed storage costs}$$
$$I = \text{fixed income}$$
$$r = \text{risk-free interest rate}$$
$$u = \text{proportional storage cost}$$
$$i = \text{proportional income}$$
$$y = \text{convenience yield}$$
$$rf = \text{foreign interest rate}$$

VALUING AN EXISTING FORWARD OR FUTURES POSITION

So far we've talked about calculating a forward price or futures price for the purpose of initiating a new contract. At inception, the value of a forward and otherwise identical futures are both the same: zero. After inception their values must be calculated differently, due to the daily settlement inherent to futures contracts, which does not take place with forwards.

Forward Contract Value

The value of a forward contract after inception is the present value of the difference between its delivery price and the delivery price of a theoretical new contract, i.e., the current forward price. This applies to any forward contract. Think of this "theoretical new contract" as just one for which we calculate a delivery price—in order to get a forward price—and it has the same underlying, quantity, and delivery date, and any other feature of the forward contract we wish to value. Its delivery price, like all forwards at inception, is equal to the forward price F. So we have two forwards, one in our hands and one in our heads, whose only difference is the amount the long party will pay on delivery: F versus K.

The value of the contract in our hands is thus the present value of the difference between F and K, as shown in Formulas 8.11 and 8.12.

$$ForwardValue_{LONG} = PV(F - K) = (F - K)e^{-rt} \qquad (8.11)$$
$$ForwardValue_{SHORT} = PV(K - F) = (K - F)e^{-rt} \qquad (8.12)$$

Why do we discount? Because the difference between F and K is a future value, and we're interested in a present value. So we need to discount it to today.

Consider our previous example where you executed a 6 month forward contract with your brother to buy 100 shares of MGrove stock at a delivery price of $15.66 per share. Three months have gone by and MGrove is currently trading for $15.80. What is the value of your position? Intuitively we can expect the value to be positive, as we have a contract to purchase for $15.66 what is currently trading for $15.80. Let's see if that bears out.

First we calculate a forward price using a spot price of $15.80 and time to delivery T of 3 months, or 0.25 years. (The risk-free interest rate r has not changed.) Here then are the inputs:

$$S = 15.80 * 100 = 1580$$
$$r = .03$$
$$t = .25$$

Here's the current forward price:

$$F = Se^{(r-i)t}$$
$$F = 1580 * e^{(.03)(.25)}$$
$$F = 1591.89$$

The forward price (i.e., the fair-market delivery price for a hypothetical new forward contract) is $1591.89. Now we have what we need for the long forward value formula:

$$F = 1591.89$$
$$K = 1565.58$$
$$r = .03$$
$$t = .25$$

Putting the formula to work we have:

$$Value = (F - K)e^{-rt}$$
$$Value = (1591.89 - 1565.58)e^{-.03(.25)}$$
$$Value = 26.11$$

The value of our contract is $26.11.

There's an easier way to calculate the value of a forward contract when there are no costs or benefits to holding the underlier. That is, no cost of carry except for interest. It's just the difference between the spot price of the underlier and the present value of the delivery price, as shown in Formulas 8.13 and 8.14.

$$Forward Value_{LONG(NO\ C.C.)} = S - PV(K) = S - Ke^{-rt} \quad (8.13)$$
$$Forward Value_{SHORT(NO\ C.C.)} = PV(K) - S = Ke^{-rt} - S \quad (8.14)$$

In the previous example, there were no costs of carry except interest. Here then are the inputs to valuing that contract using this different approach:

$$S = 1580.00$$
$$K = 1565.58$$
$$r = .03$$
$$t = .25$$

Putting it all together we have:

$$S - Ke^{-rt}$$
$$= 1580.00 - 1565.58e^{-.03(.25)}$$
$$= 26.11$$

Same result as before.

Futures Contract Value

The value of a futures contract is rather different from the value of an otherwise identical forward contract because the payoff from a futures contract is realized at the end of every trading day. The value of a forward, recall, is generally realized at the end of the contract's term. So at any time, a futures contract's value is driven solely by how much its futures price has changed since yesterday. The value of a futures, then, is the difference between the current futures price and the futures price at the end of the previous trading day when everyone settled up.

Recall the Royal Mill and their 10 futures contracts to buy wheat. Say one day the futures price on those contracts closed at $3.10. By the middle of the next day, the futures price was at $3.20. What is the value of their position then?

$$Futures\ Value_{LONG} = Number\ of\ Contracts * Bushels\ per\ contract$$
$$* (F_{NOW} - F_{YESTERDAY})$$
$$= 10 * 5000 * (3.20 - 3.10)$$
$$= \$5000$$

At the moment their futures position has a market value of $5000. This does not reflect, however, profits realized and collected previously. Recall the futures price was 3.00 when Royal Mill put on these contracts, so prior to now they'd already collected $5000 using the same math.

To calculate the value of an existing futures contract, we simply need the current futures price and the futures price from the previous day. The value is just the difference between the two. For position value we, of course, need to know the number of contracts involved, and whether one is long or short. Here's the formula for the value of a long position:

$$F_{long} = (FP_{now} - FP_{previousclose}) * number\ of\ contracts$$

where FP_{now} is the futures price as calculated right now, $FP_{previousclose}$ is the futures price at the end of the previous trading day, and F_{long} is the fair market value of one long futures contract right now. Whether the value is positive or negative depends on whether the futures price has increased or decreased.

Another example: Say you are long 1000 corn futures. The current futures price is 2.82 per bushel. The futures price at yesterday's close was 2.85. You can tell already your position has negative value because the futures price is dropping; you are committed to buy at a price greater than you would have to with a brand new contract. And sure enough…

$$F_{long} = (FP_{now} - FP_{previousclose}) * number\ of\ contracts$$
$$F_{long} = (2.82 - 2.85) * 1000$$
$$F_{long} = -30.00$$

The formula for a short futures position is only slightly different. Here are both Formulas, 8.15 and 8.16, together:

$$F_{long} = (FP_{now} - FP_{previousclose}) * number\ of\ contracts \qquad (8.15)$$
$$F_{short} = (FP_{previousclose} - FP_{now}) * number\ of\ contracts \qquad (8.16)$$

And this all leads us to something rather peculiar about futures: they are never literally "cancelled." Once you execute a contract, you are stuck with it till delivery. Alarming? No worries. To get out of a futures position (i.e., to rid yourself of its obligations and payoff potential) you simply execute a new, offsetting contract. Say again you are long 1000 corn futures. The current futures price is 2.82 and the futures price at yesterday's close was 2.85, just like above. Because you are losing money on the position—recall you're down 30.00—you decide to short 1000 (at 2.82) to get out and not lose any more. By the end of the day the futures price has dropped even further, to 2.80. Now consider the value of your two positions at settlement (for the short position we use the futures price at the time of execution instead of the previous closing price).

$$F_{long} = (FP_{now} - FP_{previousclose}) * number\ of\ contracts$$
$$F_{long} = (2.80 - 2.85) * 1000 = -50.00$$
$$F_{short} = (FP_{execution} - FP_{now}) * number\ of\ contracts$$
$$F_{short} = (2.82 - 2.80) * 1000 = 20.00$$
$$F_{long} + F_{short} = -50.00 + 20.00 = -30.00$$

There you have it. The same result as before. At the end of the day you are just where you were when you decided to bail, even though prices continued to decline. Now in subsequent days the two positions' settlements will cancel each other exactly, so you are effectively out of your long position.

NO-ARBITRAGE PRICING

Hopefully by now this manner of calculating the value of a forward seems reasonable enough, as the relationship between forward prices and costs of carry seem to make sense for the reasons given. But there is a stronger proof these relationships are true based on a principle known simply as *no-arbitrage*. All derivatives are priced using this principle, which basically says this: The fair price of any derivative is the one that prevents arbitrage.

Recall from the previous chapter an arbitrageur seeks to profit from pricing errors, that is, cases in which two prices are available for essentially the same thing. The arbitrageur simply buys at the lower price and sells at the higher, making a profit with virtually no risk. Pretty cool, huh? Although this can and indeed does happen in practice, arbitrage opportunities are fleeting. Why? Because once an arbitrage opportunity is discovered, more and more trades will occur by market participants going for that riskless profit—free money is highly desirable, after all. And this trading activity itself adjusts prices such that the arbitrage opportunity goes away. If this isn't clear, recall that a fundamental determinant of prices in a large and open market is supply and demand. As demand goes up or down, so do prices. Increased trading is just increased demand, so arbitrage is self-eliminating.

How might we "arb" a mispriced forward? First consider an imaginary type of derivative we'll call a Now. A Now is just like a forward but the delivery price is spot and the delivery date is right now. Suppose we come across a Now contract on MGrove stock offered for 15.00 when the spot price of MGrove is 15.50. What do we do? Buy the Now at 15.00, take delivery of the stock, and sell it on the spot market for 15.50 and make 50 cents. Do it for a million shares and make 500 thousand. Now all that selling will drive the price down, which is why arbitrage opportunities are essentially self-destructing, but you get the basic idea.

Okay, so that's a silly example but it makes the point, and you arbitrage mispriced forwards the same way. You just have to consider the time value of money. Recall our example of a simple forward on MGrove stock? With spot at 15.50 and interest at 2 percent, the fair market 6-month forward price (also known as the "theoretical price") is around $15.65. Suppose there is a liquid market (i.e., ample buyers and sellers) for the contracts at $15.65. But suppose you come across someone offering the same 6-month forward for $15.55. Clearly that forward is priced below market. It's "too cheap" by 10 cents, and we can get that 10 cents as follows:

Now

- Buy (go long) a bunch of forward contracts at 15.50 each.
- Sell (go short) the same number of forward contracts at 15.65.

Six Months from Now

- Take delivery of MGrove stock and pay 15.50 per share.
- Deliver those shares and receive 15.65 per share.
- Pocket 10 cents profit per share.

There are other ways to arbitrage a mispriced forward (for instance using stock and cash), but in any case you always "buy low and sell high." That's what we did here, buying at 15.50 and selling at 15.65. We won't go further into arbitrage, but just know it's out there in a big way. It is an awesome and pervasive force affecting nearly every one of the gazillion prices out there in the global financial marketplace.

Contango and Normal Backwardation

Now here are some colorful terms you may run across. Recall from the previous chapter we learned what goes into a forward price, and above we noted how a futures price is calculated the same way. Now when you calculate a futures price it is going to either be greater than or less than the expected spot price on delivery, which is just today's spot price adjusted forward for interest—not for storage or any other cost of carry. When a futures price is greater than expected spot, the market is said to be in *contango*. This will tend to be the case for underliers with high storage costs such as gold and other precious metals. Look back at the forward price formulas for the math that makes this so. When a futures price is less than expected spot, the market is said to be in *normal backwardation*. Contango is more or less the "normal" situation, so "normal backwardation" just refers to the not-so-normal case.

CHAPTER 9

Pricing Swaps

THE SWAP AS A BUNCH OF CASH FLOWS

And how do we value a swap? The easiest way, and therefore the way it's often done in practice, is remarkably simple in concept: View each leg as a string of future cash flows (as if each leg were a bond) and add up their present values. That's it. Nothing difficult at all, but it can be rather tedious. You need to know the precise number of days between now and every cash flow, the precise interest rate fraction to apply to each for each accrual, and so on. But isn't this what computers are for? Precisely. To any old computer, the valuation of a swap is a snap, provided, of course, that some human gave it the right instructions. But let's not let computers have all the fun; let's compute the value of a plain vanilla ourselves with just paper and ink and our heads.

In the examples below we'll refer to spot rates and forward rates and yield curves. A *spot rate* is a rate of interest for money borrowed right now, and a *forward rate* is for money to be borrowed in the future. A *yield curve* conveys interest rates (spot or forward) for various borrowing periods. Each of these is explained in detail in the appendix, All About Interest.

And speaking of interest, it can be helpful to keep in mind that it has two important but entirely distinct roles when it comes to interest rate derivatives. Firstly, it is the underlier of these derivatives. More precisely, it is how we measure the price of the underlier, which is really just money borrowed or lent. Second, interest is used for discounting future values to present values (and occasionally vice versa). Because of this dual role of interest, we actually have two rates to keep in mind—a rate for pricing and a rate for discounting. And tangling matters even more, an interest rate whether for pricing or discounting is only for some given length of time. Interest rates vary by maturity, so when we speak of a rate we're really speaking of an entire yield curve. Anyway, just some things to keep in mind.

An Existing Swap

Consider two businesses, the Finch Corporation and Radley Incorporated, who execute a 2-year swap on March 1, 2006. Finch is using this swap to effectively convert a 3.9 percent fixed-rate loan obligation into a floating rate, perhaps believing rates will on average "float below 3.9 percent" over the life of the loan. He pays floating and receives fixed. Radley, then, pays fixed and receives floating. Now imagine today's date is May 23, 2007 or a bit less than a year before maturity. Let's calculate the value of the swap, to Finch, as of that date (the value to Radley will be the same with the sign flipped). This is a rather plain vanilla with quarterly payments and identical terms on each leg. Here are the details:[1]

Notional	1,000,000 USD
Effective date	March 1, 2006
Maturity date	Feb 29, 2008
Discount curve	USD Libor
Compounding	None
Averaging	None
Amortizing	None
Fixed Tenor	3 months
Floating Tenor	3 months
Coupon date	22nd
Stubs	Short
Day Basis	Actual/365
Calendar	New York
Adjustment	Modified Following
Fixed Rate	3.90 percent
Rate Index	USD Libor

---

[1]For simplicity we'll ignore some picayunish details often found in actual swaps, things like reset offsets and reset adjustments.

We also need "the market," that is, Libor interest rates for 3-month loans commencing at various points in the future—forward rates. These are captured nicely in a yield curve. We need two curves, actually, both a 3-month forward curve for calculating payments and a spot curve for discounting them to today. Let's borrow the curves we construct in the appendix, as shown in Figure 9-1.

And here are the spot and forward rates from the curves, going out 2 years, which we'll use in our calculations:

Term	Spot	3m Fwd
3m	3.53	3.55
6m	3.54	3.64
9m	3.59	3.67
12m	3.63	3.71
15m	3.67	3.73
18m	3.70	3.80
21m	3.75	3.81
24m	3.78	3.84

We now have the swap terms, the market, and the date on which we want to value the swap. The previous payment, on both legs, was May 22, 2007 or yesterday. So today is the first day of the new coupon

FIGURE 9-1

Libor Yield Curves

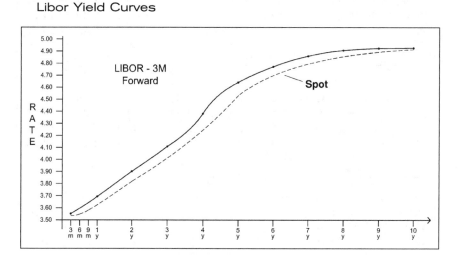

period. Now we can identify the remaining payments as our first step in calculating the value. The coupon date is the 22nd of the month, the fixed and floating tenors are both 3 months, and the swap maturity date is Feb 29, 2008. So the remaining payments must be:

Fixed Payment	Floating Payment
Aug 22, 2007	Aug 22, 2007
Nov 23, 2007	Nov 23, 2007
Feb 22, 2008	Feb 22, 2008
Feb 29, 2008	Feb 29, 2008

Figure 9-2 shows these dates on the calendar.

FIGURE 9-2

Swap Calendar

Why is the November payment on the 23rd and not the 22nd? Because the 22nd is a New York Holiday (Thanksgiving) and the Modified Following business day convention tells us to take the next business day (unless it falls into the next month, in which case we take the previous business day, but that is not the case here). Note also that the final coupon period is quite brief—just 6 days (Feb 23 thru Feb 29)—because the terms of this swap call for short stubs. Were it to call for long stubs, the Feb 22 payment would not occur. Instead, the final payment would fall on Feb 29 and the final coupon period would be longer than the 3-month tenor by 6 days.

Our job now is to calculate an amount for each payment, discount those amounts to their present values, and sum up all the PVs. Let's start with the next fixed payment. We'll use the period start and end dates, plus the fixed rate and day fraction, to calculate the interest accrual over that period. Then we'll discount it to today using the 3-month spot rate. Here's the work:

Fixed Payment 5

Notional	1,000,000
AccrualStart	May 23, 2007
AccrualEnd	Aug 22, 2007
AccrualDays	91
Payment Rate	3.90%
DayFraction	91/365
AccrualRate	.039 * 91/365
Payment FV	9723.29
Spot Rate	3.53%
Days till Payment	91
Discount Fraction	91/365
Discount Rate	.0353 * 91/365
PaymentPV	9723.29/(1 + .0353 * 91/365)
	= 9638.46

Now let's do the first floating payment. The main difference here is the rate. Instead of the fixed rate we need a Libor rate, and for this first floating payment we choose the spot rate. Why not a forward rate? Because with plain vanilla swaps the floating rate for a coupon is fixed at the start of the period, which in this case is today. Forward rates converge to spot rates, so the forward rate for money borrowed now, "on the spot," is just a spot rate. For second and subsequent floating payments, we will use forward rates. Notice too we will use a notional of negative 1,000,000 to end up with a negative cash flow. Recall that Finch pays floating (negative cash flow) and receives fixed (positive cash flow). Here's the work for the next floating payment:

Floating Payment 5

Notional	−1,000,000
AccrualStart	May 23, 2007
AccrualEnd	Aug 22, 2007
AccrualDays	91
Payment Rate	3.53%
Accrual Fraction	91/365
AccrualRate	.0353*91/365
Payment FV	−8800.82
Spot Rate	3.53%
Days till Payment	91
Discount Fraction	91/365
Discount Rate	.0353*91/365
PaymentPV	−8800.82/(1 + .0353*91/365)
	= −8724.04

Now let's work out the next floating payment, number 6. The accrual period is 3 months in length starting in 3 months, so we use the 3-month forward rate 3 months out. And remember, even though it's a 3-month *forward* rate, it's expressed as an *annual* rate so we still need that day fraction. For discounting we use the 6-month spot rate (because the payment will occur in 6 months) and a day fraction with 6 months worth of days in the numerator. Here's the work:

Floating Payment 6

Notional	−1,000,000
AccrualStart	Aug 23, 2007
AccrualEnd	Nov 23, 2007
AccrualDays	92
Payment Rate	3.55%
Accrual Fraction	92/365
AccrualRate	0.0355*92/365

continued

Floating Payment 6

Payment FV	−8947.95
Spot Rate	3.54%
Days till Payment	184
Discount Fraction	184/365
Discount Rate	0.0354 * 184/365
PaymentPV	−8947.95 / (1 + .0354 * 184/365)
	= −8791.07

Repeating this for all payments on both legs gives us a matrix like this:

Finch-Radley swap *value as of 5/23/2007 with 4 periods remaining*
from perspective of floating-payer Finch

	Pmt	Notional	Accrual Start	Accrual End	Acc Days	Pmt Rate	Year Days	Payment FV	Spot Rate	Days Till Pmt	Payment PV
fixed	5	1,000,000	5/23/07	8/22/07	91	3.90%	365	9723.29	3.53%	91	9638.46
fixed	6	1,000,000	8/23/07	11/23/07	92	3.90%	365	9830.14	3.54%	184	9657.79
fixed	7	1,000,000	11/24/07	2/22/08	90	3.90%	365	9616.44	3.59%	275	9363.18
fixed	8	1,000,000	2/23/08	2/29/08	6	3.90%	365	641.10	3.59%	282	623.79
									net fixed leg PV =		29,283.23
floating	5	(1,000,000)	5/23/07	8/22/07	91	3.53%	365	(8800.82)	3.53%	91	(8724.04)
floating	6	(1,000,000)	8/23/07	11/23/07	92	3.55%	365	(8947.95)	3.54%	184	(8791.06)
floating	7	(1,000,000)	11/24/07	2/22/08	90	3.64%	365	(8975.34)	3.59%	275	(8738.97)
floating	8	(1,000,000)	2/23/08	2/29/08	6	3.64%	365	(598.36)	3.59%	282	(582.21)
								net floating leg PV =			(26,836.29)
								swap value =			2446.94

As you can see, the fixed leg coupons net to $29,283.23 and the floating leg payments net to −$26,836.29. Combining these gives us the value of this swap to Finch: $2446.94. Finch's view, that floating rates would be below his fixed rate of 3.9 percent, is turning out correct. He is better off effectively paying a floating rate than having stayed with the fixed rate.

A New Swap

Now let's work out another swap valuation problem but for a different purpose. Instead of calculating the value of an existing swap, we will calculate the fixed rate, or swap rate, of a new plain vanilla. Recall that new swaps have a theoretical value of zero. It's just a stack of forward contracts, after all. So the job here is to calculate the fixed rate of a plain vanilla such that the swap value is zero. Sounds daunting, but once you see how it's done it will daunt no more.

The counterparties here are Lakewood Securities (a financial firm that deals in swaps) and the Cornelia Corporation. The Lakewood-Cornelia swap differs from the Finch-Radley swap in three ways: It has a fixed tenor of 6 months and floating tenor of 3 months, it calls for long stubs instead of short, and it will commence today, May 23, 2007, and run for two years. Here are all the terms:

Notional	1,000,000 USD
Effective date	May 23, 2007
Maturity date	May 29, 2009
Fixed Rate	???
Floating Rate	USD Libor
Discount curve	USD Libor
Compounding	None
Averaging	None
Amortizing	None
Fixed Tenor	6 months
Floating Tenor	3 months
Coupon date	22nd
Stubs	Long
Day Basis	Actual/365
Calendar	New York
Adjustment	Modified Following

For the market we'll use the same spot and forward curves from the previous swap. Now we'll identify the payment dates, and, of course, this time we have twice as many floating coupons as fixed coupons.

Fixed Payment	Floating Payment
	Aug 22, 2007
Nov 23, 2007	Nov 23, 2007
	Feb 22, 2008
May 22, 2008	May 22, 2008
	Aug 22, 2008
Nov 24, 2008	Nov 24, 2008
	Feb 23, 2009
May 29, 2009	May 29, 2009

Now we set up a matrix exactly like before, using a spreadsheet. But what fixed rate do we use? We'll start with a guess and see what happens. How about 3.9 percent like before?

Lakewood-Cornelia swap *proposed new swap with fixed rate = 3.9%*
from perspective of floating-payer Lakewood

	Pmt	Notional	Accrual Start	Accrual End	Acc Days	Pmt Rate	Year Days	Payment FV	Spot Rate	Days Till Pmt	Payment PV
fixed	1	1,000,000	5/23/07	11/23/07	184	3.90%	365	19,660.27	3.53%	184	19,316.53
fixed	2	1,000,000	11/24/07	5/22/08	180	3.90%	365	19,232.88	3.54%	365	18,575.31
fixed	3	1,000,000	5/23/08	11/24/08	185	3.90%	365	19,767.12	3.59%	551	18,750.93
fixed	4	1,000,000	11/25/08	5/29/09	185	3.90%	365	19,767.12	3.59%	737	18,431.08
										net fixed leg PV =	75,073.86
floating	1	(1,000,000)	5/23/07	8/22/07	91	3.53%	365	(8,800.82)	3.53%	91	(8,724.04)
floating	2	(1,000,000)	8/23/07	11/23/07	92	3.55%	365	(8,947.95)	3.54%	184	(8,791.06)
floating	3	(1,000,000)	11/24/07	2/22/08	90	3.64%	365	(8,975.34)	3.59%	275	(8,738.97)
floating	4	(1,000,000)	2/23/08	5/22/08	89	3.67%	365	(8,948.77)	3.54%	365	(8,642.81)
floating	5	(1,000,000)	5/23/08	8/22/08	91	3.71%	365	(9,249.59)	3.59%	457	(8,851.72)
floating	6	(1,000,000)	8/23/08	11/24/08	93	3.73%	365	(9,503.84)	3.54%	551	(9,021.72)
floating	7	(1,000,000)	11/25/08	2/23/09	90	3.80%	365	(9,369.86)	3.59%	642	(8,813.35)
floating	8	(1,000,000)	2/24/09	5/29/09	94	3.81%	365	(9,812.05)	3.59%	737	(9,148.87)
									net floating leg PV =		(70,732.54)
									swap value =		**4,341.32**

No good, the swap has a nonzero value of $4341.32 to the floating payer, so the fixed rate must be too high. Let's try 3.6 percent.

Lakewood-Cornelia swap *proposed new swap with fixed rate = 3.6%*
from perspective of floating-payer Lakewood

	Pmt	Notional	Accrual Start	Accrual End	Acc Days	Pmt Rate	Year Days	Payment FV	Spot Rate	Days Till Pmt	Payment PV
fixed	1	1,000,000	5/23/07	11/23/07	184	3.60%	365	18,147.95	3.53%	184	17,830.65
fixed	2	1,000,000	11/24/07	5/22/08	180	3.60%	365	17,753.42	3.54%	365	17,146.44
fixed	3	1,000,000	5/23/08	11/24/08	185	3.60%	365	18,246.58	3.59%	551	17,308.55
fixed	4	1,000,000	11/25/08	5/29/09	185	3.60%	365	18,246.58	3.59%	737	17,013.31
										net fixed leg PV =	69,298.95
floating	1	(1,000,000)	5/23/07	8/22/07	91	3.53%	365	(8,800.82)	3.53%	91	(8,724.04)
floating	2	(1,000,000)	8/23/07	11/23/07	92	3.55%	365	(8,947.95)	3.54%	184	(8,791.06)
floating	3	(1,000,000)	11/24/07	2/22/08	90	3.64%	365	(8,975.34)	3.59%	275	(8,738.97)
floating	4	(1,000,000)	2/23/08	5/22/08	89	3.67%	365	(8,948.77)	3.54%	365	(8,642.81)
floating	5	(1,000,000)	5/23/08	8/22/08	91	3.71%	365	(9,249.59)	3.59%	457	(8,851.72)
floating	6	(1,000,000)	8/23/08	11/24/08	93	3.73%	365	(9,503.84)	3.54%	551	(9,021.72)
floating	7	(1,000,000)	11/25/08	2/23/09	90	3.80%	365	(9,369.86)	3.59%	642	(8,813.35)
floating	8	(1,000,000)	2/24/09	5/29/09	94	3.81%	365	(9,812.05)	3.59%	737	(9,148.87)
									net floating leg PV =		(70,732.54)
									swap value =		**(1,433.59)**

Closer, but still no cigar. But by continuing to try new fixed rates we soon find that 3.6745 percent gives us a value of zero.[2] So the correct swap rate for the Lakewood-Cornelia swap is 3.6745 percent.

Lakewood-Cornelia swap   *proposed new swap with fixed rate =* **3.6745%**
from perspective of floating-payer Lakewood

	Pmt	Notional	Accrual Start	Accrual End	Acc Days	Pmt Rate	Year Days	Payment FV	Spot Rate	Days Till Pmt	Payment PV
fixed	1	1,000,000	5/23/07	11/23/07	184	3.67%	365	18,523.37	3.53%	184	18,199.51
fixed	2	1,000,000	11/24/07	5/22/08	180	3.67%	365	18,120.69	3.54%	365	17,501.15
fixed	3	1,000,000	5/23/08	11/24/08	185	3.67%	365	18,624.04	3.59%	551	17,666.62
fixed	4	1,000,000	11/25/08	5/29/09	185	3.67%	365	18,624.04	3.59%	737	17,365.26
									net fixed leg PV =		70,732.54
floating	1	(1,000,000)	5/23/07	8/22/07	91	3.53%	365	(8,800.82)	3.53%	91	(8,724.04)
floating	2	(1,000,000)	8/23/07	11/23/07	92	3.55%	365	(8,947.95)	3.54%	184	(8,791.06)
floating	3	(1,000,000)	11/24/07	2/22/08	90	3.64%	365	(8,975.34)	3.59%	275	(8,738.97)
floating	4	(1,000,000)	2/23/08	5/22/08	89	3.67%	365	(8,948.77)	3.54%	365	(8,642.81)
floating	5	(1,000,000)	5/23/08	8/22/08	91	3.71%	365	(9,249.59)	3.59%	457	(8,851.72)
floating	6	(1,000,000)	8/23/08	11/24/08	93	3.73%	365	(9,503.84)	3.54%	551	(9,021.72)
floating	7	(1,000,000)	11/25/08	2/23/09	90	3.80%	365	(9,369.86)	3.59%	642	(8,813.35)
floating	8	(1,000,000)	2/24/09	5/29/09	94	3.81%	365	(9,812.05)	3.59%	737	(9,148.87)
									net floating leg PV =		(70,732.54)
									swap value =		**0.00**

Now recall Lakewood is not entering into this swap to convert a preexisting fixed-rate loan to a floating rate. They are a swaps dealer, contracted by Cornelia to make this swap. Let's say Lakewood is willing to do this swap for a fee of $10,000. Cornelia could write a check for that amount and do the swap at 3.6745 percent, or the parties could adjust the fixed rate to 4.1940 percent instead. This gives the swap a present value to Lakewood of $10,000, which to them is nearly as good as a check. Here's the matrix:

---

[2]Computers are very good, of course, for this kind of trial-and-error calculation and are only too happy to do it for us. In this case we used the Excel Solver function to get our result in the blink of an eye.

Lakewood-Cornelia swap   *proposed new swap with fixed rate =* **4.1940%**
from perspective of floating-payer Lakewood

	Pmt	Notional	Accrual Start	Accrual End	Acc Days	Pmt Rate	Year Days	Payment FV	Spot Rate	Days Till Pmt	Payment PV
fixed	1	1,000,000	5/23/07	11/23/07	184	4.19%	365	21,142.16	3.53%	184	20,772.52
fixed	2	1,000,000	11/24/07	5/22/08	180	4.19%	365	20,682.55	3.54%	365	19,975.42
fixed	3	1,000,000	5/23/08	11/24/08	185	4.19%	365	21,257.07	3.59%	551	20,164.28
fixed	4	1,000,000	11/25/08	5/29/09	185	4.19%	365	21,257.07	3.59%	737	19,820.32
								net fixed leg PV =			80,732.54
floating	1	(1,000,000)	5/23/07	8/22/07	91	3.53%	365	(8,800.82)	3.53%	91	(8,724.04)
floating	2	(1,000,000)	8/23/07	11/23/07	92	3.55%	365	(8,947.95)	3.54%	184	(8,791.06)
floating	3	(1,000,000)	11/24/07	2/22/08	90	3.64%	365	(8,975.34)	3.59%	275	(8,738.97)
floating	4	(1,000,000)	2/23/08	5/22/08	89	3.67%	365	(8,948.77)	3.54%	365	(8,642.81)
floating	5	(1,000,000)	5/23/08	8/22/08	91	3.71%	365	(9,249.59)	3.59%	457	(8,851.72)
floating	6	(1,000,000)	8/23/08	11/24/08	93	3.73%	365	(9,503.84)	3.54%	551	(9,021.72)
floating	7	(1,000,000)	11/25/08	2/23/09	90	3.80%	365	(9,369.86)	3.59%	642	(8,813.35)
floating	8	(1,000,000)	2/24/09	5/29/09	94	3.81%	365	(9,812.05)	3.59%	737	(9,148.87)
								net floating leg PV =			(70,732.54)
								swap value =			**10,000.00**

THE SWAP AS A PORTFOLIO OF FRAs

Now back to our original Lakewood-Cornelia swap with a zero value. To make it zero we chose a fixed rate of 3.6745 percent. Sound familiar? Sound like a forward rate? It should. A swap can be viewed as a portfolio of a particular type of forward contract known as a forward rate agreement. And doing so can really help us understand how swaps are related to—and are in fact just a special collection of—another fundamental derivative.

The Forward Rate Agreement

The *forward rate agreement* or FRA is an agreement between a buyer (the "borrower") and seller (the "lender") to execute a loan at a certain rate for a certain future time period. FRAs are typically cash-settled, meaning the loan doesn't really take place, but this doesn't matter. Their true purpose is to provide a price guarantee. In fact a FRA is just the same forward contract we learned about earlier, where the underlier this time is borrowed money.

How might we use a FRA? One way is to reduce uncertainty about a single future interest rate payment based on a floating rate of interest. Say we have some preexisting obligation in 3 months' time to pay 6 months of interest on $100,000 using the 6-month Libor rate then in effect. Let's also say we *want* to pay 3.25 percent no matter what Libor turns out to be. We can achieve this by buying a forward contract known as a "3 by 9" FRA with a delivery price of 3.25 percent. With such a FRA in place, we are obligated to pay 3.25 percent, and the short party is obligated to accept 3.25 percent for a 6-month loan commencing in 3 months.

Now imagine three months have gone by and 6-month Libor is 3.5 percent (an annual rate, recall, for a 6-month loan). Our original obligation requires us to pay, we'll say, $1750 (i.e., .035 * .5 * 100,000). Remember we only want to pay $1625 (i.e., .0325 * .5 * 100,000). No worries! From our cash-settled FRA we will receive "25 basis points" from the short party, or $125 (i.e., [.035 − .0325] * .5 * 100,000). So we shell out the $1625 and combine it with this $125 to make our $1750 payment.

Now imagine 3 months have gone by and 6-month Libor is instead 3 percent. Our original obligation requires us to pay $1,500 (i.e., .03 * .5 * 100,000). Hey this is $125 less than we are willing to pay! A little bonus? No. Our 3 * 6 FRA requires us to pay 25 basis points, or $125 (i.e., [.0325 − .03] * .5 * 100,000). So we still shell out the $1625 but this time pay $125 on the FRA and the balance on the loan.

There we have two scenarios, one in which rates were higher than we would have liked and the other in which they were less, and in both cases we paid exactly what we wanted to pay. That's what forwards are for.

And what if we had this same obligation, to pay 6-month Libor on $100,000, every 3 months for the next 2 years? Perhaps it is our quarterly payment on a floating-rate loan. Could we not, today, execute a whole stack of FRAs? a 3 * 9 and 6 * 12 and 9 * 15 and so on? Sure could. Then, every 3 months, no matter where Libor fixes, we know our net payment would be based on a 3.25 percent annual rate, effectively converting our floating-rate obligation into a fixed-rate obligation. This, of course, is just what a swap does. A position in one swap, then, will pay off exactly the same way as a position consisting of a stack, or portfolio, of FRAs. And when two positions have the same payoffs, their present value must be identical due to arbitrage. So lo and behold, this is how we know that a swap is equivalent to a portfolio of FRAs.

Let's look again at the Finch-Radley swap as a series of cash flows:

Finch-Radley swap
from perspective of floating-payer Finch

value as of 5/23/2007 with 4 periods remaining

	Pmt	Notional	Accrual Start	Accrual End	Acc Days	Pmt Rate	Year Days	Payment FV	Spot Rate	Days Till Pmt	Payment PV
fixed	5	1,000,000	5/23/07	8/22/07	91	3.90%	365	9,723.29	3.53%	91	9,638.46
fixed	6	1,000,000	8/23/07	11/23/07	92	3.90%	365	9,830.14	3.54%	184	9,657.79
fixed	7	1,000,000	11/24/07	2/22/08	90	3.90%	365	9,616.44	3.59%	275	9,363.18
fixed	8	1,000,000	2/23/08	2/29/08	6	3.90%	365	641.10	3.59%	282	623.79
									net fixed leg PV =		29,283.23
floating	5	(1,000,000)	5/23/07	8/22/07	91	3.53%	365	(8,800.82)	3.53%	91	(8,724.04)
floating	6	(1,000,000)	8/23/07	11/23/07	92	3.55%	365	(8,947.95)	3.54%	184	(8,791.06)
floating	7	(1,000,000)	11/24/07	2/22/08	90	3.64%	365	(8,975.34)	3.59%	275	(8,738.97)
floating	8	(1,000,000)	2/23/08	2/29/08	6	3.64%	365	(598.36)	3.59%	282	(582.21)
							net floating leg PV =				(26,836.29)
									swap value =		**2,446.94**

Now let's recast it as a portfolio of FRAs:

Finch-Radley FRAs
from perspective of fixed-rate seller Finch

value as of 5/23/2007 with 4 contracts remaining

Pmt	Notional	Accrual Start	Accrual End	Days	Contract Rate	Forward Rate	Pmt Rate	Year Days	Pmt FV	Spot Rate	Days Till Pmt	Payment PV
5	1,000,000	5/23/07	8/22/07	91	3.90%	3.53%	0.37%	365	922.47	3.53%	91	914.42
6	1,000,000	8/23/07	11/23/07	92	3.90%	3.55%	0.35%	365	882.19	3.54%	184	866.72
7	1,000,000	11/24/07	2/22/08	90	3.90%	3.64%	0.26%	365	641.10	3.59%	275	624.21
8	1,000,000	2/23/08	2/29/08	6	3.90%	3.64%	0.26%	365	42.74	3.59%	282	41.59
										portfolio value =		**2,446.94**

Here we have four FRAs, each with a contract rate (a.k.a. "delivery price") of 3.9 percent. Finch is the short party, "selling money" at that interest. The payment rate each period is the difference between this delivery price and the current forward rate for the corresponding accrual period. The first payment rate, for example, is 3.9 percent–3.53 percent or 0.37 percent. Otherwise the math is the same as before, giving us a net portfolio value of $2446.94—same as the swap. (Recall this portfolio of FRAs has been in effect for 12 months. When it was initiated, the net value was, of course, zero as with a swap.)

Pretty cool, huh?

CHAPTER 10

Pricing Options

Option valuation is trickier than valuing a forward, futures, or swap because each of those contracts involves a transaction we know with certainty will occur. So how in the world do we value an option, involving a future transaction that may or may not occur? What is the fair market price of an instrument whose payoff is so wildly uncertain, depending as it does on the completely unpredictable price path of the underlier?

The basic idea involves the construction of an imaginary portfolio of nonoption instruments—whose prices you can easily obtain—such that the portfolio payoff replicates that of the option. The price of such a portfolio gives you the price of the option because two things with the same payoff must have the same value to prevent arbitrage. To create such a portfolio, you need a model of how the underlier price changes. The binomial tree method, one of two option valuation methods we'll explain in detail, provides instructions for creating the replicating portfolio using a price path for the underlier that follows a "tree" pattern with very simple branches. The Black-Scholes method grows directly out of the binomial tree method and basically uses a tree with an infinite number of branches.

EYEBALL OPTION PRICING

Before we get into formal methods, let's see how to get some rough idea of an option's value using just our eyeballs, very simple math, and common sense to arrive at so-called "boundary conditions" for option values.

Option Value versus Stock Value

The first thing to recognize when assessing the value of an option is that an option can be worth no more than a corresponding position in the underlier. Consider the call option. The lower the strike price, and the longer the time to expiry, the greater its value. The lowest a strike price can go is zero and the longest time to expiry is infinity, and what's the value of a call option with a strike price of zero and no expiration? Such an option let's you have the stock at any time for free, as if you own it already. So its value is just the stock price. A call, then, can be worth no more than a long position in the stock. And like so many things with options, the same logic in pseudo-reverse says a put can be worth no more than a short position in a stock.

Intrinsic Value and Time Value

You can further get a rough idea of an option's value by assessing its *intrinsic value* versus *time value*. Intrinsic value is the difference between the strike price and the current stock price, or zero, whichever is greater. A 50-strike call option when the stock is trading at 53 has an intrinsic value of 3. A 50-strike put option when the stock is trading at 53 has no intrinsic value. Like so:

$$Intrinsic\ Value\ of\ a\ Call = MAX(S - K, 0)$$
$$Intrinsic\ Value\ of\ a\ Put = MAX(K - S, 0)$$

Time value comes from the "optionality" you get by holding an option. Some refer to it as the "insurance" value. This is why a 50-strike put when the stock is trading at 53, which has no intrinsic value, has *some* value, because who knows where the stock price will go before the option expires? Maybe the option will go in-the-money. And if it does you're entitled to some payoff. If it doesn't you're out no more than the premium. That opportunity for upside and shield from downside is worth something, and that something is known as time value. And the more the time before expiration, the more valuable this optionality becomes—ergo, "time" value.

All options have some time value. If the option is in-the-money, it also has some intrinsic value. Like this:

OTM *Option Value = Time Value*
ATM *Option Value = Time Value*
ITM *Option Value = Time Value + Intrinsic Value*

Notice that only in-the-money options can have intrinsic value?

You can use the idea of intrinsic value to get some idea of the value of an option with a quick glance. If it's a call, just subtract exercise price from stock price. If the result is positive, that's the intrinsic value. If it's a put, just subtract stock price from exercise price. If the result is positive, that's the intrinsic value. An option is always worth *at least* its intrinsic value. More on this below.

So now we have a boundary condition for option values. An option value must lie between its intrinsic value and the value of the underlying stock. Graphically, using the same X-Y grid as a payoff diagram, the value of an option must lie in the shaded region in Figure 10-1.

FIGURE 10-1

Call Option Value Boundaries

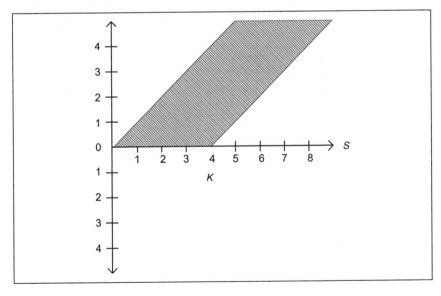

There are further boundary conditions for option values (e.g., the value is at least the difference between stock price and the *present value* of the exercise price), but now you know the basic idea. And with it you can easily figure in your head the range in which an option value sits. Consider our cZED62 from before. When the stock ZED trades at 69, you know its value is at least 7 (intrinsic value, i.e., 69 – 62) but no more than 69. With ZED at 74, the option value is at least 12 but no more than 74. With ZED at 60 the option value is at least 0—notice it's out-of-the-money— but no more than 60. As you can see, when an option is in-the-money, most of its value comes from intrinsic value. A corollary of this fact, one you can add to your top-of-the-head toolkit, is that an out of the money option is likely to be closer to 0 than stock price.

Granted these are huge ranges, but they at least get you into the ballpark of where the actual value sits. Now let's move inside the park.

BASIC BINOMIAL OPTION PRICING

Earlier in the book we learned about arbitrage, one of our basic assumptions about the financial universe stating that two things with the same payoff must have the same price. And in Chapter 5 we saw an example of position synthesis, or replication, where two positions with different assets can provide the same payoff and therefore have the same present value or price. And on the very first pages of Chapter 1, we introduced the idea of abstraction. This tried-and-true approach to learning starts by putting the mind on a simple case known to be true, often by making simplifying if unrealistic assumptions, then adds small facts also known to be true until you have in your head a rather more complicated but useful truth. We shall now combine these concepts of arbitrage, replication, and abstraction to calculate the price of an option.

In the sections that follow we'll apply two different methods for pricing an option. The first is the *binomial tree method*, and it's remarkably easy to understand when you start with the simplest case and move gradually from there. You can use and understand this powerful method with no more than algebra in your mathematical quiver. The second is the *Black-Scholes* method and it grows directly and intuitively out of the binomial model. Once you get the binomial model, it's not a big deal to get what Black-Scholes is all about. Black-Scholes depends on calculus, but you certainly don't need to know calculus to use it. Black-Scholes also applies an additional powerful concept of risk-neutrality, and we'll explain that just before we need it. Now we don't cover two methods just for educational purposes. We really need them both in the real world. Black-Scholes only works for European options and certain American ones. American put options, for example, require something like the binomial method.

A One-Step Binomial Tree

So consider again the stock *ZED* and a call option *cZED62*, which expires in 6 months with a strike price of 62. Imagine *ZED* is trading for 60 on the spot market. We are going to calculate the value of, or price, this *cZED62*. We'll first price *cZED62* by making a seemingly ridiculous assumption that the price of *ZED* can change to one of only two possible values over a given period of time. It will either increase by 10 percent and trade at 66, or decrease by 10 percent and trade at 54. We call this model a *one-step binomial tree* and it is, of course, unrealistic. But stick with me. Now if *ZED* rises to 66 the payoff of *cZED62* will be 4. Should *ZED* fall to 54, then *cZED62* will, of course, expire worthless, that is, have a payoff of 0. Here's the situation graphically in Figure 10-2 as a one-step (the price changes only once) binomial (two possible prices) tree (what mathematicians call the pattern in the figure—they don't get out much).

$$\text{Payoff of } cZED62 \text{ if } ZED = 66$$
$$MAX(0, S - K)$$
$$MAX(0, 66 - 62)$$
$$MAX(0, 4) = 4$$

$$\text{Payoff of } cZED62 \text{ if } ZED = 54$$
$$MAX(0, S - K)$$
$$MAX(0, 54 - 62)$$
$$MAX(0, -8) = 0$$

The payoff of *cZED62* is uncertain and depends entirely on whether *ZED* moves to 66 or 54. We want to know the price of this

FIGURE 10-2

One-Step Binomial Tree

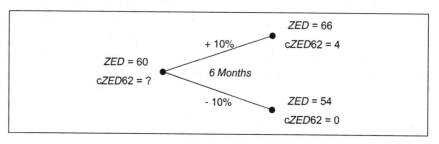

option with no more information than what we have already. And how do we do that? By creating a *replicating portfolio*, using components we *can* price, whose payoff mimics the payoff of *cZED62*. And due to the law of no-arbitrage, two positions with the same payoff must cost the same. So whatever the price of the replicating portfolio, that must also be the price of the option.

We build a replicating portfolio by purchasing some quantity of *ZED* stock and borrowing some quantity of money. We'll explain in a bit how we arrive at these quantities, but for now just take them as given. You can think of our replicating portfolio as long a stock and short a bond because "shorting a bond" is just a fancy way of saying "borrowing some money." To be exact, we will borrow 17.47 at the risk-free rate of 6 percent for 6 months. We will use these borrowed funds, plus 2.53 of our own money, to buy .3333 shares of *ZED* for 20 (i.e., .3333 * 60 = 20 = 17.47 + 2.53). Here's the composition of our replicating portfolio *RP* mathematically, with the quantity of *ZED* represented by the Greek letter delta (Δ) and the borrowed money represented by the letter *B* (it's a negative *B*, remember, because it's like shorting a bond):

$$RP = \Delta ZED - B$$

While we're here, let's calculate the cost of creating this portfolio, or its value at inception, using the delta and bond quantities mentioned above:

$$RP = \Delta ZED - B$$
$$RP = .3333(60) - 17.47$$
$$RP = 2.53$$

And this makes sense, as 2.53 is the amount of our own money we had to come up with to create the replicating portfolio; remember we borrowed the 17.47. So the value of the replicating portfolio at time zero is 2.53.

Imagine that 6 months have gone by. Your debt has grown to 18.00 (i.e., $17.47e^{(.06)(.5)}$) and you need to pay it back. And ZED is trading for either 66 or 54. Consider what you'll do with your replicating portfolio:

If *ZED* is trading for 66
- Sell your .3333 shares and collect 22.00 (i.e., .3333 * 66).
- Use 18.00 of it to repay your debt and pocket the remaining 4 dollars.

If *ZED* is trading for 54
- Sell your .3333 shares and collect 18.00 to exactly pay off your debt (.3333 * 54 = 18.00).
- Pocket nothing.

So as you see in Figure 10-3, if ZED moved to 66 your payoff was $4 and if it moved to 54 your payoff was bupkes. These are the exact same payoffs had you bought a cZED62 instead of constructing the replicating portfolio.

$$\text{Payoff of } RP \text{ if } ZED = 66$$
$$\Delta S - Be^{rt}$$
$$(.3333)66 - 17.47e^{(.06)(.5)}$$
$$22 - 18 = 4$$

$$\text{Payoff of } RP \text{ if } ZED = 54$$
$$\Delta S - Be^{rt}$$
$$(.3333)54 - 17.47e^{(.06)(.5)}$$
$$18 - 18 = 0$$

So the replicating portfolio clearly, well, replicates a position in the option. So the value of the cZED62 at time zero must have been 2.53, the cost of building the portfolio. In other words, a position in the option was equal to a position in the replicating portfolio. That is:

$$cZED62 = \Delta ZED - B$$

FIGURE 10-3

Replicating Portfolio Payoff on a One-Step Binomial Tree

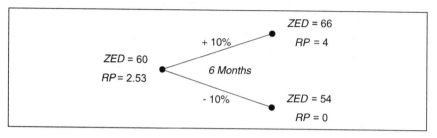

We can use this equation directly to calculate the price of the option. Like so:

$$cZED62 = \Delta ZED - B$$
$$cZED62 = (.3333 * 60) - 17.47$$
$$cZED62 = 20 - 17.47$$
$$cZED62 = 2.53$$

So the theoretical value of $cZED62$ is 2.53. Notice this is consistent with the range we identified in the previous section of 0 to 60, or the range between intrinsic value and stock price. Notice 2.53 is much closer to 0 than 60, consistent with our intuition that out-of-the-money options are closer in value to 0 than stock price.

Now let's tackle this delta factor. It tells us how much stock we need such that the sensitivity of the replicating portfolio to a change in the underlier is the same as the sensitivity of the option to a change in the underlier. Delta, then, is also a measure of the option's sensitivity to changes in its underlier. Delta is also known as an option's *hedge ratio* for reasons we'll cover later. In our one-step tree, delta is given by the ratio of two differences: the difference between possible option values over the difference between possible stock prices. We can express this mathematically by using S_u for the stock price after an up move, S_d for the stock price after a down move, C_u for the option value after an up move, and C_d for the option value after a down move in the stock.

$$S_u = 66$$
$$C_u = 4$$
$$S_d = 54$$
$$C_d = 0$$

$$\Delta = (C_u - C_d)/(S_u - S_d)$$
$$\Delta = (4 - 0)/(66 - 54)$$
$$\Delta = 4/12 = 1/3$$
$$\Delta = .3333$$

We can further generalize the formula, thus making it more useful later on, by representing the 1 plus stock return after an up move by the letter u and 1 plus the stock return after a down move by the letter d. See Formula 10.1 A *return* is a proportional representation of how much an investment earns. In our one-step tree the return is either 10 percent or −10 percent. So 1 plus return is how much of your original investment you have left, in proportional terms, after an investment period.

$$u = 1 + 0.10 = 1.10$$
$$d = 1 + (-0.10) = 1 - 0.1 = .9$$
$$\Delta(uS - dS) = C_u - C_d$$

$$\Delta = (C_u - C_d)/[S(u - d)] \tag{10.1}$$
$$\Delta = (4 - 0)/[60(1.10 - .9)]$$
$$\Delta = 4/12 = 1/3$$
$$\Delta = .3333$$

Now the bond factor. We can rejigger the generalized formula for delta to arrive at Formula 10.2 for B. It uses the same inputs as the delta formula, plus the risk free interest rate represented by the letter r:

$$r = .06$$
$$B = (dC_u - uC_d)/[e^{rt}(u - d)] \tag{10.2}$$
$$B = (dC_u - uC_d)/[e^{(.06)(.5)}(u - d)]$$
$$B = (.9(4) - 1.10(0))/[e^{(.03)}(1.10 - .9)]$$
$$B = 3.6/.2061$$
$$B = 17.47$$

Putting this all together, we get the one-step binomial option pricing formula 10.3 for a call option.

$$C = \Delta S - B \qquad (10.3)$$

where

$S = stock\ price$
$\Delta = (C_u - C_d)/[S(u - d)]$
$C_u = call\ value\ after\ up\ move$
$C_d = call\ value\ after\ down\ move$
$u = 1 + stock\ return\ after\ up\ move$
$d = 1 + stock\ return\ after\ down\ move$

and

$$B = (dC_u - uC_d)/[e^{rt}(u - d)]$$

An Alternative Approach

Now we consider an alternative approach when using a one-step binomial tree to price an option. It's a tad less intuitive but does the same thing: It gives us the price of our cZED62. And it will help demonstrate another fundamental concept of derivative pricing, the concept of risk-neutral pricing. So let's switch gears to this alternative approach.

In our first climb up the binomial tree, we created a replicating portfolio, or "synthetic option," as it is sometimes known, by borrowing money and buying stock. This is known as a "levered position" as it entails *leverage*, which simply means you borrow money to buy something. Buying something with borrowed money is, of course, more risky than buying something with your own money. If the value of the thing you bought falls below what you owe, you can get into a heap of trouble right quick. And when you think about it, buying something with a call option is more risky than buying it outright. If the value of the underlier falls below the strike price and the option expires, you lose 100 percent of your investment. This, in a nutshell, is one of the reasons we model an option position with levered stock positions.

We did not know which payoff of the synthetic option would actually occur, but it did not matter; the payoff would exactly mimic the payoff of the real option. And we could easily price the components of the portfolio, which is all we needed to get a price for the option. Our alternative approach constructs a replicating portfolio in which the payoff *is* certain, but includes a component we can't price directly. It expresses the valuation problem by asking, "What is the value of a position of one *long cZED62*?" It answers that question by constructing a replicating portfolio consisting of some quantity delta of the stock *ZED* as before, plus a *short* position in the option *cZED62*, such that the payoff of the portfolio is certain whether the spot price of *ZED* moves up 10 percent to 66 or down 10 percent to 54. So here we don't directly know the cost of the portfolio (it includes the option, after all, the thing we want to price in the first place) but this time we *do* know the payoff with certainty. In other words, we have just one variable—the price of the option—which it turns out we can solve for with algebra.

Now we're already familiar with the (really important) concept of delta. In our formulas it is just some proportional quantity of stock. For example, a delta of .50 is one half a share. A delta of .07 is seven one-hundredths of a share, a delta of 1.0 is exactly one share, and a delta of 0 is no shares. (Of course, you can't really buy fractions of shares; in practice you multiply delta by a multiple of 10 to get a whole number of shares.) Using delta, along with a positive sign to represent a long position and negative sign to represent a short position, the contents of the replicating portfolio can thus be represented like this:

$$+(\Delta * ZED) - cZED62$$

or

$$+\Delta ZED - cZED62$$

Say you own this portfolio. The positive sign in front of ΔZED signifies a long position in some quantity delta of *ZED* stock. You've bought some *ZED* so any future payoff of that stock is yours. In other words, its payoff is positive from your perspective. It's your asset, if you will. The negative sign in front of *cZED62* signifies a short position in *cZED62*. You've sold, or written, this call option, and any positive payoff to that option belongs to the other party. Its payoff is negative from your perspective. It is your liability.

Rewriting things just a bit we can express the value of the portfolio—in other words, the cost of creating this portfolio—with a simple algebraic expression:

$$RP = \Delta ZED - cZED62$$

This says the value of the portfolio is equal to the cost of delta shares of ZED less the cost of one $cZED62$ option. We have then three unknowns: RP, ΔZED, and $cZED62$. If we can figure out two of them we can deduce, or solve for, the third. Let's start with delta. To find it using this new approach, imagine that 6 months have gone by. We need a delta such that the value of the portfolio is the same whether ZED is trading for 66 or 54. In algebraic terms, then, we want the following equation to be true:

$$\Delta 66 - 4 = \Delta 54 - 0$$

where $\Delta 66 - 4$ is the payoff with ZED trading for 66 and $\Delta 54 - 0$ is the payoff with ZED trading for 54. With a pinch of algebra we can solve this equation for delta:

$$\Delta 66 - 4 = \Delta 54 - 0$$
$$\Delta 66 - \Delta 54 = 4$$
$$\Delta (66 - 54) = 4$$
$$\Delta 12 = 4$$
$$\Delta = 4/12 = .3333$$

Same delta as before. But let's plug this delta back into the equation above to be extra sure it works:

$$\Delta 66 - 4 = \Delta 54 - 0$$
$$(.3333)66 - 4 = (.3333)54$$
$$18 = 18$$

Yep. This proves the value of delta is correct. And as a little bonus, it also tells us the value of the portfolio at expiration under either scenario is 18. We'll use this factoid in a moment. First let's see what our formula looks like at time zero now that we know delta. And we know from before the spot price of ZED is 60.

$$RP = \Delta ZED - cZED62$$
$$RP = (.3333)60 - cZED62$$
$$RP = 20 - cZED62$$

Now we're down to two unknowns, portfolio value and the price of *cZED62*. Can we figure out the portfolio value? Sure can. Recall from above that the value of this portfolio in 6 months is 18 whether the stock moves to 66 or 54. So the portfolio value is just the present value of 18. Can we calculate the present value of 18? Sure can. We just need a period of time and an interest rate. The period is, of course, 6 months. But what interest rate should we use? We know the payoff of this portfolio with complete certainty, that is, without risk. So the discount rate should be the risk-free interest rate. Let's say it's 6 percent and use continuous compounding as before.

$$PV(18) = 18e^{-(.06)(.5)}$$
$$PV(18) = 17.47$$

So the present value of the payoff is 17.47, which must be the portfolio value. That is:

$$17.47 = 20 - cZED62$$

Now we have just one unknown, the value of *cZED62*, and can solve for it with just a smidge more algebra:

$$17.47 = 20 - cZED62$$
$$cZED62 = 20 - 17.47$$
$$cZED62 = 2.53$$

The correct price of this option, also known as its *fair market value* or *theoretical value*, is 2.53. Same result as before.

And how can we verify this price? By imagining the construction of a portfolio using this option price and delta and seeing what happens under both of the two possible price paths for the stock. Recall the portfolio contents and costs of its components:

$$RP = \Delta ZED - cZED62$$
$$RP = (.3333)60 - 2.53$$

Imagine it is time zero. We just follow the above formula like a recipe and any cash required we borrow at the risk-free interest rate:

1. Sell *cZED62* and collect the 2.53 premium.
2. Borrow 17.47 at 6 percent.

3. Use the premium and borrowed funds to buy .3333 *ZED* for 20.00 (i.e., .3333 * 60).

Imagine that 6 months have gone by. Your debt has grown to 18 (i.e., $17.47e^{(.06)(.5)}$). You need to pay this back. And *ZED* is trading for either 66 or 54.

If *ZED* is trading for 66: The option is in the money, so you must sell the holder *ZED* for 66 or cash settle by paying them 4.00.

- Sell your .3333 *ZED* for 22 (i.e., .3333 * 66).
- Use 18 of the 22 to repay your debt.
- Use the remaining 4.00 to cash settle the option.

If *ZED* is trading for 54: The option is worthless so you owe nothing to option holder, but you still must repay your debt.

- Sell your *ZED* on the spot market and collect 18 (i.e., .3333 * 54).
- Use the proceeds to repay your debt.

In either case you break even. Nothing exciting about that, but it does prove the value of our option is correct. Still not convinced? Recall that arbitrage is not allowed in our land of derivatives. If we can demonstrate how one *could* perform an arbitrage if the price is *not* 2.53, then we further demonstrate the correctness of our price.

So imagine then you had the opportunity to buy *cZED62* for less than 2.53, let's say 2.43. We can prove such a price is cheap by 10 cents by demonstrating how you can make money no matter what by just doing this:

1. Borrow .3333 shares of *ZED* and sell them (this is *short selling*) for 20 (i.e., .3333 * 60).

2. Use 2.43 of your proceeds to buy one *cZED62*.

3. Invest the remaining 17.57 at 6 percent.

Imagine that 6 months have gone by. Your investment has grown to 18.10 (i.e., $17.57e^{(.06)(.5)}$). Cash it in. Now you need to return those *ZED* shares you borrowed no matter what.

If *ZED* is trading for 66: The option is in the money so you will want to buy *ZED* for 66 or cash settle by receiving 4.00.

- Cash-settle your *cZED62* and collect 4.00. Now you have 22.10 on hand (i.e., 18.10 + 4).
- Use 22 to buy .3333 shares of *ZED* (i.e., .3333 * 66). Return them to your *ZED* lender.
- Keep the remaining .10 as your profit.

If *ZED* is trading for 54: The option is worthless so you do nothing with it, but you do need to return those shares of *ZED* you borrowed.

- Use 18 of your 18.10 to buy .3333 shares of *ZED* on the spot market (i.e., .3333 * 54). Return them to your *ZED* lender.
- Keep the remaining .10 as your profit.

You make a dime no matter what. In other words, you've made a riskless profit, that is, an arbitrage. And derivative valuation is based on the assumption that arbitrage opportunities don't exist. Now you can debate that assertion long into the night, and point out one example after another of market inefficiencies and real arbitrage profits that people have really made, but when the sun comes up the next morning and computers all over the planet start calculating the values of derivatives, trust me, they will assume arbitrage opportunities cannot exist. At least not for long.

We could also examine the case where you find an opportunity to buy *cZED62* for more than 2.53, let's say 2.63, and prove such a price is "rich" by 10 cents by demonstrating how to make another riskless profit through arbitrage. We just do things in reverse: Write the option and buy the stock. At the end of the period we again pocket a dime no matter what.

I know one thing you might be thinking about now: "So you made 10 cents—big whoop." Yes it might seem a lot of bother for a dime until you consider that most U.S. equity option contracts entitle the holder to buy or sell 100 shares of the underlier. So the price of the contract would really be 100 * 2.63 or 26.30, and the payoff 100 * 0.10 or 10.00. And, traders often buy or sell not just one contract (a *one-lot*) but hundreds of contracts as a single trade. So multiply that 10 dollars again, say, by 500, and now you've made a profit of $5000.00. Do 20 or 30 or 100 trades like this in a day, and you can make a lot of whoop in a hurry.

A Multistep Binomial Tree

I know what else you might be thinking: "Stock prices don't change like your little tree." Right. "This binomial tree thing is bogus." No, it's just that we're still working with an abstraction and need to get more concrete. As we've demonstrated the method so far, underlier prices can follow one of just two possible paths. That's not a good model of reality, as clearly the number of possible price paths is way more than two. But we can improve our model—that is, make it more like reality—by simply shortening the branches and adding more of them. A two-step tree, for instance, has three leaves (each is a possible prices for ZED) and four possible price paths.

In Figure 10-4 we've divided the one, 6-month step into two, 3-month steps. As before, the price of ZED at the outset can move to one of just two values, either up by 5 percent or down by 5 percent, to one of the two middle nodes. At each of those nodes,

FIGURE 10-4

Two-Step Binomial Tree

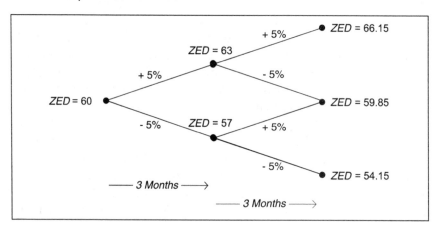

ZED can again either go up by 5 percent or down by 5 percent, ultimately taking us to one of the three end nodes. So there are four possible paths, and notice how the two middle paths take you to the same node, because increasing then decreasing by 5 percent is the same as decreasing then increasing by 5 percent. This idea that more paths take you to the "middle" of the possible end prices than to the "edges" is an important phenomenon that we'll get back to when we cover probability distributions.

Notice our two-step tree is really just three, one-step trees. So we basically iterate through the tree, working right to left, till we are at the starting node. In other words, to calculate the price of an option with this tree, we create a replicating portfolio just as before, but whose payoff is certain no matter which of the *four* paths are taken, then back out the price of the option from the present value of that payoff. We basically need an option value at each node, and we get those by repetitively applying the one-step process. If you're interested, we walk through all the steps in the Advanced Binomial Option Pricing appendix, as well as provide the generic formulas.

Taking It to the Limit

If you took a look at the appendix, you saw how the math can get a little hairy. But hopefully you are at least reasonably convinced that binomial trees really do allow us to price options, and the deeper the tree (to mix a metaphor) the better the price. A tree that perfectly models reality, one that provides for *every* possible price path, would require an infinite number of steps. And wouldn't you just know there's a way to do basically just that—by turning to the friendly field of calculus and its awesome concept of the limit. The Black-Scholes model for option valuation, which we'll turn to next, is based in part on this idea.

There's an important practical ramification of this idea of deeper and deeper trees that also demonstrates nicely the imperfection of pricing something in the real world with a theoretical model. Think back to how we priced an option by building a replicating portfolio on the one-step tree. That replicating portfolio is only good for that one step of the tree. Once we know which of the two paths the price is taking, we need to get rid of the old replicating portfolio and build a new one. Same thing at the next step, and the next step, all the way to the end. Liquidating and recreating this portfolio is known as *dynamic replication.* And as the number of steps goes past a couple or three, it starts getting tough to really do that, with the transaction costs and time involved and what not. And when the number of steps goes to infinity with Black-Scholes it's truly impossible. This dynamic replication requirement is one of the things that makes option pricing more difficult than forward pricing. With forwards you can set up a replicating portfolio and forget about it. Not so with options. But, alas, both the binomial tree method and Black-Scholes assume not only that you can do it, but that you can do it for free! Oh well.

Risk-Neutral Valuation

Here's another sidebar worth noting before we get to Black-Scholes, but it is just a sidebar, and not something you have to understand to apply Black-Scholes. In our option pricing examples so far we've relied heavily on no-arbitrage arguments to prove that our calculations are correct. In the financial universe, this law against arbitrage is like the law against exceeding the speed of light in the physical universe. It's just, well, the law. There's another idea with nearly equal standing in this land and it goes by the name of *risk-neutral valuation.* This idea says that the theoretical value of any derivative—any derivative, not just an option—is equal to the expected value of the derivative's payoff in a risk-neutral world, discounted at a risk-free rate of interest. An *expected value* is just some value in the future considering some probability. A *risk-neutral world* is one in which investors don't care about risk. Neither are they risk-adverse nor risk-inclined. Hedgers in reality *do* wish to mitigate risk, and speculators, of course, seek out risk to potentially profit from it. So this risk-neutral assumption seems wildly bogus at first glance. But as happens every so often in the world of thinkers, one can prove this assertion. And it's an assertion worth proving because doing so allows us to greatly simplify our pricing calculations by using a risk-free rate, as we've been doing all along. The Advanced Binomial Option Pricing appendix illustrates the basic proof of risk-neutrality.

BLACK-SCHOLES OPTIONS PRICING

Step back for a minute and think about how we approached the problem of option valuation using the binomial tree method. We constructed a model of how the real world operates (stock price changes follow a binomial tree), then observed facts from the model (a carefully constructed portfolio gives the same payoff no matter which path is followed, etc.). It's a bit like testing a new design for an aircraft wing. Before building a pair for real and sticking them onto a plane for a real flight, the designers typically build a model of the proposed new wing, place it in a wind tunnel, crank up the air, and observe facts about how air flows around the wing. If it's a good model, they can reasonably assume air will flow over the real wing in a similar way. That is, the facts they observe from the model in the wind tunnel will apply to the real world—with some consideration, perhaps, for the differences between the wind tunnel and the real sky. The point is, the better the model, the more reliable the facts. And this is where Black-Scholes comes in. It uses a better wind tunnel.

The basic idea behind Black-Scholes is the really the same basic idea behind the binomial tree method: The value of an option equals the price of a leveraged stock portfolio that replicates the payoff of the option. The binomial tree method constructs such a portfolio supposing that a price path follows a tree (from its "trunk" to one of its "leaves") with a fixed number of branching levels, where at each branch the stock price can change to one of two possible new prices. Given enough branches, the binomial tree is not a bad model for price changes in the real world. Black-Scholes uses an even better model by essentially supposing a tree with an *infinite* number of branches. Really!

The method we call "Black-Scholes" is named for Fisher Black and Myron Scholes, who in the 1970s along with Robert Merton developed the Black-Scholes formula for pricing European options on nondividend paying stock. Their work was a real groundbreaker in the world of finance, so much so that in 1997 it earned Scholes and Merton the Nobel Prize.[1] There are actually

---

[1]Fisher Black had passed away by then, and Nobels are not given posthumously.

two main components to Black-Scholes: the *Black-Scholes formula* for pricing an option, which we'll explain entirely in the sections that follow, and the *Black-Scholes partial differential equation*, which we'll summarize briefly for the mathematically curious. Partial differential equations or "PDEs" are one of the workhorses of calculus. They express how things change with respect to various contributing factors. The Black-Scholes PDE expresses how an option price and its factors change with respect to one another between two points in time, where the length of time between those points is infinitesimally small. It's given by Formula 10.4.

$$\frac{\delta f}{\delta t} + rS\frac{\delta f}{\delta S} + \frac{1}{2}\sigma^2 S^2 \frac{\delta^2 f}{\delta S^2} = rf \qquad (10.4)$$

This eyeful basically says that over this ultrateeny period of time, the change in price is a function the option price f, stock price S, stock volatility σ (a measure of the "changiness" of the stock price), time t, and the risk-free interest rate r. You can read the symbol δ as "the change over an infinitesimally small period of time in the value of" so the term

$$\frac{\delta f}{\delta t}$$

for example, expresses the ratio between very small changes in option price to very small changes in time. The equation makes a number of assumptions, which we'll detail in a later section, mostly with respect to how stock prices change over time. Bottom line, we've got this equation that says how all these factors are related to one another. What we want, of course, is an option price or a value for f in the PDE. The Black-Scholes formula gives us such a value by "solving" the Black-Scholes partial differential equation for f.

Now we won't go any further into the Black-Scholes partial differential equation. That's the stuff of books way more mathy than this one. But we will explain the formula because this handy recipe is followed billions of times each day in the world of derivatives, so it's worth a few pages. If you understood the basics of the binomial tree method, then Black-Scholes will even make some sense. And because, well, it's just cool.

Volatility

The Black-Scholes formula has five inputs, and one of them, volatility, we've not yet covered. *Volatility* is a measure of how a stock return changes. Recall that *return* is the growth rate (or "shrink rate" if negative) of a stock price over time.[2] So we're talking here about a stock's return and not its price. Now if a stock's return changes a lot—frequently and by significant amounts, in either direction—its volatility is said to be high. If it doesn't, then its volatility is said to be low. Volatility is given as a number between 0 and 1 and pertains to some period of time. So if you see a stock with an annual volatility or "vol" of .30, you can read it as saying the stock return changes 30 percent (up or down) over the course of a year. The return of stock with a vol of .05 changes 5 percent. And so on. Technically, volatility is the standard deviation from the probability distribution of stock returns (we'll discuss probability distributions below), but just think of volatility as a measure of how "changy" a stock price is.

Volatility is an absolutely crucial ingredient in the option price recipe—arguably *the* most critical. And yet, wouldn't you know, it's the one factor we cannot observe. It's true. Nobody can tell you the current volatility of any stock, anywhere, at any time. Dang! But we must have one and there are, fortunately, a couple of ways to get one. First, we can calculate *historical volatility* by calculating it from past stock price changes. Unfortunately, one of our bedrock assumptions is that past price changes cannot foretell future price changes so anything derived from past price changes is really, well, dubious at least. A second source, a more reliable source, is *implied volatility*. Calculating this is a neat trick and you might even think it bogus. But it actually works. And besides, if everyone is doing it, if everyone is punching the same number into their Black-Scholes calculator, it sort of doesn't matter, right? Sort of.

We get implied volatility by observing the market prices—the prices at which traders are *actually* buying and selling options—and deducing the volatility from those prices. Think of it

---

[2]$Stock\ Return = 1 + (EndPrice - StartPrice)/(StartPrice).$

this way: Black-Scholes requires five inputs and produces one output. If we have the output from some other source and four of the inputs, we can deduce mathematically or "imply" the missing input using algebra. Ignore for a minute the complicated Black-Scholes formula and picture a trivial formula like this:

$$x = a + b$$

If we're given a and b we, of course, just add them to find x. But if we're given, say, x and a, we can find b by just rearranging the formula into this:

$$b = x - a$$

So we subtract the given a from the given x to find b. Basic algebra. Same idea for implied volatility. We observe the output of Black-Scholes (the market price of an option) and four of its inputs (stock price, strike, time, interest rate) and plug those into a rearranged version of the Black-Scholes formula to get volatility. Now I'm tempted to show you such a rearranged version of Black-Scholes, but trust me it's just a big pile of *not* so basic math you can find elsewhere if you really need it. The point is we get implied volatility by seeing a market price and asking: What volatility factor would we have to plug into Black-Scholes to produce that price? But you may be asking a different question right about now: What's the point? What's the point of a formula to calculate an option price if you just use the market option price anyway? And it does perplex. But remember there's more than one option traded for a given stock, and it's the stock volatility we're after. You might have 10 call options on IBM, for instance, differing only by strike price (one option to buy at 50, another to buy at 55, and so on.) Say we're interested in the 50-strike call. Could we not imply the volatility of IBM from the market price of the 55-strike, and plug that into Black-Scholes for the price of the 50-strike? Yes! It's the volatility of the underlier we're after, so "backing out the vol input" from Black-Scholes doesn't seem quite so stupid after all.

But this leads us to another conundrum worth noting, the so-called "constant-volatility" assumption of Black-Scholes, which stems from the Black-Scholes assumption about how stock prices change. Intuitively, a stock should have just one volatility at a time, right? It's like the speed of a car. You can't be driving at both 60 and 65 mph at the same time, no more than you can weigh 195 and 205 at the same time. You would think the implied volatility from options differing only by strike price would be the same. But alas they typically are not. And here we approach the misty lands at the edge of Black-Scholes territory. For if you were to imply the volatility from, say, the market prices of seven otherwise identical calls on *ZED*, you are likely as not to get seven different volatilities for *ZED*. Graphically it might look like Figure 10-5.

Weird, huh? This says *ZED* has a volatility of, well, take your pick! And notice it looks a bit like a smile? It lends one of the names given to this phenomenon, the "volatility smile." Now they don't always turn out this way, and a snarl or sneer is as likely as a smile, but the point is you don't get a straight line as you would expect. The phenomenon is more formally known as *skew*. And whence

FIGURE 10-5

Volatility Smile or Skew

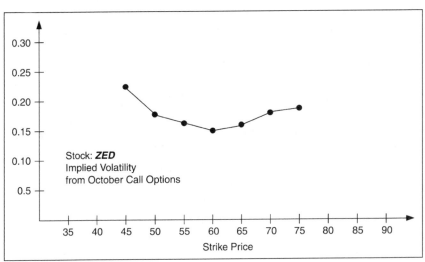

derives this peculiar thing? Well, the first thing you might wonder, as many do, is if the problem is with Black-Scholes. Considering some of its assumptions we'll see later—constant interest rates, lognormal stock price distributions, etc.—it's no surprise its results lead to things like skew. (It's *not* a perfect formula for the real world, clearly, but it's nearly so given its well-defined assumptions, and that's a lot.) Skew might also point to some rather intuitive, if difficult to quantify, possibilities such as investor preference for one strike over another. If demand for, say, a deep ITM option is different from a deep OTM, you would expect the market to bear different prices, and this is something Black-Scholes doesn't consider.

So the way people deal with this skew thing is to modify the model (i.e., build a different wind tunnel) for stock price changes. They price options with models different from Black-Scholes, models with names like *jump-diffusion* and *stochastic volatility* to name a couple. And they consider things such as *kurtosis,* having to do with the "peakiness" and "tail thickness" of a distribution. Now we shan't go down any of these those roads in this slender text, but at least you know some people do, people who might while away their minutes at the coffee pot talking about things like "leptokurtotic distributions" with their colleagues.

Oh, and one more important and related thing: Not only do implied volatilities exhibit weirdness across options with different strikes, they also do not line up when you sample the same option—option with the same strike—across different expiration months, or terms. Same intuition as before: You would expect the implied volatility from two market options who differ only in expiration to be the same. But alas you do not, getting instead something often termed *volatility term structure* and graphically looking something like Figure 10-6.

So now we have volatility anomalies across two dimensions—strike space and term space. These two anomalies are so closely related and have such similar practical effects that they are often merged into one, three-dimensional graphical representation. The resulting image is known as *volatility surface* and is simply a representation of implied volatility across strike space and term space at once. Vol surfaces look something like Figure 10-7.

FIGURE 10-6

Volatility Term Structure

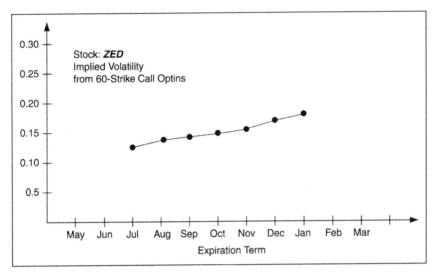

FIGURE 10-7

Volatility Surface

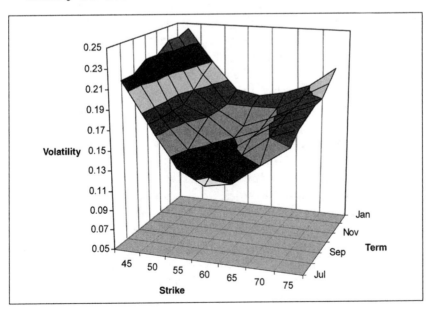

The Five Option Price Factors

Table 10-1 shows all five inputs to the Black-Scholes option pricing formula, that is, the five factors affecting the price of an equity option:

TABLE 10-1

Black-Scholes Pricing Factors

S	Stock Price
K	Strike Price
T	Time to Expiration
σ	Volatility
r	Interest Rate

Whether you care about how Black-Scholes works or not, if you plan to work with options it's a good idea to get real comfortable with these factors and how each affects the price of an option. Let's summarize those effects by examining what happens to the value of an option as each of these factors increases or decreases.

Stock Price (S) Increasing stock price increases the value of a call and decreases the value of a put. Makes sense, right? A call is an option to buy at a set strike, so the more you would have to pay *without* the call, the better off you are as a holder of the option. A put is an option to sell at a set strike so the relationship is, of course, reversed. You want your strike price to be more than you could get by selling spot, so as the stock price increases the value of a put option decreases.

Strike Price (K) This is just the above in reverse. Increasing strike price decreases the value of a call and increases the value of a put. Remember, the difference between stock price and strike price chiefly determines the value of an option, so increasing the strike price is like decreasing the stock price, and decreasing strike price is like increasing stock price. And we already know how stock price changes affect the option value from above.

Time to Expiration (T) Increasing time to expiration increases the value of calls *and* puts. The more time remains, the more values the underlier can potentially take on, so the more likely it is for an option to expire in the money. Just consider the extremes: Whether

TABLE 10-2

Effect of Factor Changes on Option Prices

Change in Factor	Effect on Call Value	Effect on Put Value
Increase S	Increase	Decrease
Increase K	Decrease	Increase
Increase T	Increase	Increase
Increase σ	Increase	Increase
Increase r	Increase	Decrease

you are holding a call or a put, you'd certainly like an option that never expires more than one that expires tomorrow, right?

Volatility (σ) Like time to expiration, increasing volatility increases the value of both calls and puts. The intuition is the same as well. The more "changy" a stock price, the more likely it is that an option on that stock will expire in the money, whether a call or a put. Volatility, you should know, is *the* most interesting price factor to option traders. So much so that "trading options" is often known as "trading volatility" because that's the most dynamic of price inputs. Now stock prices also change continuously and unpredictably, but options are all about probability. And as we will see below, volatility, as the standard deviation from a probability distribution, is literally an indicator of the probability of future stock price values.

Interest Rate (r) Increasing interest rates increases the value of a call and decreases the value of a put. The intuition isn't as obvious as with other factors because it involves opportunity costs. Here's the thing: Say you have a choice between buying a stock for 50 or buying a 50-strike call option and you buy the option. This means you have 50 bucks (less the price of the premium) to put into an interest-bearing savings account. While waiting to exercise the option, that savings earns interest. The higher the interest rate, the more you earn—for holding an option instead of buying the underlier. Now suppose you have a choice today between selling a stock for 50 or instead buying a 50-strike put. If you choose the option, you *don't* have that 50 to invest like the call holder does. While waiting to exercise the option, you don't earn any interest. So the higher the interest rate, the greater the opportunity cost of earning interest. The higher the interest rate, the more you *don't* earn. So a call holder benefits by higher interest, while the put holder takes a hit.

Table 10-2 is a summary of the effect of the five pricing factors on the price of an option. This is information worth getting to the top of your head if you plan to work with options.

The Black-Scholes Formula

Conceptually you can think of Black-Scholes as just another a function, taking inputs and generating output. For a call value, then, it's like this:

$$Call\ Value = BlackScholes(S, K, t, \sigma, r)$$

And in mathematical terms, here is the Black-Scholes Formula 10.5 for the value of a European call option on a nondividend paying stock, using the factors above and some mathematical expressions we'll explain in a minute:

$$c = SN(d_1) - Ke^{-rt}N(d_2) \qquad (10.5)$$

where c is the value of a European call option, S is current stock price, K is strike price, $N(\ )$ is the cumulative normal distribution function (more on this below) and d_1 and d_2 are these guys:

$$d_1 = \frac{\ln\left(\dfrac{S}{K}\right) + (r + \sigma^2/2)t}{\sigma\sqrt{t}}$$
$$d_2 = d_1 - \sigma\sqrt{t}$$

Ay, caramba! What a mess!! Well, sure it's mathy, but they don't give out Nobels for pound cake recipes. And it's not so bad if you take it one piece at a time. First, though, just take a look at the Black-Scholes formula together with the binomial tree formula to see a resemblance:

Black-Scholes: $c = SN(d_1) - Ke^{-rt}N(d_2)$

Binomial tree: $c = S\Delta - B$

The two formulas say basically the same thing! The value of a call option is equal to that of a portfolio consisting of some long position in stock (Δ shares in the binomial tree model, $N(d_1)$ shares in Black-Scholes) and some short position in a bond (B in the binomial tree model, $Ke^{-rt}N(d_2)$ in Black-Scholes). And a short position in a bond, recall, is just the borrowing of some money. Black-Scholes gives more precise quantities of stocks and bonds for the replicating portfolio, for a more precise option value.

We can appreciate how Black-Scholes gets its precision by examining and understanding the formula. As always, feel free to jump off here and skip ahead. We're about to get into some statistics and calculus, and no problem if those aren't your cups of tea. No need to know this stuff for most purposes. But if you're still curious and don't mind some math, let's go for it.

The Normal Distribution

First let's figure out this *cumulative normal distribution* function, or $N()$ in the formula. It tells us how many shares of stock we need to buy (S) as well as how much money to borrow as some portion of the discounted strike price (Ke^{-rt}). Now the arguments to $N() - d_1$ and d_2—just think of them as some numbers. What does the cumulative normal distribution function return for a given input X? What does $N(X)$ tell you? A statistician would tell you it gives the probability of a normally distributed random variable having a value less than X. A mathematician would tell you it gives the area beneath the normal probability distribution curve to the left of X. And here's a refresher in case those last two sentences mean nothing to you:

The basic thing to understand here is a *probability distribution*, which is a tool for telling us about the expected values of some *random variable* or *RV*. A random variable represents the numerical result from a *sampling*. There are a bazillion candidates for random variables out there. Consider the weight of a pumpkin—that's a perfectly autumnal *RV*. How much does a ripe pumpkin weigh on average? What's the likelihood of it weighing more than 10 pounds? Less then 2 pounds? A probability distribution *exists* to answer questions just like these.

Imagine spending one autumn visiting pumpkin stands and selecting pumpkins at random for weighing. You record each weight in pounds, then count the pumpkins at each weight. A nice

FIGURE 10-8

Sampling Histogram

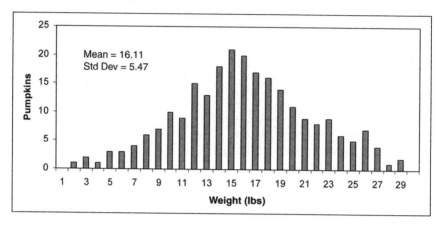

way of presenting your data is a *histogram* where the height of each bar gives the number of pumpkins having a certain weight. So the X-axis is for weight and the Y-axis is for counts, as in Figure 10-8.

Now just by looking at our histogram, we can glean some facts about the pumpkins. The highest bars are around 15, telling us this is the average or *mean* weight. (It's 16.11 to be precise.) Another less intuitive fact is something called *standard deviation*, which measures how "bunched up" the data points are around the mean. To understand this important statistic, first remember that each bar of the histogram is like a stack of pumpkins. Think about any one of these pumpkins, say one of the pumpkins in the 7 stack. Now consider the difference between the mean weight (say 15) and the weight of this pumpkin (7), which is just 8 (i.e., $15 - 7$). A pumpkin on the 19 stack has a difference of -4 (i.e., $15 - 19$). Imagine calculating this difference for every pumpkin, squaring all the results (to make them all positive values) and taking the average of your results. That average is known as the *variance*. For these pumpkins it turns out to be 29.94. Now take the square root of variance, to undo the effect of squaring and return things to the original units. The result is the standard deviation, or for these pumpkins, 5.47.

The important thing to remember about standard deviation is best illustrated graphically. It measures the "bunchiness" or

FIGURE 10-9

Sampling Histogram with Greater Dispersion

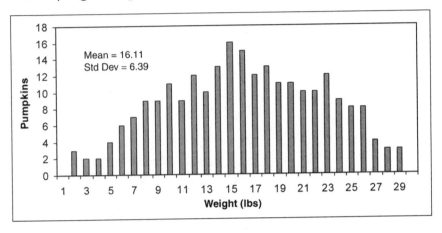

dispersion of a random variable. Figure 10-9 shows another hypothetical pumpkin sampling. In this new distribution, you can see how pumpkin weights are, on average, farther from the mean, which is again 16.11. Thus although the mean is the same, it has a higher standard deviation of 6.39. The greater the standard deviation, the greater the dispersion.

Now everything we've said so far about pumpkin weights pertains only to this particular sampling. But if the random variable samples meet certain conditions—that they are identically distributed (every sampling has the same probability characteristics) and independently distributed (the weight of one pumpkin does not affect the weight of any other pumpkin)—then we can safely say *any* pumpkin has a weight that is *normally distributed*. This essentially means if you were to sample every single pumpkin at every stand, a "histogram" of the precise (not rounded) weights would be shaped as in Figure 10-10.

The normal distribution is perhaps the most widely used probability distribution of them all and is sometimes called a bell curve distribution for its shape. Again, think of the normal as a histogram for an entire *population* of random variable values, as opposed to just the *sample* pumpkins. Population mean is typically

FIGURE 10-10

Normal Distribution

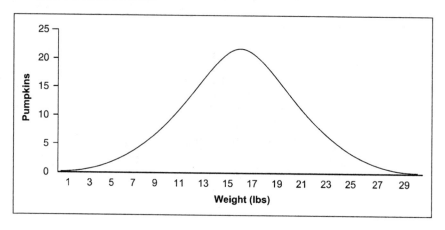

FIGURE 10-11

Population Mean and Standard Deviation

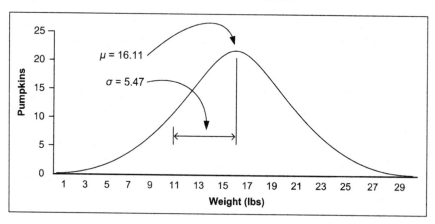

denoted by the Greek letter mu, or μ. Population variance is typically depicted by the symbol σ^2 or "sigma-squared," and standard deviation by σ or "sigma" as shown in Figure 10-11.

Now let's move on to the good stuff. First, recall the numbers along the X-axis (horizontal) represent possible values for the

FIGURE 10-12

Area Beneath the Normal Curve

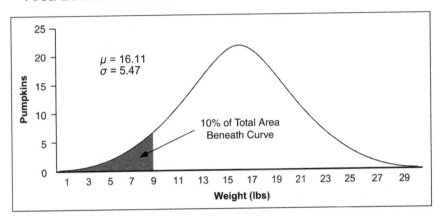

random variable. In our case, these are pumpkin weights. The height of the curve over a given point is the proportional number of pumpkins having that weight. We can see that quite a few pumpkins weigh around 15, whereas only a few weigh more than 25 pounds. Now the key thing to observe from a distribution is *the area beneath the curve*, which translates directly into a probability of the random variable taking on some value or another. Let's start with an extreme case. What is the probability that a random variable will take on some value, any value? Why it's 100 percent of course, or the entire area under the curve, or just "1" if you will. And what do you suppose is the probability of the random variable taking a value less than or equal to the mean, or 15? Well, because half the pumpkins weigh less than the mean and half have more, it's reasonable to say there is a 50 percent probability of that being the case. And what is the area beneath the curve to the left of the mean? Fifty percent. So it turns out this is true for any value of X. The probability of the random variable taking on a value less than X is just the area beneath the curve to the left of that point. In our pumpkin distribution, for example, the area beneath the curve to the left of 9 pounds is 10 percent of the total areas. Thus, there is a 10 percent probability that a pumpkin chosen at random will weigh no more than 9 pounds. See Figure 10-12.

The area to the left of the 21-pound mark happens to be 81 percent, which is the probability of a pumpkin weighing no more than 21 pounds. For $X = 26$ the area is 96 percent. And this brings us to the *raison d'etre* for this little lesson. That area beneath a curve, which measures the probability of a random variable taking on some value less than the X-value at which the area stops, is known as the *cumulative normal distribution*.

Calculating an area beneath a curve is where the calculus comes in—*integral calculus* in fact, as the area beneath a curve is known as the integral of the function the produces it.[3] Now you can imagine that there are many possible normal distributions. And calculating integrals is a lot of work, even for computers. To reduce this drudgery someone a long time ago imagined a normal distribution with a mean of 0 and standard deviation of 1. Such a distribution is known as the *standard normal distribution,* and the cumulative normal distributions for the standard normal have been calculated for scads of X-values and documented in numerous textbook appendices and programmed into a great many computer programs and calculators. And how does this help us? It turns out that the cumulative normal of any normal distribution can be easily calculated from the cumulative normal from the standard normal distribution. Whoo hoo! A labor-saving device if ever there was one.

Summarizing a bit, the cumulative normal distribution function $N(X)$ returns for a given value X the area beneath the normal distribution curve to the left of X. This area is equal to the probability of a normally distributed random variable having a value less than X. The cumulative normal distribution for any normal distribution is derivable from that of the standard normal distribution. In the Black-Scholes formula, $N(d_1)$ tells us that the number of shares of stock in a replicating portfolio is equal to the probability of a standard normally distributed random variable having a value equal to d_1. Voila.

And that's all you need to know to understand what's going on in the formula. But while we're here, let's jump off the path and point out how we can connect the pumpkin thing with the option

---

[3]The other type of calculus you might recall is *differential calculus,* which is concerned with the slope (rise over run) of the curve at a single point.

pricing thing. Imagine you stumbled across this undocumented button on your kid's computer that did something slightly out of the ordinary. Let's say, hmm, let's say it turned back time for the entire earth for exactly one day. Reasonable? Okay. Now imagine you sample the closing price of the stock ZED one day. Then you press the button, wait for a day, and again sample the closing price of ZED. It's different from before because that's just how random processes work. So you do this again and again several hundred times (it's kinda fun, right?), then use your data to calculate mu and sigma and use those to plot yourself a distribution curve just like we did with pumpkin weights. Now you have a probability distribution for stock prices.

For better or worse, we don't have world replay buttons on our computers like that. But Black, Scholes, and Merton essentially imagined they *did* have such a button and made an important assumption about the resulting curve. Did they assume stock prices were normally distributed? Not exactly. We won't go into all the reasons why, but they assumed stock price *returns* are normally distributed, which happens when stock *prices* are log-normally distributed. And we'll explore that further when we cover all the Black-Scholes assumptions below.

APPLYING BLACK-SCHOLES

Now back to the formula:

$$c = SN(d_1) - Ke^{-rt}N(d_2)$$

That $N()$ function is really the trickiest part of Black-Scholes. The rest, calculating the d_1 and d_2 values, is just algebra. There are some square roots and exponents and Euler's number e in there. And the natural log function $ln()$ is something your calculator is only too happy to calculate for you. The function $ln(x)$, you might recall, as the inverse of the natural exponential function, returns the number you need to raise e to in order to get x.

$$d_1 = \frac{ln\left(\frac{S}{K}\right) + (r + \sigma^2/2)t}{\sigma\sqrt{t}}$$

$$d_2 = d_1 - \sigma\sqrt{t}$$

So let's fill up the tank and fire up this Nobel-prize winning contraption. Say we want to again value our old friend cZED62, a European call option on the stock *ZED* that expires in 6 months with a strike price of 62, this time using Black-Scholes. We'll use the exact same factors as before plus a volatility factor. Let's choose .15. Here's the math:

$$S = 60$$
$$K = 62$$
$$t = .5$$
$$\sigma = .15$$
$$r = .06$$

Call Value = *BlackScholes*(S, K, t, σ, r)

$$c = SN(d_1) - Ke^{-rt}N(d_2)$$

$$d_1 = \frac{ln\left(\dfrac{S}{K}\right) + (r + \sigma^2/2)t}{\sigma\sqrt{t}}$$

$$d_1 = \frac{ln\left(\dfrac{60}{62}\right) + (.06 + .15^2/2).5}{.15\sqrt{.5}}$$

$$d_1 = \frac{ln(0.9677) + 0.0356}{0.1061}$$

$$d_1 = 0.0267$$

$$d_2 = d_1 - \sigma\sqrt{t}$$

$$d_2 = 0.0267 - .15\sqrt{0.5}$$

$$d_2 = -0.0793$$

$$c = SN(d_1) - Ke^{-rt}N(d_2)$$
$$c = 60N(0.0267) - 62e^{-(.06)(.5)}N(-0.0793)$$
$$c = 60(0.5107) - 62(.9704)(0.4684)$$
$$c = 30.64 - 28.18$$
$$c = 2.46$$

Black-Scholes tells us the fair market value of this option is 2.46. Compare this with the 2.53 from the one-step binomial tree. And it, of course, falls in the range of 0 to 60, which we identified using the rough method. And again we see the value falling much closer to the bottom of that range, as we expect with most out-of-the-money options.

Black-Scholes Assumptions

Black-Scholes is darn good but not perfect. It's still based on a wind-tunnel test that draws facts from a model—a very good model, but still a model. We can tell how the model differs from the real world by examining the assumptions made by Black-Scholes about stock price changes. There are three biggies.

First is the Black-Scholes assumption about how stock prices change over time. As you noticed above, it assumes stock returns are normally distributed. Not prices, mind you, but returns. Normally distributed random variables can take values less than zero and stock prices are always positive—so they can't be normally distributed. But stock *returns* can be negative and, thanks to something in mathland known as the *central limit theorem*, assuming they are independently and identically distributed, we can say they are normally distributed—that is, histograms of very large samplings will take on the familiar bell curve shape. One can also assert, as Black-Scholes does, that returns are normally distributed by assuming stock price paths follow a *stochastic* or "essentially unpredictable" process. Think of process in this sense as the path created as the value of something, in this case returns, changes over time. Black-Scholes further assumes that returns follow a special form of stochastic process known as Brownian motion, a type of Weiner process, or a process in which the random variable changes continuously and whose changes are normally distributed.

Now it so happens there's this distribution called the *log-normal*, which essentially plots the logs (the number you have to raise *e* to ...) of a normally distributed random variable that follows a process known as *geometric Brownian motion*. And mathematically it can be shown that if a stock price is log-normally

FIGURE 10-13

Normal and Log-Normal Distribution Comparison

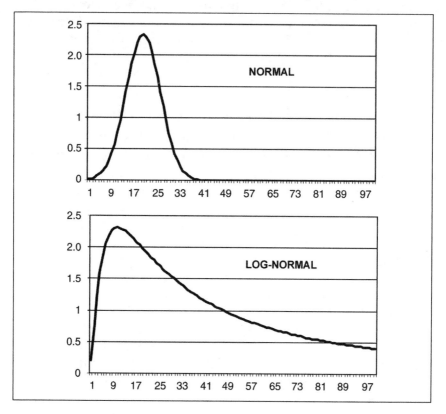

distributed, it's return is normally distributed. Bottom line, Black-Scholes assumes that stock *returns* are normally distributed by assuming that stock *prices* are log-normally so. Figure 10-13 pairs up a normal and lognormal distribution to give the basic idea.

You might wonder about the asymmetric shape of the log-normal and how that fits with reality. If you think about it, the U.S. stock market over many decades has been a bull market. Over long periods of time the value of stocks overall has increased. (Of course, over relatively short periods it can be a bear market, with stock prices decreasing.) The log-normal model, if you look at it and think about it, fits with that fact. The left-hand slope is steeper than the right, which says there are fewer price decreases than increases. So in this respect it's not a bad model of reality.

And before we leave the log-normal, here's a fact you'll want to know: The binomial distribution, the distribution produced by the binomial tree we used in the previous section, approaches the log-normal as you add levels to the tree. So there's another reason we like the log-normal and a key link between the binomial tree method of option pricing and Black-Scholes.

The normal distribution, of course, is where we get the volatility values required by the formula. Now stemming from the Black-Scholes assumption about normally distributed stock returns, it also assumes there is only *one* such distribution applicable to the price of an option, irrespective of its strike price or term. This is where the skew thing, and the warped volatility surface, gets Black-Scholes into trouble. This is often known as the "constant volatility assumption" of Black-Scholes, and like other assumptions, it just doesn't jive with what we see empirically.

The second huge assumption of Black-Scholes is that markets are frictionless. This means one can trade continuously with no transactions costs, taxes, or other encumbrances of any kind. This assumption is required by the dynamic hedging involved in maintaining the replicating portfolio of stocks and bonds. Recall from the binomial tree method that the replicating portfolio changed slightly at every step, and with a tree of infinitely small steps the portfolio changes continuously. Only a frictionless market would permit such a thing.

Third, Black-Scholes assumes constant interest rates. In other words, interest rates don't change over the course of contract. But, of course, they can and do.

Are stock prices *really* log-normally distributed? Probably not. Are markets *really* frictionless? Definitely not. Trading does involve commissions and other costs, truly continuous trading is impossible, etc. Are interest rates constant? Not usually. Still, owing to widespread acceptance of Black-Scholes, we can say clearly the markets believe that these assumptions are reasonable. Further, nobody is limited to Black-Scholes as it comes "out of the box." Indeed, a great many fine minds are forever at work modifying and extending Black-Scholes, for example, to deal with the implied volatility anomalies we discussed earlier, all in pursuit of the illusive "real" value of an option.

Why all the interest in a better and better price? Why isn't Black-Scholes good enough? Because the better your pricing *analytics*, as they are known, the better you are at spotting pricing errors in the market, that is, people offering to buy or sell at the "wrong" price. And as we'll explore further in the next chapter, and as you may have already gathered, pricing algorithms also provide hedging instructions. So if your analytics tell you that something in the market is mispriced, you can lock in the difference between the market price by hedging according to those same analytics, thus realizing an arbitrage. So arbitrage is indeed attainable even today, but you need damn good analytics to pull it off.

PUT-CALL PARITY

So far we've dealt only with call options. There is a variation of the Black-Scholes call option formula for valuing put options, given below, but it's good to know that put prices are mathematically linked to call prices due to an important concept known as *put-call parity*. To get some intuition behind the put-call-parity, imagine that you form a portfolio by buying 100 shares of a $5 stock, buying one put option to sell (100 shares of) that same stock at $5, and writing one call option to buy it at $5. If you think through a sample of possible prices for the stock, you will quickly see that the value of this portfolio at expiration is $5 no matter what. So the value of the portfolio must be the present value of $5. Algebraically, then, we arrive at the put-call parity for European options in Formula 10.6.

$$S + p - c = Ke^{-rt} \qquad (10.6)$$

where

$$S = \text{stock price}$$
$$p = \text{put option price}$$
$$c = \text{call option price}$$
$$K = \text{strike price for both call and put}$$
$$e^{-rt} = \text{discount factor}$$
$$Ke^{-rt} = PV(K) = \text{present value of strike price}$$

The put-call parity can be arranged, of course, into whatever form we like, depending on what we're after. To wit, here are four expressions of put-call parity for European options on non-dividend paying stock:

$$S = c - p + Ke^{-rt}$$
$$c = S + p - Ke^{-rt}$$
$$p = c - S + Ke^{-rt}$$
$$Ke^{-rt} = S + p - c$$

So owing to the put-call parity and math we shall not delve into, 10.7 is the Black-Scholes formula for valuing European put options on nondividend paying stocks.

$$Put\ Value = BlackScholes(S, K, t, \sigma, r)$$
$$p = Ke^{-rt}N(-d_2) - SN(-d_1) \tag{10.7}$$

where, as before, $N(\ )$ is the cumulative normal distribution function and d_1 and d_2 are again these guys:

$$d_1 = \frac{ln\left(\dfrac{S}{K}\right) + (r + \sigma^2/2)t}{\sigma\sqrt{t}}$$
$$d_2 = d_1 - \sigma\sqrt{t}$$

Effect of Discrete Dividends

So far we've dealt only with options on stocks that don't pay dividends. Dividends are payments made by stock issuers to their stock holders, typically at some interval like every 3 months. Think of these as *discrete dividends* (versus continuous dividends, which we'll get to next). When a dividend is paid, it immediately lowers the value of the stock because receiving a dividend is like partially "cashing in" your investment in the issuer. Another way to think of this is that some portion of a dividend-paying stock price is the present value of all future dividend payments. Now imagine that you are pricing a call option with a 9-month term. Of course you need a stock price—but the current stock price includes the *PV* of, say, three dividend payments, *which the option holder will not receive.* A more appropriate stock price is one from which the *PV* of those three dividends has been removed, known as a *dividend-adjusted stock price*.

Now companies are free to change their dividend payments from time to time, but it so happens they don't change all that much, so at any time there is a decent consensus on the future expected dividends from a stock issuer. So to price an option on such a stock, we first calculate the present value of the expected stream of all dividends paid before option expiration. (This is easier than it sounds. Just look back to our earlier explanation of calculating present values. Do that once for each dividend and sum the results. There's your *PV* of the dividend stream.) We subtract that *PV* from the stock price, then plug this dividend-adjusted stock price into our option valuation formula in lieu of the regular stock price. If and when issuers pay dividends that deviate from expectations, or simply announce their intention to do so, this, of course, immediately affects the dividend-adjusted stock price; this is why dividend announcements and unexpected dividend payments affect option prices.

To modify the Black-Scholes formulas to work for options on dividend paying stocks, we simply replace all occurrences of the factor "*S*" (stock price) with "*S* − *PV(D)*" (dividend-adjusted stock price) where *D* represents future dividend payments to be paid before expiration. See Formulas 10.8 and 10.9.

$$Call\ Value = BlackScholes(S, D, K, t, \sigma, r)$$

$$D = Discrete\ dividends$$

$$c = (S - PV(D))N(d_1) - Ke^{-rt}N(d_2) \qquad (10.8)$$

$$Put\ Value = BlackScholes(S, D, K, t, \sigma, r)$$

$$p = Ke^{-rt}N(-d_2) - (S - PV(D))N(-d_1) \quad (10.9)$$

$$d_1 = \frac{ln\left(\dfrac{S - PV(D)}{K}\right) + (r + \sigma^2/2)t}{\sigma\sqrt{t}}$$

$$d_2 = d_1 - \sigma\sqrt{t}$$

Effect of Continuous Dividends

Think of discrete dividends as money that "drips" out of the underlier at some regular interval. Not only can an underlier drip like this, but some underliers "leak" money continuously. The value of foreign currency, for example, when priced in local currency, decreases continuously by the foreign risk-free interest rate. Or a stock index, with a great many component stocks all dripping discrete dividends on their own schedules, can be seen as leaking a continuous stream. For option pricing, we think of these leaks as *continuous dividends*. Just like discrete dividends, they affect the price of an option by effectively lowering the value of the underlier. And they, too, decrease the value of the stock by the present value of the expected dividend stream over the life of the option. We use slightly different math to arrive at that present value, however, because continuous dividends are actually just like continuously compounded interest. So the dividend rate is treated like an interest rate and affects the value of the underlier. See Formulas 10.10 and 10.11.

$$Call\ Value = BlackScholes(S, d, K, t, \sigma, r)$$
$$d = Continuous\ dividend\ rate$$
$$c = Se^{-dt}N(d_1) - Ke^{-rt}N(d_2) \tag{10.10}$$
$$Put\ Value = BlackScholes(S, d, K, t, \sigma, r)$$
$$p = Ke^{-rt}N(-d_2) - Se^{-dt}N(-d_1) \tag{10.11}$$

$$d_1 = \frac{ln\left(\dfrac{Se^{-dt}}{K}\right) + (r + \sigma^2/2)t}{\sigma\sqrt{t}}$$

$$d_2 = d_1 - \sigma\sqrt{t}$$

Alternatively,

$$d_1 = \frac{ln\left(\dfrac{Se^{-dt}}{Ke^{-rt}}\right)}{\sigma\sqrt{t}} + \frac{\sigma\sqrt{t}}{2}$$

$$d_2 = d_1 - \sigma\sqrt{t} = \frac{ln\left(\dfrac{Se^{-dt}}{Ke^{-rt}}\right)}{\sigma\sqrt{t}} - \frac{\sigma\sqrt{t}}{2}$$

And here's a little bonus. You can use the continuous dividend option pricing formulas for options on two other kinds of underliers: stock indices and foreign currency. For an index, S is just the index price (i.e., an average of a bunch of individual stocks) and d is the approximate total dividend flow from all the dividend-paying stocks in the index. For foreign currency, S is the spot price in local currency (i.e., the currency you want the option value in) of one unit of foreign currency. And d is the risk-free interest rate paid in the foreign country.

AMERICAN OPTIONS AND EARLY EXERCISE

So far we've restricted our discussion of Black-Scholes to the valuation of European options, which can only be exercised on the expiration date. Americans, of course, can be exercised any time up to and including expiry. And here's the basic question: Is it ever wise to exercise an American option before the expiration date? Yes, but not as often as you might think. First, it is *never* wise to exercise early an American call option on a nondividend paying stock. It *may* be optimal to exercise early an American call or put on a dividend-paying stock, depending mostly on the size of the dividend. And it may be optimal to early exercise an American put on a nondividend paying stock if it's deeply in the money.

Consider the case of a nondividend paying stock. Imagine holding 100 American call options with a strike price of 30 on a stock currently trading for 50, and the options don't expire for another 3 months. If you exercise, you get to buy 10,000 shares of stock (remember each option is to buy 100 shares) for $300,000 instead of the going price of $500,000—saving a whopping $200,000! Who could pass up an opportunity like that? You should. Why? Because there are two alternatives to exercise in which you are better off.

First, you can simply sell the option and lock in a profit of *more* than $200,000. That's just the intrinsic value, recall, so you know the option must be worth more than that. And this is cash you get to keep no matter what; if you exercise and hold, remember, the stock price can tank and take those gains with it. If you exercise and sell immediately, the most you get is intrinsic value. So selling the option is always better than exercising.

If you can't sell the option, you can still take that $300,000 and, rather than using it to purchase stock, invest it at the risk-free rate. After 3 months the stock price will either be above the $30 strike price or below it. If it is above, cash in your investment, use $300,000 to buy the stock, and pocket the interest as a bonus. If it is below, cash in your investment and use some portion of the $300,000 to buy the stock, and again pocket the interest. In either case you are better off (because of the interest) than if you had exercised and held the stock.

You still might be thinking: What if I believe the stock price is sure to fall? Shouldn't I exercise and sell immediately if I can't sell the option, to at least lock in the intrinsic value? If you really believe the stock price will fall, then you should sell the stock short. If the stock price falls as you expect, you make money from the short stock position—and you haven't given up the opportunity to exercise your option.

In the case of American options on dividend-paying stocks, it may be optimal to exercise early, just before or after the dividend payment, in order to get the dividend and future dividends. (Remember, it goes to the stock holder.) The basic idea for a call is to compare the present value of all remaining dividends with the sum of the option value and the interest you will lose on K by exercising. If the former exceeds the latter, go for it. You only do this immediately before the dividend pays because doing so earlier gains you nothing and gives up optionality. Because option value and foregone interest changes over time, you need to reevaluate for early exercise before every dividend. While it may not be wise to exercise before the next dividend, it could be wise to exercise just before the next or a later one.

In the case of an American put on a dividend-paying stock, the same intuition applies but in reverse. And you make the decision just *after* a dividend is paid. If the present value of interest on the strike price—which, remember, you don't get if you don't exercise—is greater than the PV of remaining dividends and option value, you should exercise. Here you don't mind giving up remaining dividends and optionality because you'll make more by selling the stock and investing the proceeds.

Unlike an American call on a nondividend paying stock, it turns out it may be optimal to exercise an American put on a nondividend paying stock—if it is very deep in the money. Imagine, for instance, that a stock price is nearly zero and the strike price of your put is $5. You'll never get more than $5 because the stock price can't go below zero. And you might as well collect the payoff now so you can put it to work earning interest.

WHICH METHOD TO USE?

Black-Scholes cannot be applied to all types of options; for some you must use a tree method. Here's the lowdown:

For European calls and puts on nondividend-paying stocks, use Black-Scholes in its simplest form. For European calls and puts on dividend-paying stocks, use Black-Scholes modified for discrete or continuous dividends, whichever the case may be, using the formulas laid out earlier.

For American calls on dividend-paying stocks, you can arrive at an approximate option value using Black-Scholes by applying it twice and taking the maximum of the two results. On the first application you assume exercise (just before the dividend date) and for the second you assume no exercise. It's just an approximation; the tree method is a better choice.

For American puts, Black-Scholes is simply not a choice. You must use a the binomial tree method because an analytical method for pricing an American put option simply does not exist. An *analytical* solution is one in which you plug factors into a function and get a result. A nonanalytical method is more of a brute-force or trial-and-error approach, which the tree method really is once you think about it. A faithful explanation of why no analytical solution exists would go well beyond the scope of our little book. It's an example of a "free boundary" problem and these things are *hard*— like trying to predict precisely where water will flow when poured from a bucket onto a flat surface. If you can solve this one, the Nobel committee is waiting to hear from you.

Incidentally, there is an extension of the binomial method known as the *trinomial method*, often used in practice for pricing options. It's the same basic idea as the binomial but instead of assuming a stock can change to one of two prices at each node, we assume it can also remain unchanged—so there are three possible values, ergo the name. It makes for a more complicated tree, but as it turns out the math can actually be simpler, and therefore faster to perform in a time crunch. And when it comes to option pricing, there is always a time crunch.

And while we're on the subject of alternative methods, we should touch briefly on the *martingale* approach to pricing. Like Black-Scholes, it is based on a "continuous-time" model, meaning time intervals are infinitesimally small. (Time intervals in the "discrete-time" binomial and trinomial models are also small, but not infinitesimally so.) As it relates to the pricing of derivatives, a martingale is a stochastic (unpredictable) price process with no discernable trend. Using the martingale approach, you apply formulas and constructs assuming stock prices are martingales, that is, moving with no trends. Only they don't. Over time, stock prices tend to drift up. And discount bond prices are expected to increase as well. So there are these transformations you can apply to make derivative underlier prices behave like martingales, and these are known as *equivalent martingale measures*. We won't go into these, but at least you know now that Black-Scholes with its partial differential equation is not the only game in town when it comes to cool pricing models.

PRICING OPTIONS ON FUTURES

The first thing to remember here is that a futures price (like a forward price) is just a spot price adjusted for carry. So options on futures are like options on stock, but the value on expiration is not the difference between exercise and stock prices, but between exercise and a futures prices.

Should you hold a call option on a futures with a strike price of 35, and the futures price on expiration is 39, exercising the option gives you $4. It also gives you a long position in the futures, which you can either unwind immediately (for little or no cost) or hold if you so choose. The option writer is obligated to take a correspond-ing short position in the futures. Should you hold that futures option and the futures price at expiration is 34, your option expires worthless. Oh well. Same thing in reverse for a put option. Your option is in the money when its strike price exceeds the futures price, and is otherwise out of the money, or at the money if strike happens to equal the futures price.

Now, to calculate an option on a futures contract, we use Black-Scholes with just two changes. First, the underlier is a futures contract potentially initiated at time t (expiration) and going on to a delivery date we'll call t' (read "t prime"). So the futures contract we might do at expiration is $F(t, t')$. Now notice we have three dates: the date when the option is executed, which we'll denote t_0 or "t zero", t when the option expires and the futures commences, and t' when the futures contract delivers. The first change to the formula, then, is to replace the S factor with $F(t_0, t')$. Second, to account for daily interest received on a replicating portfolio including lent funds in the amount of $F(t_0, t')$, we treat the underlier as if it has a continuous dividend, using the risk-free interest rate for the "dividend" rate. Using Black-Scholes in this way, modified this way for future options, is known as *Black's model*.[4] Here is Black's model in Formulas 10.12 and 10.13.

$$Call\ Value = Black(F(t_0, t'), d, K, t, \sigma, r)$$
$$F(t_0, t') = \text{underlier futures price}$$
$$d = \text{continuous dividend rate}$$
$$c = F(t_0, t')e^{-dt}N(d_1) - Ke^{-rt}N(d_2) \qquad (10.12)$$
$$Put\ Value = Black(F(t_0, t'), d, K, t, \sigma, r)$$
$$p = Ke^{-rt}N(-d_2) - F(t_0, t')e^{-dt}N(-d_1) \quad (10.13)$$

$$d_1 = \frac{ln\left(\dfrac{F(t_0, t')e^{-dt}}{Ke^{-rt}}\right)}{\sigma\sqrt{t}} + \frac{\sigma\sqrt{t}}{2}$$

$$d_2 = d_1 - \sigma\sqrt{t} = \frac{ln\left(\dfrac{F(t_0, t')e^{-dt}}{Ke^{-rt}}\right)}{\sigma\sqrt{t}} - \frac{\sigma\sqrt{t}}{2}$$

---

[4]Fischer Black devised it.

Hedging a Derivatives Position

HEDGING SWAPS AND OPTIONS

Consider the options dealer or market-maker, who as a matter of course buys and sells derivatives all day long, taking on new exposures with every new trade. If they do nothing, on some of the exposures they will likely gain and on some they will lose, depending on how the market moves thereafter. But in general the dealer is not interested in making upside profits—that's the dominion of the speculator. The dealer wants to make money on every trade no matter what, and is willing to forego upside along with downside in order to make that happen. And they do so by hedging, managing the exposure created by taking on a new position in a derivative. Notice how this contrasts with our "classic" hedger from the earlier chapter who used derivatives to hedge an exposure stemming from some nonderivative.

We'll examine derivatives risk management from the perspective of two market-makers: the swaps dealer and options dealer. The swaps dealer can hedge nicely with offsetting positions in interest rate futures or bonds, and the options dealer can hedge most of their exposure with offsetting positions in the underlier. We choose the swaps dealer and options dealer because they illustrate two very different hedging requirements. The swaps dealer (and any dealer of forward-based derivatives) can manage risk with a *static* hedge. This essentially means they can form the hedge position and more or less forget about it until it's time to close it. The options dealer, on the other hand, can only manage risk with a *dynamic* hedge. This is a hedge position that must be monitored and adjusted nearly continuously for as long as the hedge is required.

Hedging a Swap

Imagine you're a swaps dealer who just executed a 1-year, fixed-for-floating Libor swap with some business using the swap to effectively convert a preexisting floating rate debt into a fixed rate. As the party to receive fixed, you are said to have "sold" the swap. (The party who pays fixed is said to "buy.") The swap has a notional of $1 million and fixed rate of 3.5 percent. Its coupon frequency is 3 months, so every quarter for the next 2 years you will make a payment based on a floating rate of interest on an imaginary $1 million loan, and receive a payment based on a rate of 3.5 percent or $8750 (i.e., $1,000,000 * .035/4$). You are thus exposed to changing interest rates. Should they increase, so will the net of your payments and receipts, effectively causing you a loss. And should they decrease, so will your payments, effectively making you money. How the heck do you manage that exposure? And how, by the way, do you make some money whether interest rates rise or fall?

To get your mind around swap hedging, first thing you do is chop the big problem into a bunch of smaller problems. Remember, a swap is equivalent to a portfolio of forwards. In other words, executing this 2-year quarterly swap is economically equivalent to taking short positions in a series of 3-month Floating Rate Agreements or FRAs—one for each of the swap coupons. On each FRA expiration date you would make a payment if rates exceed the delivery price or receive a payment should rates be below. Just like your swap obligation.

Now all you need is some hedging instrument with the same payoff characteristics as your FRAs, something in which you can take offsetting positions such that every 3 months you will receive money should rates increase and make a payment should they fall. The Eurodollar Futures Contract, an exchange-traded instrument whose underlier is Libor and whose payoff characteristics

FIGURE 11-1

Short Swap Payoff

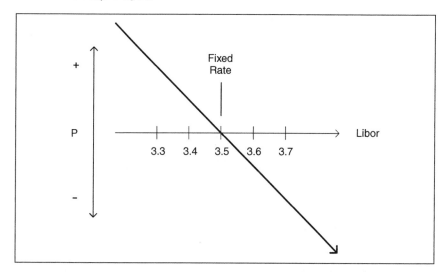

are similar to that of a FRA, is just such a hedging instrument. Another instrument is a government bond that makes quarterly payments and whose price changes are correlated with Libor, such as U.S. Treasury bonds. Both Eurodollar Futures and U.S. Treasuries are used a zillion times a day by swaps dealers around the world to hedge their exposures.[1]

So let's use futures to hedge the swap. We'll look first at just one coupon period in the middle of the swap, but the idea is the same for the entirety of any plain-vanilla swap. Let's express the swap coupon in terms of a payoff diagram for the swap dealer in Figure 11-1.

By virtue of the swap, the dealer has a short position (hence the idea you are the seller of the swap) on forward Libor at a delivery price of 3.5 percent or $8750 as we calculated above, and a delivery date 12 months out. Now short forward positions always make money when the spot price is below delivery price. So, for

---

[1]Futures that expire within 4 or 5 years tend to be much more liquid than futures for periods further out, so dealers tend to use them for so-called "front-terms." For periods further out, bonds tend to be the favored hedging instrument.

FIGURE 11-2

Long Eurodollar Futures Payoff

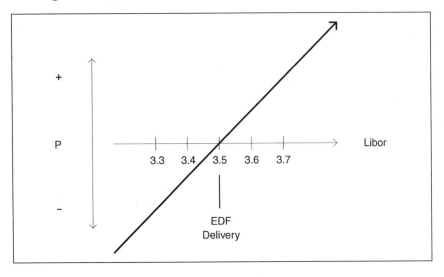

example, should Libor settle at 3.4 percent, they make a gain of
$250 (i.e., 1,000,000 * (.035/4 − .034/4)). By the same reasoning and
math, they will lose $250 should rates increase to 3.6.

Now consider the payoff of a long position in a Eurodollar
futures contract with a delivery date 12 months out and delivery
price of 3.5 percent. Eurodollar futures, or EDFs, have a notional of
$1 million. The actual underlier is 3 months of Libor interest, so in
dollars the delivery price is $8750—just like our coupon. Here's the
long EDF payoff in Figure 11-2.

Now we're getting somewhere. A combined short position in
the swap coupon and long position in the EDF gives us a net exposure in Figure 11-3.

No more worries about rising interest rates. But wait! The
dealer isn't writing a swap just for the fun of it. They would like to
make some money for their trouble. So instead of an EDF with a
delivery price of 3.5, let's use 3.4 instead. That shifts the futures
payoff line to the left, which raises the net payoff, as in Figure 11-4.

The dealer can now bank on a profit whether interest rates rise
or fall. And what if they take the other side of the swap, and receive

FIGURE 11-3

Net Swap and Eurodollar Futures Payoff

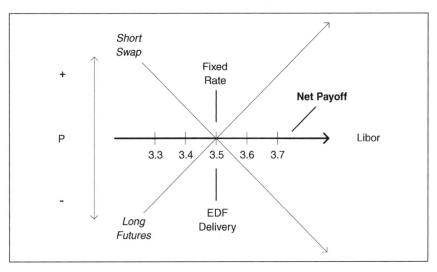

FIGURE 11-4

Net Swap and Eurodollar Futures Payoff with Dealer Profit

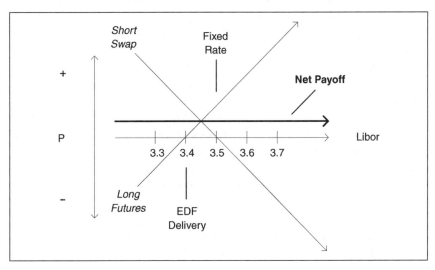

FIGURE 11-5

Net Long Swap and Short Eurodollar Futures Payoff
with Dealer Profit

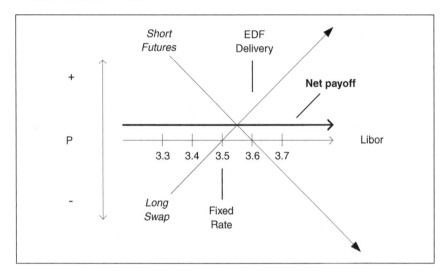

floating and pay fixed? Same hedge, different side. Instead of long futures positions, they take short futures positions with delivery prices slightly higher, for positive net payoffs, as in Figure 11-5.

Now a couple of practical points are in order because swaps in practice aren't hedged exactly as we see above, but the idea is the same. First, you can't exactly choose the delivery price of a new futures contract. Recall that it's set such that the initial value of the contract is zero. You can, though, adjust the fixed rate of the swap you are willing to sell. And this is how it works in practice; the fixed rate is set some number of basis points away from the "break-even rate" such that the dealer makes some money. Second, we've seen just one coupon of a multicoupon swap. And due to the term structure of interest rates, each coupon is bound to have a different break-even rate, but we want a single fixed rate for the entire swap, right?

If this intrigues you, then take a look back at the swaps chapter and see how we chose the break-even fixed rate, or swap rate, by setting up each leg of the swap as a series of cash flows, one using forward interest rates (which generally differed from one coupon to the next) and another using a fixed rate, which we chose by trial-and-error till we found the break-even rate. Constructing a swap in this fashion also makes it easy to deal with different tenors on each leg. Bottom line, the swaps dealer is likely to make money on some coupons and lose money on others, but the net payoff across all coupons will work out as if the dealer makes a few bucks on each one just like our simple example above.

The dealer can also adjust the fixed rate to make some set target profit. Recall that in the Lakewood-Cornelia swap, Lakewood was in the same position as our swaps dealer above, receiving fixed and paying floating. They fiddled with the fixed rate till the present value of the swap came to $10,000, which was their "fee" in essence for doing the swap. Here are the cash flows:

Lakewood-Cornelia swap
from perspective of floating-payer Lakewood

proposed new swap with fixed rate = **4.1940%**

	Pmt	Notional	Accrual Start	Accrual End	Acc Days	Pmt Rate	Year Days	Payment FV	Spot Rate	Days Till Pmt	Payment PV
fixed	1	1,000,000	5/23/07	11/23/07	184	4.19%	365	21,142.16	3.53%	184	20,772.52
fixed	2	1,000,000	11/24/07	5/22/08	180	4.19%	365	20,682.55	3.54%	365	19,975.42
fixed	3	1,000,000	5/23/08	11/24/08	185	4.19%	365	21,257.07	3.59%	551	20,164.28
fixed	4	1,000,000	11/25/08	5/29/09	185	4.19%	365	21,257.07	3.59%	737	19,820.32
									net fixed leg PV =		80,732.54
floating	1	(1,000,000)	5/23/07	8/22/07	91	3.53%	365	(8,800.82)	3.53%	91	(8,724.04)
floating	2	(1,000,000)	8/23/07	11/23/07	92	3.55%	365	(8,947.95)	3.54%	184	(8,791.06)
floating	3	(1,000,000)	11/24/07	2/22/08	90	3.64%	365	(8,975.34)	3.59%	275	(8,738.97)
floating	4	(1,000,000)	2/23/08	5/22/08	89	3.67%	365	(8,948.77)	3.54%	365	(8,642.81)
floating	5	(1,000,000)	5/23/08	8/22/08	91	3.71%	365	(9,249.59)	3.59%	457	(8,851.72)
floating	6	(1,000,000)	8/23/08	11/24/08	93	3.73%	365	(9,503.84)	3.54%	551	(9,021.72)
floating	7	(1,000,000)	11/25/08	2/23/09	90	3.80%	365	(9,369.86)	3.59%	642	(8,813.35)
floating	8	(1,000,000)	2/24/09	5/29/09	94	3.81%	365	(9,812.05)	3.59%	737	(9,148.87)
								net floating leg PV =			(70,732.54)
								swap value =			**10,000.00**

Hedging an Option

The writer of an option contract automatically takes on a risk that the option will go in-the-money and be exercised. Note that this applies to anyone who takes a short position in an option, not just dealers per se. When a long option is exercised in the money, the dealer is obligated to buy stock for more than it is worth (for calls)

FIGURE 11-6

Short Option Payoffs

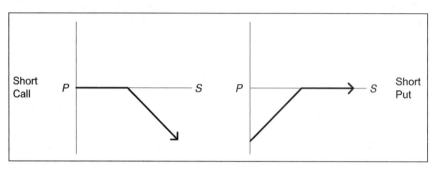

or sell stock for less than it is worth (for puts).[2] Recall the payoff diagrams for short option positions in Figure 11-6.

The payoff diagrams make the bad news perfectly clear: the exposure is huge—theoretically unlimited for written calls. The good news is the exposure can be significantly reduced by assuming offsetting positions in stock such that the net change in value of the option and stock positions remains near zero. For example, later on we'll learn about a crucial measure known as *delta*, which quantifies the sensitivity of an option price to changes in the underlier price. Delta tells the short party (e.g., the dealer) how many shares of stock they need per contract written. A delta of 60 gives the correct *hedge ratio*, or how much offsetting stock they need in the hedge position per option contract.

Now an option's delta changes with price, which changes all the time, illustrating why options require dynamic hedging. Delta tells you how to construct the hedge, but it changes continuously, so the contents of a hedge must be adjusted all the time. Whoa! Is it even possible to hedge an option? A perfect hedge is indeed practically impossible, but it turns out option dealer doesn't need a perfect hedge, just a reasonably good one.

---

[2] As in previous chapters, our discussion of option hedging will focus on equity options, but the same concepts apply to many other kinds of option as well.

Synthetic Options

A position that offsets the payoff of an option is often known as a *synthetic option*, as it replicates the payoff of the option using instruments other than the option itself. How do we make one? Recall first how we priced an option by constructing an imaginary replicating portfolio, a portfolio whose payoff mimicked that of the option. The price of the replicating portfolio gives the price of the option because two portfolios with the same payoff must cost the same due to arbitrage. If you think about it, then, to hedge an option position, one could simply create an actual replicating portfolio based on the theoretical portfolio presumed by the pricing formula and take the opposite side of it. And this is true in theory. But in practice it's virtually impossible because the composition of the replicating portfolio presumed by the pricing formula changes all the time—at each branch of the tree using the binomial method and continuously using Black-Scholes. Changing the composition of a portfolio means trading, and trading costs money (broker fees, etc.), so the transaction costs of a continuously changing portfolio quickly approaches infinity. And that's a bit more money than most of us have to spend.

While we cannot construct a perfect replicating portfolio, we can construct an approximate replicating portfolio by quantifying the sensitivities of an option price to its input factors—sensitivities known as *the Greeks*—then constructing a portfolio with those same sensitivities. It's not perfect and requires constant maintenance, but zillions of these portfolios are constructed every day, so it can't be all bad. A perfect options hedge is nearly impossible in practice because there are multiple factors affecting an option price, and each Greek addresses just one of them. So you can be perfectly hedged with respect to one Greek but exposed with respect to another. Option hedging can be quite a juggling act.

THE GREEKS

To understand what the Greeks are all about, first recall the five inputs to an option pricing formula: strike price, underlier price, volatility, time to expiration, and interest rates. Four of these (all except strike price) change all the time over the life of an option, hence we say the option price is sensitive to changes in each of those factors. The Greeks tell us how the price of an option changes as these pricing input factors changes, providing instructions for constructing the synthetic option. Table 11-1 provides their common names and what they measure.

Only four of these, by the way, are actually letters in the Greek alphabet. "Vega" is not a true Greek but somehow was adopted as one. For the purist, the Greek letter for sensitivity to volatility is *kappa,* which you might see in some academic texts. And don't be tripped up by the coincidence of there being five Greeks and five factors to an option price. There is no Greek for strike price (because it never changes), and there are two Greeks related to underlier price.

Calculating the Greeks is a rather complicated affair that we won't delve into, but for the mathematically curious, each is a partial derivative related to the Black-Scholes partial differential equation. Using the Greeks, thankfully, is a much less complicated affair than calculating them. But to use them we first need to understand precisely what each of them tells us. Every Greek expresses a ratio of a change in one thing to a change in another thing, as depicted in Table 11-2.

A delta of .50 (often expressed as simply "50" without the decimal point) tells us that for a $1 increase in the underlier price, the price of the option increases by 50 cents. Vega, theta, and rho also tell us how the option price changes per unit change in underlier volatility (1 percent change), time to expiration (1 day) and the

TABLE 11-1

The Five Greeks and Corresponding Sensitivities

Greek	Measures option price sensitivity to changes in:
Delta	Underlier Price
Gamma	Underlier Price
Vega	Underlier Volatility
Theta	Time to Expiration
Rho	Interest Rates

TABLE 11-2

The Greeks as Ratios

Greek	Ratio	Example
Delta (Δ)	Change in *option price* / Positive change in *underlier price*	.50/$1.00 = .50 = "50"
Gamma (Γ)	Change in *delta* / Positive change in *underlier price*	3/$1.00 = "3"
Vega (V)	Change in *option price* / Positive 1% change in underlier *volatility*	.35/1% = .35 = "35"
Theta (Θ)	Change in *option price* / One day change in *time-to-expiration*	.05/1 day = .05 = "−.05"
Rho (P)	Change in *option price* / Positive 1% change in *interest rates*	.02/1% = ".02"

risk-free interest rate (1 percent), respectively. Gamma is a bit different. It expresses how *delta* changes with underlier price. A gamma of 10, for example, tells us the delta of an option changes by 10 units per $1 change in the underlier. In a bit we'll see why that's so important. While we're here, notice how delta and vega are much greater numbers than the rest. This is true for most options, and tells us the two greatest sensitivities are to underlier price and volatility. As such, most option hedgers spend most of their time worrying about these.

Table 11-3 contains an assortment of facts about, and properties of, the Greeks. These can come in handy if you ever need to apply them for real.

Greeks and Option Pricing

One of the interesting things about the Greeks is where they come from. They are, in essence, by-products of the option pricing formulas. In the Black-Scholes pricing formula, for example, delta is just $N(d_1)$ for calls, and $N(d_1) - 1$ for puts. And this connection between hedging and pricing makes sense when you consider that pricing an option is based on the idea of a replicating portfolio. For now, just think of the Greeks as values you can use to construct

TABLE 11-3

Properties of the Greeks

Greek	Ratio	Facts
Delta Δ	$\dfrac{\text{option price}}{\text{underlier price}}$	<ul><li>Typically expressed as a percent without the sign ("50"). Intuition: Delta 50 means option price changes at a rate 50% of that of the underlier.</li><li>Positive for long calls: 0 to 100. Negative for long puts: 0 to -100.</li><li>Approximately 50(-50) for ATM calls(puts), near 100(-100) for deep ITM, near 0 for deep OTM.</li><li>Can view as "probability of option expiring ITM."</li><li>As underlier price increases, call delta approaches 100 and put delta approaches 0. With decrease, call delta approaches 0 and put delta approaches -100.</li></ul>
Gamma Γ	$\dfrac{\text{delta}}{\text{underlier price}}$	<ul><li>Typically expressed as % without the sign ("3").</li><li>Positive for long positions (calls or puts), negative for short positions.</li><li>Typical range: 0 to 10 for long, 0 to -10 for short.</li><li>Greatest when ATM. Near 0 for deep ITM or OTM.</li></ul>
Vega V	$\dfrac{\text{option price}}{\text{volatility}}$	<ul><li>Typically expressed as % without the sign ("35").</li><li>Positive for long positions (calls or puts), negative for short positions. Just like gamma.</li><li>Greatest for ATM, smallest for ITM and OTM.</li><li>Decreases as expiry approaches (opposite of theta).</li></ul>
Theta Θ	$\dfrac{\text{option price}}{\text{time-to-expiration}}$	<ul><li>Technically expresses rate of loss with passage of time so is always positive. By convention, expressed in dollars gained or lost per day ("$-.05$").</li><li>Positive for long positions (calls or puts), negative for short positions.</li><li>Relative size negatively correlated with gamma: Large positive gamma goes with large negative theta, and vice versa.</li><li>Grows as expiry approaches. (Opposite of vega).</li></ul>
Rho P	$\dfrac{\text{option price}}{\text{interest rate}}$	<ul><li>Typically expressed in dollars gained in option value per 1% increase in risk-free interest rates (".02").</li><li>Positive for long calls, negative for long puts.</li><li>Typically so small it's ignored in practice.</li></ul>

a hedge portfolio, values someone else has been kind enough to calculate for you.

The Delta Hedge

Delta hedging is the basic routine for the option market-maker, or dealer, and it goes like this: The dealer expresses a willingness to buy an option for some *bid* price less than model price, or to sell it for some *ask* or *offer* price greater than model price, where *model price* (MP) is simply the theoretical value produced by a pricing method such as Black-Scholes. The difference between a bid and model price, or offer and model price, is commonly known as "edge." Someone comes along, say a hedger, and buys the option at the offer. The dealer now has a position in the option. They immediately establish a *delta-neutral* hedge position in the underlier, then adjust that hedge over time to remain delta-neutral. When the two positions are closed, if the hedge was successful then the dealer realizes the edge (or something close to it, if the vega and other sensitivities weren't too outrageous) as their profit. We'll walk through an example with numbers in just a minute.

Delta hedging is also, by the way, the daily grind for the option arbitrageur. But instead of quoting bids and offers, they scan the market for "mispriced" options, or option bids above model price and offers below. When they spot one, they take a position in it. Like the dealer, they immediately establish a delta-neutral hedge position, which they adjust over time to remain delta-neutral. When the positions are closed, the arbitrageur realizes the edge as their profit.

Now you might be thinking, "What's the difference between a so-called 'mispriced option' and an option bid or offered by the dealer?" Think of an option dealer's offer price as analogous to a car dealer's retail price, where model price is analogous to cost. Car dealers as a matter of course sell cars for some price greater than cost, and the option dealer is doing the same. So market-makers publish bids below MP and offers above, for the benefit of "customers" willing to pay the edge. Arbitrageurs essentially look for market-makers who place bids above MP and offers below MP by mistake, who are then forced to pay the difference whether they want to or not. It's like a car dealer who mistakenly sells a car for less than what they paid for it. They lose the difference. And the car buyer gets a great deal.

So imagine a 30-strike call option whose model price one morning is 1.85. You are a dealer and offer it for 2.00, for a theoretical edge of 1.50 per contract (recall each contract is for 100 shares of the underlier). Someone comes along and buys 20 calls from you. Your goal now is to realize the theoretical edge of 300.00 (i.e., 20 * 1.50). The option delta is 79. This tells you for a delta-neutral hedge you need 79 shares of the underlier for each contract. So you buy 1580 shares of the underlier (i.e., 79 * 20). Throughout the day you monitor delta and adjust your hedge accordingly by buying or selling stock. At the end of the day, say your option holder exercises and you close out your stock position. Your P/L or "profit/loss" on the option trade is negative, meaning you lose money. But your P/L on the stock is positive by a greater amount. The net of option and stock P/L is your profit. Let's see the numbers:

		Opts	Strike Price	Option P/L	Stock Price	Delta	Stock Buy (Sell)	Stock Position	Stock P/L
9 am	Dealer writes 20 calls @2.00 (MP = 1.85) and buys stock	20	30	4,000	31.50	79	1580	1580	
10 am	Delta goes down; dealer sells stock				31.00	78	(20)	1560	(10)[3]
11 am	Delta goes down; dealer sells stock				30.50	60	(360)	1200	(360)
12 pm	Delta goes down; dealer sells stock				30.00	54	(120)	1080	(180)
1 pm	Delta goes up; dealer buys stock				31.00	78	480	1560	
2 pm	Delta goes up; dealer buys stock				32.25	98	400	1960	
3 pm	Delta goes up; dealer buys stock				33.50	99	20	1980	
4 pm	Holder exercises. Dealer settles the option and sells all stock	20	30	(8,000)	34.00		(1980)	0	4,850[4]
	Total P/L			(4,000)					4,300

At the end of the day on the option trade you lost 4000 (the call option went well into the money), but on the stock transactions you gained 4300 for a net gain of 300—exactly the theoretical edge. Now for the purposes of this example, we've simplified the deltas and stock prices by rounding and restricted our update intervals to

---

[3]For our purposes we only realize P/L when we sell stock. To calculate it, we simply multiply the number of shares by the change in stock price while we held it. For example, 20 * (31.00 − 31.50) = −10.

[4]Notice the 1080 shares were purchased at four different prices. Here's the P/L calculation: $1{,}080 * (34 − 31.50) + 480 * (34 − 31) + 400 * (34 − 32.25) + 20 * (34 − 33.50) = 4{,}850$.

TABLE 11-4

Option Positions and Underlier Hedge Positions

Option Position	Hedge Position
Short Call	Long Underlier
Short Put	Short Underlier
Long Call	Short Underlier
Long Put	Long Underlier

hourly, but otherwise this is how to delta-hedge a written call with a long position in the underlier. You just might need to do it more often, using stock prices and deltas more precise than these. Hedging a written put, by the way, works the same way, but you maintain a short position in the stock instead a long position as we did above. And for hedging long positions in calls and puts, it's just the reverse. (Remember, dealers buy options as well as write them, and they hedge long options in the same way to capture the edge.) Table 11-4 sums it up.

A long position in the underlier simply means you buy stock and hold it. A short position means you "short sell" the stock. To sell a stock short, you literally borrow shares belonging to someone else and immediately sell them on the open market. After some period of time, you purchase new shares and return them to the lender. If the price of the stock has fallen over that period, you make money; it if has risen you lose money. Short selling is very different from simply "selling" stock that you own, as we did in the delta hedging example just above. Short selling is traditionally used by the speculator who believes a stock price will fall.[5] It just so happens it's also an indispensable tool for the options hedger. Figure 11-7 shows payoff diagrams for both long and short stock positions to illustrate.

This is an appropriate point to revisit what we mean exactly by "model price." In the most practical sense to the options dealer or arbitrageur, it is simply *the price of an option they can synthesize*

---

[5]The speculator can also, as you know, buy put options.

FIGURE 11-7

Long Underlier and Short Underlier Payoffs

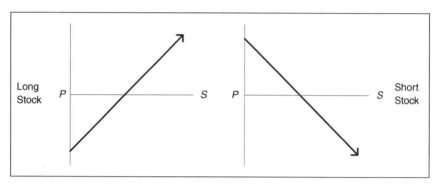

with confidence. And the "better" a model price in this sense, the better they are in quoting, or spotting mispriced options. Consider the example above. We supposed a model price of 1.85, but if a dealer believed the model price was really 1.75, they could make not $300 but $500 on the trade—provided they could synthesize the hedge. Alternatively, a dealer who believed the model price was 1.95 might not even bother doing the trade at all. (In reality, disagreements in model prices are generally not so wide as these simple examples.) This is why the better your model, the better you will be as a dealer or arbitrageur. It also explains why firms spend great gobs of money in developing ever-better pricing models, or *analytics*. It also illustrates *model risk*, or the risk that your pricing analytics are simply wrong. Suppose a dealer mistakenly believes a model price to be 1.50 when it's really 1.30, and buys 500 contracts at 1.40 thinking they can make $5000 in edge, when really they will *lose* $5000. Ouch.

Now there are complicating factors that make delta-hedging a bit more complicated in practice than in our example above. For one, we disregarded transaction costs. And if your hedge requires a short sale of stock, regulations in the United States dictate that short selling is permitted only after an "up tick" (increase) in the stock price. This was put in place to prevent traders from rampant short selling in a declining market, which itself can quickly turn a decline into a crash.

Using Gamma

Gamma is a measure of how delta changes with underlier price. The delta of a high-gamma option changes more rapidly than that of a low-gamma option. The practical effect to the option hedger is straightforward: the higher the gamma, the more quickly an option becomes unhedged as the underlier price changes. It's a speed thing. If gamma is high, you'd better monitor your hedge like a hawk. If it's low you'll have a bit more time.

Using Vega

Vega indicates how the price of an option changes with underlier volatility. This means you can have a perfect delta-hedge all day long and still lose money if the volatility of the underlier changes significantly. Oops. So what is the option hedger to do? Plenty, and most of it goes way beyond the scope of an introduction to derivatives. There are derivatives whose underlier is a *volatility index*, and these can certainly be used to hedge baskets of options or options whose prices are highly correlated with the market, but for a simple option on a single underlier, these often are of little help. Another tool is the *spread trade*, an option strategy in which you take simultaneous positions in different options (say, both November *and* December options with otherwise identical features), such that the value of the combined position is sensitive to changes in volatility. These so-called "calendar spreads" can be effective because changes in volatility are closely related to the passage of time. The greater the time to expiration, the greater the probability of underlier price changes. Anyway, that's the basic idea.

Using Theta and Rho

Theta and rho measure, respectively, the sensitivity of an options price to changes in time and changes in the risk-free interest rate. Thankfully, these sensitivities tend to be far smaller than sensitivities measured by delta and vega, so the option dealer need not worry about these quite as much. Still there are ways to hedge theta and rho. For example, a calendar spread discussed above can be used for theta, as can a position in a bond—another instrument whose value is closely related to the passage of time. Bonds are also sensitive to changes in interest rates, so they can be used as well for rho hedging. Another liquid instrument for rho hedging are interest rate futures such as Eurodollar futures—the same ones we used for hedging swaps in the previous section.

OTHER ASPECTS

So what other fun stuff goes on in the heady world of financial risk management? One thing you might hear about is the idea of *value-at-risk*, or VAR. Risk managers and regulators tend to like VAR because it gives a concrete answer to a mushy question: What's the most money a position might lose? VAR is an example of a general topic of *scenario analysis* which involves analyzing potential future scenarios to help you prepare for or avoid them. To be precise, VAR expresses the maximum loss you can expect to incur over a given time period T with probability P. For example, a swaps dealer might run some VAR calculations at the end of the day and see that the most they can expect to lose over the next 30 days, with 95 percent probability, is 12.5 million dollars. If they are uncomfortable with a VAR greater than, say, 10 million, then they probably want to unwind some of the portfolio to bring it down. A portfolio manager might use VAR to compare two nearly identical investment opportunities, to see which one has greater risk. And industry regulators can use VAR to set capital requirements, or how much money a financial institution is required to keep on hand to weather adverse market conditions. An agency might recommend (or enforce) that a swaps dealer keep "five times VAR" in reserves.

How is VAR calculated? Mostly by *simulation*. Recall how the value of a financial instrument depends on some set of factors. A floating-rate loan is affected heavily by changing interest rates, an option is affected by underlier price and volatility and such, and so on. One popular type of simulation is known as *monte carlo*. This involves running a computer program that supposes different values for those factors (typically using randomly generated numbers in some form or another) and calculating the value of the position under those factors. Then it does so again using different factor values. Then again, and again and again. The key, of course, is to run as many simulations as possible. The more you try, the better you can make inferences about the future.

It's no wonder, of course, why risk management is so important in the world of derivatives. As the sheer number of derivatives positions increases, so does the global risk. There are shelves full of books now just on "derivatives disasters," and we'll look at some of them in the postscript. The good news is each disaster provides both a wake-up call to the importance of risk management, and valuable real-world—not hypothetical—examples of what can happen. And if you spend any time looking at the disasters, you'll notice not all of them had to do with the type of risk we've covered so far in this chapter. There's more than one type of risk.

The exposures we've dealt with are all examples of *market risk*, sometimes called *price risk*, or the risk associated with changing market prices. But there are other types of financial risk that tools like our forwards, futures, swaps, and options are ill-suited to handle. One of these is *operational risk*, or the risk that flaws in a firm's internal processes and policies could cost it substantial sums of money. Consider the trading firm that lets a rogue trader rack up huge speculative positions on behalf of the firm due to insufficient oversight. If those speculations don't pay off, the firm can suffer dearly. When we discussed option hedging you probably got a sense of *model risk*, or the risk that your pricing models aren't right. This can really mess up a hedge! Another type is *legal risk*, or the risk that laws could change that affect your ability to manage an existing position. Another huge one is *credit risk*, or the risk that your counterparty doesn't honor their responsibilities and will leave you with a loss. That's no fun.

So why do we have derivatives? Derivatives exist because so does financial uncertainty. We don't know what the future will bring and we certainly don't know what things will cost, or whether or not everyone will fulfill their financial obligations. Derivatives quantify uncertainty, thereby letting us put exposures into reasonably tangible packages that can be measured, managed, priced and—most important—traded. That's their power. Derivatives allow the efficient transfer of risk from one party to another. When applied wisely, derivatives are simply the coolest gadgets for getting things done that you can possibly imagine. When applied not so wisely, derivatives can be the most costly trouble-maker our economic universe has ever known.

For better or worse we just can't seem to get enough of these "wild beasts of finance" to use Alfred Steinherr's moniker. The global market is colossal and gets colossally larger every day. How big is it? Putting a monetary figure on this market is like measuring a cloud with a yardstick. Where do you put it? And when? Want to know that there are more than 80 million option contracts in effect? That the notional values of outstanding interest rate derivatives total more than $160 *trillion* U.S. dollars—and climbing all the time? It's a big place, this world of derivatives; trust me on this. And you'll just get a headache googling for truly meaningful statistics.

DERIVATIVES AS ENABLERS

Most applications of derivatives, you'll be happy to know, are remarkably safe and nothing to get alarmed over. They are, if you will, good things. They just help folks do what they otherwise might not. A farmer may want to plant wheat but fear that the price of what will decline while it's growing, forcing the farmer to sell it for less than what it cost to grow. A commodities future, one of the oldest of all derivatives, lets the farmer lock in the price of wheat before the first seed hits the soil. A manufacturer may want to borrow money to build a plant but can only do so at a floating rate of interest, raising the possibility of financial insolvency should interest rates float too high. An interest rate swap lets them convert that debt to a fixed rate, removing that risk. And on and on and on.

The whole of derivatives affects not just individual industries and institutions. It also acts as a network of financial fibers connecting very different corners of the economy with one another: A farmer sells wheat forward on the futures market to lock in a return from their planting investment. The miller buys wheat forward on the same futures market to lock in a future profit, and does a swap with a commercial bank to convert the debt from purchasing a machine to grind that wheat from a floating rate to fixed. The bank uses long Eurodollar futures to hedge the swap. A hedge fund combines short Eurodollar futures and long U.S. Treasury bonds to arbitrage pricing discrepancies between those two instruments. A global pharmaceutical firm uses protective puts on Treasury bonds to hedge the bond portion on their pension fund, and buys Japanese yen forward on the FX market to lock in the U.S. dollar price of a future purchase from a Japanese supplier. A French commercial real estate developer sells yen forward to lock in the recent appreciation of property they hold in Osaka. And so on.

DERIVATIVES AS DISABLERS

When things go wrong with derivatives, they tend to go wrong in a big way. If there were an Academy Award for derivative disaster spectacles, there'd be no shortage of nominees each year. "And the Oscar goes to . . . Barings Bank!" Complexity and risk spell occasional disaster in many worlds, not just finance. Aeronautics and aviation come to mind, as does the practice of thoracic surgery and the manufacture of chemicals. Mistakes can be painful. Fortunately we tend to learn a lot from mistakes and sometimes—not always— we learn to avoid repeating them.

What have we learned from derivatives disasters? Mostly we've learned it's the commonsense stuff that gets us in trouble, stuff like not anticipating future cash flow requirements, giving managers too much power, and lending gamblers obscene amounts of money to fund their bets. And those aren't just hypotheticals.

Those three mistakes were spectacularly demonstrated by three names destined to go down in the history of derivatives: Metallgesellschaft, Barings Bank, and Long Term Capital Management.

In the early 1990s, MGRM, a division of the large industrial complex Metallgesellschaft, sold oil forward to OTC counterparties for terms going out as long as 10 years. At fixed prices. They hedged their short forward contracts with stacks of long futures contracts—with terms often going out only a few months. And this extreme difference in terms is what got them into trouble. As the futures did what futures do, their payoff neutralized any loss or gain from buying oil spot to make good on their forwards. Basic hedging. And every month they would put on new futures hedges for future obligations, as part of their "stack-and-roll" hedge. The strategy was theoretically sound over the long run, but when oil prices dropped sharply they simply didn't have enough cash on hand to satisfy margin calls on their futures positions. Recall that long futures positions lose money when prices decline, and the MGRM positions were huge. The corresponding gains on the oil forwards just weren't sufficient for making up the difference. Before long there was simply not enough cash to keep the thing going, so they shut it down. But the size of their positions made doing so all at once very costly, as it involved numerous "unwinds" at a substantial loss. In the end they watched something like $1.5 billion U.S. dollars go down the proverbial toilet.

In the mid 1990s, the venerable Barings Bank suffered the "rogue trader" syndrome. This is where a trader puts on speculation trades that exceed reasonable risk tolerances, trades that turn out to be bad bets. Plenty of places have suffered from rogue traders. But Barings suffered with particular pain because the trader, Nick Leeson, was also in essence his own manager— approving his own speculation on the Japanese stock market from his base in Singapore and hiding the losses from his managers. Normally, firms strictly separate their "front office" (where trading happens) from their "back office" (where settlements, accounting, and related functions take place). According to government studies of the debacle, Mr. Leeson apparently employed a short straddle on the Nikkei 225 stock index. Recall that the payoff of a short straddle is like an inverted "V" with unlimited losses possible should the underlier go above or below a certain level. When the

Nikkei fell more sharply than he expected, the position lost money. Lots of it. When he placed an equally aggressive bet that stocks would rise—in hopes of compensating for his straddle losses before anyone found out—things just got terribly worse. By the time the parent company found out what their wayward child was up to, the losses on the Nikkei trades exceeded the entire capital of the bank by something like a billion U.S. dollars. The 250-year-old bank was forced to declare bankruptcy. Leeson spent a few years in jail, after which he gave speeches on the dangers of rogue traders for a reported $100,000 a crack. Barings is gone for good.

In the late 1990s, the hedge fund Long Term Capital Management was having a grand time, showering their investors with annual returns of close to 40 percent. Their principle strategy appears to have been arbitrage, using sophisticated analytical models to detect the subtlest of pricing discrepancies in the government bond markets. Some of those bonds were issued by Russia, which just happened to default on their bonds. Oops. Now LTCM had hedged their long bond positions with short positions on the Russian currency the ruble because in theory those currency positions would increase in value when the long bond positions tanked. But the ruble tanked so hard that their currency counterparties basically shut down. And Russia itself suspended all trading in its currency.

Now this ruble issue was a decidedly bad thing for LTCM, but what really made matters bad—not just for LTCM but for the system as a whole—was that LTCM had borrowed nearly all of its money to do this cool arbitrage. At one point LTCM had a stake in the market of well over $100 billion U.S. dollars. And their equity was something like *half* a billion dollars. This is an extraordinary leverage ratio and is not unlike buying a million-dollar house with a down payment of 5 thousand dollars. So now you've got all these lenders with a great deal of skin in the game. And then you've got something called a "flight to liquidity" in the global fixed-income markets, such as the U.S. Treasury markets, where everyone seemed to be putting their money in response to the Russian bond crisis. The intricacies of LTCMs position were such that it was not "hedged" against the negative effects of the flight to liquidity, so it found itself against the ropes with no hope of recovery. But the system couldn't just let this fighter die because they had lent it all that money, and besides they too were exposed to the ill effects of the same liquidity crisis. And with all the interdependencies among players in the capital markets game, if every lender simply tried to call in its debts, you'd have defaults and bankruptcies rippling through the system like cracks in a shattering piece of glass.

So what happened? The Federal Reserve Bank of New York, for all intents and purposes an arm of the U.S. government, got a bunch of banks together in a conference room and convinced them to write checks totaling $3.5 billion dollars. This "gift" was injected into the system to prevent a catastrophic meltdown but still did not cover everyone's losses. Nobody can say for sure, but banks took additional write-offs totaling another billion or so of losses that year, so it's not a stretch to put the overall price tag of the LTCM folly at around $5 billion dollars. Not exactly chump change.

As demonstrated most colorfully by the LTCM disaster, the web of interdependency spun by derivatives—and the funding of derivatives positions—is perhaps the cause for greatest concern when it comes to these wily financial instruments. Checks and balances, whether from industry sensibility or government mandate, are clearly essential to keeping the bad things from overpowering the good things.

INTEREST AND INTEREST RATES

Think of *interest* as the price of money. You want to borrow a million bucks to expand your business? It'll cost you some interest. You want to loan some money to the U.S. government, by purchasing a bond, so they can build roads or wage wars? They will pay you interest. For our purposes, interest is the money paid by the borrower of money to its lender. It doesn't always seem that way because "paying for" money is different from paying for, say, cantaloupes. You don't generally pay for cantaloupes with cantaloupes, but you do pay for money with money. Also, you don't so much purchase money as rent it. The grocer doesn't expect to see his cantaloupe again, but bankers most certainly expect to be reunited one day with their money.

The way we measure interest is, of course, the *interest rate*. The interest rate specifies a cost of borrowing money for some unit of time. A one-bedroom Chicago apartment might go for $900 per month. A tanning booth might rent for $39 per hour. A million bucks from Citibank might go for $65,000 of interest per year. Of course, interest rates aren't expressed in dollar amounts but rather in percentages. So the price of a million from Citibank is expressed not as $65,000 per year but as 6.5 percent per year. This ability to express a cost as a percentage of the thing we buy turns out to be quite a convenience, and is possible, of course, because we pay for money with money.

With interest rates, the unit of time is always one year. Well, not always but trust me, you can go the rest of your life assuming every interest rate you ever hear is for one year and you'll be just fine. Of course, we work all the time with units of time smaller or greater than one year—monthly payments, quarterly accruals, and so on—and later on we'll get into that. But the interest rate itself expresses an annual rate, that is, the rate for one "annum" or year.

And what does this mean exactly, this 6.5 percent per year, or six and one-half percentage points? The term is from the Latin *per centum* or "per hundred" and is indicated by the percentage sign: %. So a rate of 6.5 percent is six and one-half dollars for every \$100 borrowed. How many hundreds are in a million? Ten thousand. Multiply this by 6.5 and there's your \$65,000.

$$6.5 \text{ percent of } 1,000,000 = ?$$
$$6.5\% = .065 = 6.5 \text{ per } 100$$
$$1,000,000 \div 100 = 10,000$$
$$10,000 * 6.5 = 65,000$$
$$6.5 \text{ percent of } 1,000,000 = 65,000$$

There's another unit to know when it comes to measuring interest and it's called the *basis point* or "BP" or "bip." It turns out a percentage point is way too big to be practical in a world where a billion-dollar deal is no big deal. In this world we deal in hundredths of percentage points, and one-hundredth of one percent is what we call a basis point. One hundred basis points equals one percentage point, and vice versa. So when we speak of "25 basis points" we simply mean one-quarter of a percent, or 0.25 percent. Five basis points is 0.05 percent or one twentieth of 1 percent. Here are some more examples:

$$1 \text{ basis point} = .01\% = .0001$$
$$25 \text{ basis points} = .25\% = .0025$$
$$100 \text{ basis points} = 1\% = .01$$
$$150 \text{ basis points} = 1.5\% = .015$$
$$1.5\% + 25 \text{ basis points} = 1.75\% = .0175$$

If you are familiar with U.S. coinage, it can help to think of 1 percent as one dollar and one basis point as one penny. Then when you see 25 bp you think of a quarter, and "five bips" brings to mind a nickel, which you know without thinking is one twentieth of a dollar.

$$100 \text{ basis points} = \text{"one dollar"}$$
$$25 \text{ basis points} = \text{"one quarter"}$$
$$10 \text{ basis points} = \text{"one dime"}$$
$$1 \text{ basis point} = \text{"one penny"}$$

However you do it, you need to be comfortable thinking in terms of basis points because this numerical sliver can itself be too big to be practical. So we speak about hundredths or even thousandths of basis points. This isn't so ridiculous when you're a large derivatives dealer with trillions of dollars worth of contracts on your books.

$$1 \text{ basis point} * \$100 = \$0.01$$
$$1 \text{ basis point} * \$1 \text{ million} = \$100$$
$$1 \text{ basis point} * \$1 \text{ billion} = \$100 \text{ thousand}$$
$$1 \text{ basis point} * \$1 \text{ trillion} = \$100 \text{ million}—!!$$

FLOATING INTEREST, RATE INDEXES, AND LIBOR

Interest rates in practice are expressed as fixed or floating. A *fixed rate* is an interest rate that does not change over the life of a loan. If your bank lends you $100,000 for 10 years at 7 percent, with interest payments due monthly, neither you nor the bank can expect that rate to change over that 10 years (unless you renegotiate the loan).

In a *floating-rate* loan, the interest rate does change over the life of the loan. Say your bank lends you $100,000 for 10 years under the condition you will make monthly payments not at a fixed rate, but at a changing rate known as *Libor*. Pronounced "lie-bohr" or "lee-bohr," Libor is an example of a *rate index*. Indeed, in the land of rate indices, Libor is king. A rate index is just a price index like the ones we introduced earlier, providing an average price from a survey of related things. Like other price indices, a rate index can, and very often is, employed as a derivative underlier.

With respect to swaps and other interest rate derivatives, think of a rate index as an "undisputed thermometer" that monitors some aspect of an ever-changing environment and reports it as a number. A real thermometer monitors temperature; a rate index monitors interest rates. Like temperature, interest rates change continuously and unpredictably. If you borrow money at Libor, the exact amounts of your future payment obligations are unpredictable at the time you take out the loan. Nobody uses the word "unpredictable," with all its negative connotations, so instead we use the euphemistic term "floating." So much nicer on the ear.

Libor is short for London Inter Bank Offer Rate. (I should write LIBOR to be precise, but why shout?) Every business day in London, at 11:00 a.m. local time, the British Bankers Association publishes a set of interest rates, "fixing" or "setting" Libor for the day for a number of different currencies. For loans denominated in U.S. dollars, they publish U.S. Libor rates. For loans denominated in Pounds Sterling, they publish GBP Libor rates. And so on. In swap parlance these daily events are also known as "resets." Once fixed for the day, they do not change until the next fixing day, when they can indeed change. From day to day the rates change unpredictably, but once fixed there is no quibble over the daily proclamations of those helpful British bankers. Perfect ingredients of a rate index.

So back to your $100,000 loan. If it "floats with Libor," each month when your interest payment is due (we ignore principal payments for now) the rate with which to calculate that payment is "read" from the Libor thermometer. If it's 6.02 percent one month, you owe roughly $501.67 (one twelfth of $100,000 * .0602). If the next month it's 5.26 percent you owe $438.33. (Rates went down. Bonus!) And so on. Figure A-1 depicts a sample of actual 1-month Libor rates taken at monthly intervals just to show how wildly rates can float from month to month.[1] And don't be confused by the terminology. These "1-month rates" are still expressed as annual or "1-year rates." They just pertain to money *borrowed* for 1 month.

Rate indices such as Libor are profoundly useful in the stormy world of finance, as they are reliable, precise, and undisputed. While real thermometers may sometimes stop functioning, and different observers might quibble whether the mercury is at 70 and one-half or 70 and three-quarters, rate indices for all practical purposes are unambiguous and undisputed. In addition to Libor, another common index is based on the *prime rate*, a rate of interest offered by a bank to its most creditworthy customers. Every business day of the year, for example, Citibank publishes its prime rate. And every day you can obtain an average, or index, of such primes and base a

---

[1]For the curious, these are Eurodollar deposit rates sampled monthly by the U.S. Federal Reserve, starting in April 1995.

FIGURE A-1

One-Month Libor Rates

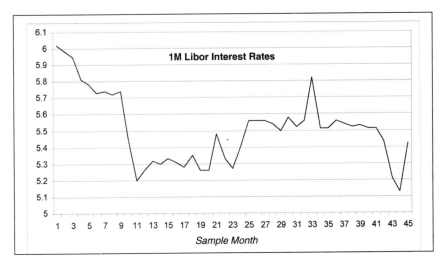

1M Libor Interest Rates

Sample Month

loan on that rate. You can count on it being there, you know exactly what it is, and you don't have to wonder whether it's correct or not. Other indices include *commercial paper* rates, indicating rates at which businesses will pay to borrow funds, and numerous indices analogous to Libor for other financial centers besides London.

TERM STRUCTURE AND YIELD CURVES

For any given index on any given day, there is no single interest rate. An index is in fact like an entire set of thermometers. This is because interest rates vary by *term* or *maturity*, or the length of time money is borrowed. An annual Libor rate for a 3-month loan is almost always different from the annual Libor rate for a 1-year loan. So we have 3-month Libor, 6-month Libor, 12-month Libor, and so on. This variation in interest rate by time-to-maturity is known as the *term structure of interest rates*. Having so many different rates for a single index can be rather unwieldy, but thankfully we have an indispensable device known as a *yield curve* for dealing with term structure. And Figure A-2 shows what a yield curve looks like.

FIGURE A-2

Libor Spot Yield Curve

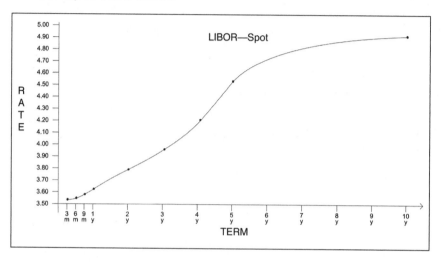

A yield curve illustrates term structure by depicting, for one index, different rates of interest—or yield—for different terms, all at a glance. This curve tells us that money borrowed for 3 years can be had for an annual rate of around 4.00 percent, while money borrowed for 6 years will cost you around 4.7 percent. So think of "yield" as another word for "interest rate." The word comes from the world of bonds where bond issuers (borrowers) raise money by "selling" bonds to investors (lenders), who are thereafter known as bond holders. Issuers pay money to holders (money costs money, recall), and those payments constitute the return, or gain, or yield to the investor. Yields are expressed as some percentage of the amount invested. Sound familiar? A yield is just an interest rate.

CONSTRUCTING A SPOT CURVE

The best way to understand a yield curve is to construct one. Now there are two fundamental types of interest rates in the land of derivatives, spot rates and forward rates, and two corresponding types of curve, spot curves and forward curves. *Spot interest rates* apply to money borrowed now and *forward interest rates* apply to money borrowed in the future. We'll cover forward rates and curves in the next section. Right now let's construct a spot curve to illustrate this whole yield curve thing. We start with a fictitious but plausible set of U.S. Libor rate fixings. Let's say it's 11:00 a.m. in London, and the BBA publishes the following rates for the following terms:

US Libor Rate Fixings

3 month	3.53
6 month	3.54
9 month	3.59
1 year	3.69

Here we have four spot interest rates, or prices of money. You want to borrow today for 3 months? That'll be 3.5275 percent per year, or 0.8819 percent for 3 months if we keep it simple (3 months = 3/12 of a year, or 1/4 or .25, and 3.5275 * .25 = 0.8819%) You want it today for 6 months? The rate goes up one basis point to 3.5375 percent, or 1.7688 percent for the half year. You want it today for a year? That rate is 3.69 percent.

To construct this yield curve, we simply plot these points on a simple graph where the X-axis (horizontal) represents the term, or time-to-maturity, of a theoretical loan starting today. The Y-axis (vertical) represents the interest rate. So Figure A-3 shows our plot, with the points connected by straight lines.

Now this is not much of a "curve," being so elbowed and incomplete, although it does convey some sense that interest rates increase with time-to-maturity. But it doesn't give a rate for, say, a 5-year loan. After all, the longest Libor term is 1 year. A common way of handling this is to extend the curve with yields from various Eurodollar Futures or U.S. Treasury securities, or both.

A Eurodollar Futures Contract, or *Eurodollar* for short, is an exchange-traded derivative obligating the long party to borrow $1 million not today but on some future date, for a period of 3 months, at the prevailing 3-month Libor rate as of that future date. Notice we're referring now to a future loan, so the rates involved are forward rates and not spot rates. The Eurodollar, especially front-term Eurodollars for borrowing 3, 6, and 9 months

FIGURE A-3

Beginnings of a Libor Spot Curve

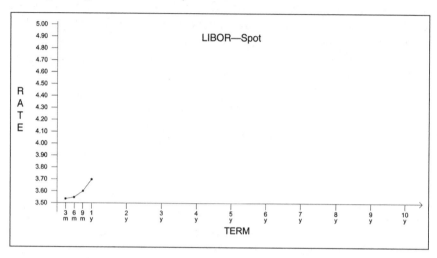

down the road, are highly liquid.[2] The prices at which they trade, then, can be seen as indicators of where people expect the BBA to publish Libor rates in the future. Because interest is just the price of money, the price of a Eurodollar is just an interest rate in disguise.

Where were we? That's right, looking for spot rates with which to extend our yield curve. Now the Eurodollars give us futures prices. And by applying a "futures-forward adjustment" involving math we won't delve into, from a futures price we can deduce a forward price.[3] And from such forward rates we can deduce spot rates with which to extend our spot curve past the 12-month term available from the BBA.[4]

---

[2]You'll see this lingo used all the time in the securities markets. "Front term" or "front month" contracts expire earlier than do "back term" or "back month" contracts, and tend to be more liquid.

[3]Recall that a futures is just an exchange-traded forward, whose value is affected by the daily marking to market, and with some fancy math we can "back out" that effect.

[4]Quick example: If 3-month spot is 2.5 percent and the 3-month rate 3 months forward is 2.6 percent, the implied 6-month spot rate must be the arithmetic average or 2.55 percent. Any other rate would permit arbitrage.

Here are some spot rates we might infer from the Eurodollars market:

Eurodollar Implied Spot Rates

3 month	3.53
6 month	3.54
...	
18 month	3.72
21 month	3.75
...	
45 month	4.03
48 month	4.07

Now we have perfectly defensible interest rates for loans going out 4 years. Incidentally, liquid futures markets of all kinds are used like this all the time, whenever we need an indicator of expected future prices. Does it matter if the expectations come true? No. You cannot tell future prices from futures prices. But as long as we have an indicator of *expected* prices, and liquid markets for securing obligations based on those expectations, we're all set. And as you can imagine, front-term futures prices tend to be more reliable than those in the back-terms as futures prices converge to spot prices as we get closer to their maturity dates. It's like weather forecasting. A 1-day forecast is more likely to come true than a 1-week forecast, and a 1-hour forecast is probably even better.

Extending our curve with Eurodollar 2-year, 3-year, and 4-year rates gives the growing curve in Figure A-4.

Now the liquid Eurodollar terms still take us only 4 years into the future. To get spot rates for longer terms, we can turn to the market for U.S. Treasury securities. These are more liquid, therefore more reliable for price discovery than Eurodollars going out beyond 4 years. These *treasuries*, as they are known, consist of bills, notes, and bonds[5] issued by the U.S. government for varying

---

[5]The distinction is primarily in maturity. Bills go out to a year and pay interest only at maturity; instruments like this are sometimes known as "zero-coupon" instruments or just "zeros." Notes go out to 10 years, bonds go beyond 10 years, and both notes and bonds make period coupon payments to their holders (i.e., lenders).

FIGURE A-4

Partial Libor Spot Curve Going Out Four Years

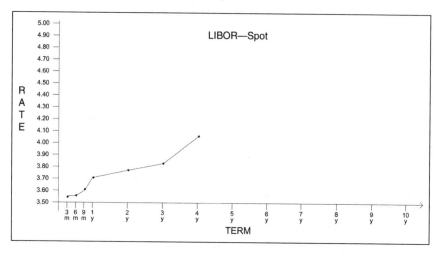

terms. Treasury notes and bonds are loans to the U.S. Treasury, which makes interest or *coupon* payments semiannually (every 6 months) at a fixed coupon rate. As marketable securities, once issued they are heavily traded on secondary markets. This just means bond holders actively buy and sell (trade) them, and the price at which they trade determines their effective interest rate or yield, which can be wildly different from the coupon rate.

By the way, does it seem bizarre a coupon rate and effective rate can be different? Here's how it happens: Say you buy a 5-year treasury with a face value of $100,000 (the amount you lend to Uncle Sam) and a coupon rate of 4.75 percent (the annual interest rate for semiannual interest payments). If you hold this bond to maturity, you can look forward to a stream of cash flows over the next 5 years based on the 4.75 percent rate. Now if you add up the present values of these cash flows, you will get $100,000, or face value. Imagine that you buy one of these from the U.S. Treasury, and right away someone buys it from you on the secondary market for $101,200. Now they can look forward to those cash flows based on the coupon rate—whose present value is just $100,000! They clearly paid a premium for your bond—i.e., more than the PV of its cash flows. It's as if they bought a bond that pays a coupon of something less than 4.75 percent. In fact I'll do the math for you and tell you they effectively bought a bond that pays an annual rate of 4.53 percent annual rate. And this is how we deduce spot interest rates from treasury prices.

And while we are spinning tangents, do you notice that the 3-month treasury rate of 3.38 is 15 basis points lower than the 3-month Libor rate of 3.53? This is a great example of a *credit spread*, which we'll speak more of later on. Libor rates are intended for commercial loans, whereas treasuries are for loans to the United States Treasury. All other factors equal, a commercial loan is more likely to default than a U.S. Treasury loan. A lender demands a risk premium for this increased credit risk, which in this case is 15 bips.

Now back to the matter at hand. Let's say U.S. Treasury yields look like this on the same day as our Libor rate fixings above:

U.S. Treasury Rates

3 month	3.38
6 month	3.37
1 year	3.44
2 year	3.76
5 year	4.53
10 year	4.92
20 year	5.53
30 year	5.44

When we add Treasury rates to the Libor curve, for the 5-year and 10-year points, we get something like Figure A-5.

Our nascent curve now covers a longer set of maturities, but still it doesn't give an exact rate for a term between the given points, say for a 3-year loan. You might think you can simply read up from the 3-year point and stop when you hit the line, and this will indeed give you an approximation, but mathematicians will tell you there is a better way to make this curve more useful. It's called *curve smoothing*. To get an idea for curve smoothing, just imagine taking a pencil and eye-balling a smooth line that connects the dots and extends the lines beyond the first and last dots. Now it might look like the curvy thing in Figure A-6.

Now we have a yield curve. And while it's a theoretically correct curve, it's a bit wavy to be useful. In practice we like a

FIGURE A-5

Complete Libor Spot Curve Before Smoothing

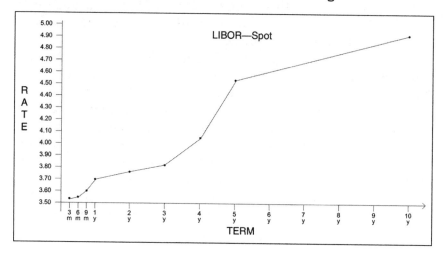

FIGURE A-6

Complete Libor Spot Curve with Some Smoothing

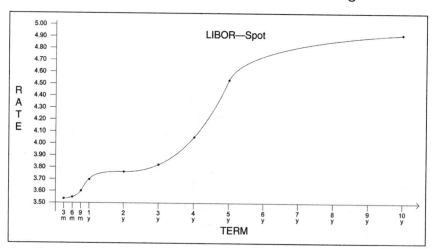

smoother curve and are even willing to adjust the sample points a bit to fit a nice smooth line, as in Figure A-7.

You can, of course, adjust even further and end up with a line so smooth is it perfectly straight. But that's too smooth. How

FIGURE A-7

Complete Libor Spot Curve with More Smoothing

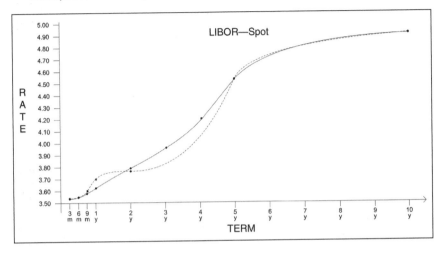

smooth is smooth enough? Here we will step off the bus because to go further requires a generous helping of math. It turns out there are a number of formulas or *algorithms* for smoothing a curve given a sample of points. Some are in the public domain, widely known and taught in school, and some are highly proprietary or secret to their creators. (In addition to curve smoothing, the choice of inputs is also proprietary. Do we use the 1-year Libor or 1-year U.S. Treasury rate? Do we take rates from the spot market or futures market? And so on.) They are secret because things like this—drawing better yield curves and developing better algorithms—are the sort of thing that helps you make money in the world of derivatives. For our purposes, we'll stick to the one shown in Figure A-8.

THE FORWARD RATE AND FORWARD CURVE

A spot rate is an interest rate for money borrowed now. It's the rate (price) available right now on the spot market for money and is the type of rate depicted in our spot curve above. If you ask your bank

FIGURE A-8

Libor Spot Yield Curve

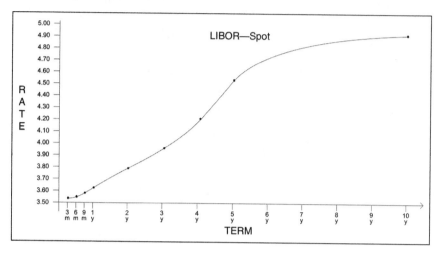

for a 6-month loan commencing immediately, the rate they will quote you is a spot rate. A *forward rate* is an interest rate for money borrowed for some future period of time. If you ask your bank for a 6-month loan commencing not today but one year from now, they will quote a forward rate. This is a rate (price) at which the bank agrees today (guarantees) to lend you money in one year's time. Sound familiar? It should! The forward rate is just the delivery price of a forward contract whose underlier is borrowed money. (Such contracts are known as *forward rate agreements*, introduced earlier.)

A forward curve looks just like a spot curve, but the rates depicted are for a loan commencing some time hence. And different lag periods get their own forward curves. So on any given day for any given index, you will have a spot curve, a 3-month forward curve (for loans of varying maturities commencing 3 months later), a 6-month forward curve, 12-month curve, and so on. Here's the main thing: forward rates are derived from spot rates. And forward curves, therefore, are derived from spot curves. For any given spot curve, there is only one possible 3-month forward curve, one possible 6-month forward curve, and so on. So the first step in constructing a forward curve is always the construction of a spot curve. You can't make toast without bread, and you can't make a forward curve without a spot curve.

Forward Rates from Spot Rates

Say you want to borrow $10,000 6 months from now for a period of 3 months. The 6-month spot rate is 3.5 percent and the 9-month spot rate is 3.55 percent. What is the 3-month forward rate for a loan commencing in 6 months, or 6 × 9 ("six by nine") rate? It's 3.71 percent. How come? Imagine two hypothetical scenarios. In scenario A you borrow for 9 months at 3.55 percent. In scenario B you borrow for 6 months at 3.5 percent, then take out a new, 3-month loan at the then-current 3-month spot rate. Both scenarios should cost the same because they both give you the same thing: a 9-month loan of 10 grand. This means the 3-month spot rate in 6 months—the 6 by 9 rate—is the one that makes both scenarios cost the same. In other words, it's the rate that makes the present value of one scenario's interest payments equal to the present value of the other scenario's interest payments. (Any other rate would allow arbitrage, which you'll recall is simultaneous trading to make a riskless profit from pricing discrepancies, and the correct price for anything in the land of derivatives is the one, and only one, that prevents arbitrage.) The rate that does that is 3.71 percent. Here's the math if you don't believe me (to simplify a bit, we assume interest payments are made in advance):

Scenario A
9-month loan today

Notional	10,000.00
9-mo spot rate	3.55%
Day fraction	9/12 = 0.75
9-mo interest rate	2.66%
Interest payment	266.25
Months till payment	0
Discount factor	1
Interest payment PV	266.25
Total interest PV	266.25

Scenario B
6-month loan today

Notional	10,000.00
6-mo spot rate	3.50%
Day fraction	6/12 = 0.5
6-mo interest rate	1.75%
Interest payment	175.00
Months till payment	0
Discount factor	1
Interest payment PV	175.00

3-month loan in 6 months

Notional	10,000.00
3-mo forward rate	3.71333%
Day fraction	3/12 = 0.25
3-mo interest rate	0.9283%
Interest payment	92.83
Months till payment	6
Discount factor	$(1/1.035)^{6/12} = 0.9829$
Interest payment PV	91.25
Total interest PV	175.00 + 91.25 = 266.25

Figure A-9 shows what a complete 3-month forward curve might look like, given using spot rates from our spot curve, and a bit of smoothing:

FIGURE A-9

Libor Forward and Spot Yield Curves Superimposed

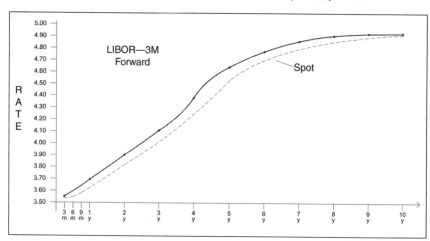

Here's another factoid for you: Notice that the forward curve is above the spot curve at all points? This is always the case for upward-sloping spot curves. When spot curves slope downward (it happens), the forward curve is below spot. That's all academic, of course. The main thing for us is that from a curve like this, we can obtain 3-month forward rates for 3-month loans commencing at any point out 10 years. This comes in very handy when we value a swap.

In addition to conventions introduced in the Swaps chapters and previous appendix, there's yet another batch of concepts applicable to swaps and virtually all interest rate derivatives used in practice. Some of these are mathematical, and some are just conventions that have arisen over the years.

COMPOUNDING

We examined *compounding* in an earlier chapter. Swap interest rates can be specified as compounding or noncompounding. Recall that when a loan is based on a compounding rate of interest, interest is paid not only on the principal (the amount borrowed) but also on accrued interest. If you owe me interest, but don't pay it to me, then it's just like I'm loaning you more money, money that will cost you more interest. And if you don't pay me that interest, it will cost you more interest, and so on, until you finally fork over the dough. That's compounding, which can be applied to either a fixed or floating-rate loan.

AVERAGING

The concept of *rate averaging* applies to floating-rate obligations. Here, when it comes time to make a payment, the rate applied is not the current reading of the index thermometer but the average of some number of previous readings. An example illustrates it best. Say we observe the following rate fixings for 6-month Libor:

Monday	3.60
Tuesday	3.58
Wednesday	3.59
Thursday	3.60
Friday	3.57

Now say it's Friday and time to calculate a payment. For a nonaveraging obligation we choose the Friday fixing, or

3.57 percent. For an obligation based on a 5-day average rate we calculate the average of all five rate fixings, or 3.59 percent, and use that.[1] The 5-day period is just an example. You can have an obligation based on a 30-day average, 6-month average, whatever.

AMORTIZATION

Amortization is when a loan, either fixed or floating, has a principle that changes over the life of a loan. All interest rate derivatives have a *principle*, also known as the *notional* in the context of interest rate derivatives, against which an interest rate is periodically applied (as on payment dates) for the purpose of calculating some amount of interest. Perhaps you've borrowed $10 million, and each year must make a 6 percent interest-only payment. The $10 million is your notional, the amount by which the 6 percent rate is multiplied to calculate your $60,000 payment. If your loan is nonamortizing, the notional remains constant over the life of the loan, and every payment is calculated from it. If your loan is amortizing, the notional changes, or amortizes. All amortizing obligations include a schedule of notional amounts, predefined at the outset of a trade. This amortization or "am" schedule may follow some neat pattern, or it may be downright wacky, as long as both parties agree to it up front.

Here are the more common forms of amortization:

Additive

The simplest amortization involves adding to (or subtracting from) the previous level some fixed amount. Say you begin with $10 million and decrease it by $1 million each period. That's additive amortization—you're just "adding" a negative number.

Period 1:	10,000,000	
Period 2:	9,000,000	(i.e., 10,000,000 − 1,000,000)
Period 3:	8,000,000	(i.e., 9,000,000 − 1,000,000)
Period 4:	7,000,000	(i.e., 8,000,000 − 1,000,000)
etc		

---

[1]$3.60 + 3.58 + 3.59 + 3.60 + 3.57 = 17.94$ and $17.94/5 = 3.59$.

Straight-Line

This is a special case of additive amortization where the notional steps down by the same amount each period, and the final notional amount is the stepping amount. Say you amortize $1 million over four periods by $250 thousand each period. Your complete am schedule looks like this:

Period 1:	1,000,000
Period 2:	750,000
Period 3:	500,000
Period 4:	250,000

Multiplicative

Here instead of adding to the previous amount we multiply it by some amount, typically (but not always) some fractional amount between zero and 1. A multiplicative amortization schedule starting at $1 million and decreasing by 12 percent each period starts off like this:

Period 1:	1,000,000	
Period 2:	880,000	(i.e., 1,000,000 − (1,000,000 * .12))
Period 3:	774,400	(i.e., 880,000 − (880,000 * .12))
etc		

Mortgage-Style

This amortization schedule will be familiar if you've ever borrowed money to purchase real estate. Each payment consists of some notional plus interest, such that each payment is the same and all notional is repaid by the end of the loan. A four-period amortization schedule, starting at $100 million using a 7 percent "mortgage rate," with annual payments, might look like this:

	Notional	Interest	Payment (N + I)
Period 1:	22,522,811.67	7,000,000.00	29,522,811.67
Period 2:	24,099,408.48	5,423,403.18	29,522,811.67
Period 3:	25,786,367.08	3,736,444.59	29,522,811.67
Period 4:	27,591,412.77	1,931,398.89	29,522,811.67
	100,000,000.00		

Note above that mortgages are typically paid in arrears, which simply means you pay for the money after you have it for some period of time. So the interest is based on the remaining notional at the beginning of the period. In the example above, then, the first period interest is 7 percent of the full 100,000,000 notional, or the notional as of the beginning of the first period. The second period interest is 7 percent of 100,000,000 less the 22,522,811.67 paid off with the first payment. And so on.

CALENDARS

This might seem so basic it's not worth covering, but the simple and meaningful fact is this: people don't work every day of the year. We take off weekends and holidays, known as *nonbusiness days*, leaving the rest as work days or *business days*. And for reasons soon to be revealed, it is crucial for transaction counterparties to agree on which days are business days and which are not. Is Groundhog Day a business day? Boxing Day? John Lennon's Birthday?

Fortunately, there are a set of predefined calendars to make this task easier. Each calendar is named for a city—New York, London, Tokyo, etc.—and each is basically a list of weekdays not considered a business day in that locale. (Saturdays and Sundays, I am happy to report, appear to be nonbusiness days the world over.) The calendar definitions are for all intents and purposes universally accepted, so we never have to quibble over individual holidays, just the calendar. Figure B-1, for example, shows September holidays one year in New York and Tokyo.

So for any given transaction, we simply specify one or more of these calendars up front. More than one? Sure. It's not

FIGURE B-1

New York and Tokyo Holiday Calendars

	September									September					
	Su	Mo	Tu	We	Th	Fr	Sa		Su	Mo	Tu	We	Th	Fr	Sa
New York						1	2	**Tokyo**						1	2
Sep 4 : Labor Day	3	[4]	5	6	7	8	9	Sep 18 : Respect for the Aged Day	3	4	5	6	7	8	9
	10	11	12	13	14	15	16		10	11	12	13	14	15	16
	17	18	19	20	21	22	23		17	[18]	19	20	21	22	23
	24	25	26	27	28	29	30		24	25	26	27	28	29	30

uncommon for a transaction to specify as its calendar some combination of calendars, say New York and Tokyo. And, a contract might specify the New York calendar for one aspect of a trade and Tokyo for the other.

Using our examples above, if a trade is based on a New York calendar, then September 18 is a business day. But if the trade is based on a Tokyo holiday, then September 18 is not a business day. If the trade's calendar is New York + Tokyo, then September 18 again is not a business day; for multicalendar trades, a nonbusiness day anywhere is a nonbusiness day for the sake of the trade.

BUSINESS DAY CONVENTIONS

A trade's calendar tells us which dates over the life of that trade constitute business days and which do not. So what if some meaningful date, say the date on which a payment is due, falls on a weekend or holiday? Does someone come into the office? The two parties in a trade can decide to handle this situation however they want. But as with calendars, they will no doubt wish to select from a number of standard *business day conventions* at the outset of a trade. These are simply rules that specify what to do when a meaningful date falls on a nonbusiness day. The most common of these are pretty easy to grasp and are listed below.

Following	Go forward in time till you get to a business day and use that one.
Previous	Go back in time till you get to a business day and use that one.
Modified Following	Go forward in time till you get to a business day and use that one—unless that day should take you into the next month, in which case go backward in time till you get to a business day and use that one.
No Adjustment	Someone is coming into work. Use the date as is.

Day Count Conventions

Interest rates are almost always expressed as annual rates, that is, the cost of borrowing money for exactly one year. When you see a rate "5.325 percent" you just know it applies to one year. Same with "1.25 percent" or "10 percent." When it comes time to calculate an actual amount of interest, however, the period we are concerned with is almost never 1 year exactly. Instead we want to calculate a payment due for some accrual period such as "3 months commencing April 1" or "September 3 through October 5" or "85 days starting May 17." What rate do we apply? It turns out there's more than one way to reasonably arrive at an applicable rate for a given period of time. And to bring some clarity to this gray area, there are five techniques, or algorithms, known as *day count conventions*. Some of these are more tedious than others, but all are well understood and that's all that matters. Every trade specifies one of these at the outset of a trade, to be applied when necessary to calculate interest accruals.

The whole thing boils down to fractions. If your rate of interest is 6 percent per year and you want to calculate interest for a period less than a year, clearly you need to apply only a fraction of that 6 percent. That fraction is known as a *day fraction*. This ubiquitous computational ingredient tells us how much of an annual interest rate to apply when calculating interest for some period of time. If the period of time is less than one year (typical) the fraction is less than one, if exactly one year, the fraction is equal to one, and if greater than one year (it happens) the day count fraction is greater than one.

As a math problem it looks like this:

$$Interest = (Annual\ Rate * Day\ Fraction) * Notional$$

Ignoring the real conventions for a second, imagine you want to calculate 6 percent interest on a million dollars for exactly one year. Our day fraction is of course "1:"

$$Interest = (.06 * 1) * \$1,000,000 = \$60,000$$

Now if we want to calculate interest for one half of a year, our day fraction is clearly "one-half" and we just do this:

$$Interest = (.06 * 1/2) * \$1,000,000 = \$30,000$$

The day count conventions specify what to put in the numerator (the top part) and denominator (the bottom part) of a day count fraction. Several conventions are floating around out there (some of them quite convoluted!), but here are a few of the common ones and how they work:

Actual/365[2]

Here we basically divide the actual length of the accrual period by 365 to get our day fraction. So for the numerator we need the number of days—business and nonbusiness—in the period for which we want to calculate interest. Say the period starts September 15 and ends December 14 in 2006. Looking at a 2006 calendar, we see there are 90 actual days in that period, including the end date but not the start date. So that goes into the numerator. And the denominator under this convention is 365. So under the Actual/365 convention, the day count fraction for calculating the applicable rate of interest for the period September 15, 2006 through December 14, 2006 is 90/365. Multiplying this fraction by 6 percent gives us the accrual rate. For notional amount of $1,000,000, then, the payment in dollars works out to be $14,794.52.

Accrual start	Sep 15, 2006
Accrual end	Dec 14, 2006
Actual days	90
Day fraction	90/365
Annual rate	6%
Accrual rate	.06 * 90/365
Accrual	1,000,000 * .06 * 90/365 = 14,794.52

Actual/360

Similar routine here, but we put 360 in the denominator instead. For notional amount of $1,000,000 and annual rate of 6 percent, the payment in dollars works out to be $15,000 on the nose.

Accrual start	Sep 15, 2006
Accrual end	Dec 14, 2006
Actual days	90
Day fraction	90/360
Annual rate	6%
Accrual rate	.06 * 90/360
Accrual	1,000,000 * .06 * 90/360 = 15,000.00

---

[2]The convention I describe here is known technically in some quarters as "Actual/365 (Fixed)" and is not to be confused with a different "Actual/365" altogether, also known as "Actual/Actual." Now you see why I'm only giving a few examples.

30/360

Also known as the *bond basis* convention, here we take the difference between the start and end date as the numerator but in a funny way. Rather than looking at a calendar and counting days, we instead assume every year has 12 months of 30 days each, for 360 days total (which we use for the denominator). To arrive at the number of days in the period, we take the ending year less starting year times 360, ending month less starting month times 30, and ending day minus starting day times one. Using DD/MM/YYYY format, which helps illustrate this thing, the payment for the period starting 09/15/2006 and ending 12/14/2006 is \$14,833.33 as follows:

Accrual start	9/15/2006
Accrual end	12/14/2006
Year difference	$(2006 - 2006) * 360 = 0$
Month difference	$(12 - 9) * 30 = 90$
Day difference	$(14 - 15) * 1 = -1$
Total difference	89 days
Day fraction	89/360
Annual rate	6%
Accrual rate	$.06 * 89/360$
Accrual	$1,000,000 * .06 * 89/360 = 14,833.33$

SWAP ATTRIBUTE SUMMARY

Below are a few words on most of the features of a plain vanilla swap starting with features that apply to a trade in its entirety, then zooming in on features of individual legs.

Trade-Level Features

A number of attributes typically apply to the trade overall, that is, both legs. These include:

Notional	What is the amount of money, or "principal," on which interest will be calculated? Recall that this amount typically does not actually change hands in a plain vanilla. It is a reference amount for interest calculation.
Effective date	When does the swap go into effect? More precisely, on what day does interest start to gather up in reserve in anticipation of a payment?
Maturity date	When does the swap end? What is the last day on which interest accrues?

| Discount curve | For present-value calculations (say, to calculate the current market value of the swap), what interest rates will we choose? And because interest rates vary by term, and a yield curve conveys a whole set of rates at once, what yield curve shall we reference for this swap? Note the discount curve need not be the same as the pricing curve discussed below.[3] |

Accrual Features

At the outset of a swap, we must specify precisely how interest will gather or *accrue* over the life of the trade. These attributes can, and typically do, pertain to both legs of the trade and include the following:

Compounding	Will interest accrue only on principal (noncompounding) or will it also accrue on interest earned but not yet paid (compounding)? If it does compound, at what frequency will it do so? Monthly, daily, continuously...?
Averaging	When it comes time to choose an interest rate from an index in order, say, to calculate a payment, do we choose a rate fixing from a single day (nonaveraging)? Or do we calculate the average of some number of daily rate fixings (averaging)? If it is averaging, how far back to we go when collecting rate fixings to average? Five days, 1 month, 1 year...?
Amortizing	Will the notional, or swap principle, remain unchanged over the life of the trade (nonamortizing) or will it change (amortizing)? If amortizing, how exactly will it change from period to period? Straight-line, mortgage-style, custom...?

Leg-Level Features

These features are typically specified separately for each leg of a trade, and often differ between legs:

| Tenor | At what frequency will cash flows occur? Three-month tenors are quite common, whereby cash flows or coupons occur every 3 months. |
| Coupon date | On which day of the month are cash flows exchanged? In other words, on which day of the month does one coupon period end and another begin? And in what month will the first coupon occur? |

---

[3]The fact a swap has both a pricing curve and discount curve illustrates one of the ways interest rate derivatives are so interesting (so to speak). Interest rates are used in two very different ways. First to provide a spot price of the underlier, and second for the purpose of discounting cash flows.

Stubs	In many cases the effective date of a trade is different from the coupon date. Or, the period of time between the effective date and first coupon date does not equal the tenor of the trade. In either case we are left with *stub* periods, or periods of time less then the tenor. We can handle these in one of two ways. We can treat this like a regular coupon and just calculate interest on some number of days less than a regular period. We call these "short stubs." Or we can add the stub to the first regular coupon, and accrue on some number of days greater than a regular coupon. We call these "long stubs." Note too that stubs can occur at the end of a trade, where again we can treat them as either long or short.
Day Basis	To apply an annual interest rate to an accrual period whose length is less than or greater than one year we need a *day fraction* for converting the rate. Which day basis convention shall we use? Common selections here are Actual/365, Actual/360, 30/360 and others.
Calendar	Of all the days between the effective date and maturity date of our swap, which shall we consider business days? Do we agree on one calendar such as New York? Or a blended calendar such as New York + London?
Adjustment	If a meaningful date such as a coupon payment date should fall on a nonbusiness day, should we use that date in our interest calculation? Or should we select a nearby date according to one of the business day adjustment conventions such as Previous or Modified Following?

Fixed Leg Features

There's really only one attribute unique to the fixed leg, but it's an important one.

Fixed Rate	What is the rate of interest, never to change over the life of the swap, for the calculation of cash flows on the fixed leg? If we had to choose just one, this would be the single most important attribute of a swap, known also as the *swap rate*. Analogous to the delivery price in a forward, it is often the "last" attribute calculated, chosen so that the initial value of the swap is zero to both parties.

Floating Leg Features

These pertain to the cash flows calculated with a changing rate of interest:

Rate Index	What is the source of a yield curve for the calculation of accruals on coupon dates. Also known as the "pricing curve" (to distinguish it from the "discount curve," which

	may or may not reference the same index), the most common rate index for swaps is Libor.
Reset Offset	For an accrual period commencing on some given day, which business day's rate fixing should we use? If an accrual period commences on a Thursday, do we use the Libor fixing from Tuesday, perhaps? This attribute is expressed as a simple integer and for Libor is typically 2 days.
Reset Calendar	When the reset offset is something other than zero, and if we find ourselves needing to move some number of days away from the accrual start date, which of those days should we consider business days? What calendar should we follow?
Reset Adjustment	If we land on a nonbusiness day when choosing a rate fixing date in accordance with the reset offset and reset calendar, what should we do? Do we follow the Previous convention? Or perhaps Modified Following?

Now keep in mind these are OTC instruments and the two parties can add whatever additional features they can agree on, tossing ISDA out the window if they'd like, making them just as complex and weird as you can imagine. But the feature above pretty much sums up those used by the vast majority of swap users.

Advanced Binomial Option Pricing

In this appendix we'll extend the basic concepts we introduced in the Pricing Options chapter. We'll walk through the nitty gritty of pricing an option using a multistep binomial tree, present formulas for option pricing with a binomial tree, and demonstrate the important concept of risk-neutral pricing using the binomial tree.

A MULTISTEP TREE

In Figure C-1 we've constructed a two-step binomial tree using the same basic setup as our one-step tree in the option pricing chapter. Now we start on the right-hand side by determining the option value at each of the end nodes. That's easy. It's just the MAX $(0, S\text{-}K)$ thing applied with three different S (i.e., ZED) values.

Now we work our way to the left and calculate the value of $cZED62$ at each of the two nodes in the middle. Look at the node where ZED equals 63. We have here a value for the underlier and the value of the option under two different future prices—just what we need to solve an option price with a one-step tree.

First we calculate delta:

$$\Delta 66.15 - 4.15 = \Delta 59.85 - 0$$
$$\Delta 66.15 - \Delta 59.85 = 4.15$$
$$\Delta(66.15 - 59.85) = 4.15$$
$$\Delta = .6587$$

Next we need the portfolio value in 3 months, when ZED is trading for 66.15 or 59.85. We need only consider one case but let's do both anyway:

$$P_{t=3m} = \Delta 66.15 - 4.15$$
$$P_{t=3m} = (.6587)66.15 - 4.15$$
$$P_{t=3m} = 39.42$$
$$P_{t=3m} = \Delta 59.85$$
$$P_{t=3m} = (.6587)59.85$$
$$P_{t=3m} = 39.42$$

FIGURE C-1

Two-Step Binomial Tree with Terminal Prices

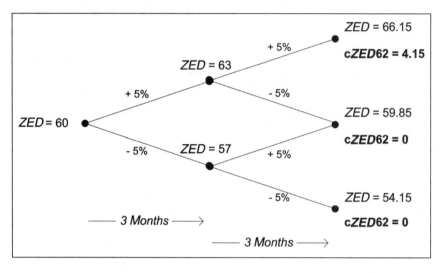

Recall what we need next? The present value of the portfolio value. Same math as before, but notice we multiply the rate by one-quarter instead of one-half because our period is now one-quarter of a year (3 months):

$$P_0 = 39.42e^{-(.04)(.25)}$$
$$P_0 = 39.03$$

Now we have values for two of three components of our portfolio and can solve for the third. Don't forget the price of ZED is 63 at this node:

$$RP = \Delta ZED - cZED62$$
$$39.03 = .6587(63) - cZED62$$
$$cZED62 = 41.50 - 39.03$$
$$cZED62 = 2.47$$

Now we need an option value for the node where ZED equals 57. First we calculate delta:

$$\Delta 59.85 - 0 = \Delta 54.55 - 0$$
$$\Delta 59.85 - \Delta 54.55 = 0$$
$$\Delta(59.85 - 54.55) = 0$$
$$\Delta = 0$$

Then we need the portfolio value in 3 months, when ZED is trading for either 59.85 or 54.55:

$$P_{t=3m} = \Delta 59.85 - 0$$
$$P_{t=3m} = (0)59.85 - 0$$
$$P_{t=3m} = 0$$
$$P_{t=3m} = \Delta 54.55 - 0$$
$$P_{t=3m} = (0)54.55$$
$$P_{t=3m} = 0$$

The portfolio in either case is worth zero. And the present value of 0 is of course 0:

$$P_0 = 0e^{-(.04)(.25)}$$
$$P_0 = 0$$

Again we have values for two of three components of our portfolio and can solve for the third:

$$RP = \Delta ZED - cZED62$$
$$0 = 0(57) - cZED62$$
$$cZED62 = 0 - 0$$
$$cZED62 = 0$$

The value of the option at this node is zero. Our tree now is shown in Figure C-2.

We're left now with a single one-step tree. The math should be familiar now so we'll jump right to the solution. The completed tree looks like Figure C-3.

This tells the option price of 1.47 is correct no matter which of the four possible price paths is actually taken by the underlier. Any other price would allow arbitrage. This price is clearly different from the 2.53 we calculated on a one-step tree. But we like it better—that is, we think it's closer to the real value—because the price path model is (ever so slightly) better using a two-step tree than a one-stepper.

Now a 3-period tree provides eight possible paths so we'll like a price from one of those trees even more. A 4-period tree allows for 16 possible paths, and so on. You can see where I'm going. The algebra works no matter how big the tree. And by using a tree with sufficiently short and numerous branches, we can model a very large number of possible price paths. And the number of paths grows

FIGURE C-2

Two-Step Binomial Tree with Prices after One Step

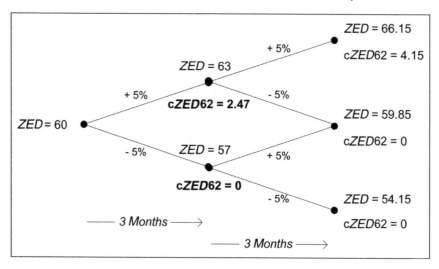

FIGURE C-3

Two-Step Binomial Tree with Price at Origination

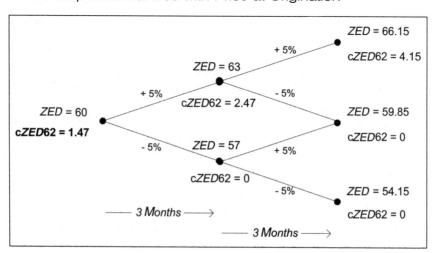

very quickly (it's just 2 raised to the number of steps). So a 20-period tree allows for over a million paths, and a 30-period tree more than a billion. Think of it this way: Nobody can predict the actual future price path of an underlying asset between now and some time in the future. But if we construct a model with a billion possible price paths, odds start getting pretty good that the actual price path will be one of, or very close to one of, those billion. So an option price that works for *any* of those billion price paths is a mighty good one.

GENERAL BINOMIAL FORMULAS

First let's summarize in a key the symbols we've seen so far. Algebra is all about representing things with symbols, right?

S : Stock price

K : Strike price

C : Call option value to the long party

u : 1 + stock return after an up move

d : 1 + stock return after a down move

S_u : Stock price after an up move
$$S_u = S * u$$

S_d : Stock price after a down move
$$S_d = S * d$$

C_u : Call value after an up move
$$C_u = MAX(0, S_u - K)$$

C_d : Call value after a down move
$$C_d = MAX(0, S_d - K)$$

ΔS : Delta shares of stock
$$\Delta = (C_u - C_d)/(S_u - S_d)$$
$$\Delta S = (C_u - C_d)/[(u - d)]$$

r : Risk-free interest rate

t : Time between steps in years

e : Euler's Number
$$e = 2.7182\ldots$$

B : Borrowed money in synthetic option position
$$B = (dC_u - uC_d)/[e^{rt}(u - d)]$$

And to this mix we need to add the symbol p for *pseudoprobability* of an up move or "uptick." Now "pseudo" just means "sorta" or "not really but it'll work." As we'll see when we explore risk-neutrality below, we're working now in a world without risk. It doesn't matter whether stock prices go up or down, so we don't need real probability just like we don't need a real interest rate. But for the math to work, we do need an interest rate for discounting, for which we use the risk-free rate. And we also need a probability, for which we use this p.

p : Pseudoprobability of an up move
$$p = (e^{rt} - d)/(u - d)$$

$1-p$: Pseudoprobability of a down move
$$1 - p = (u - e^{rt})/(u - d)$$

Now recall how we expressed the value of a call option using the components of a synthetic option or leveraged stock position:

$$cZED62 = \Delta ZED - B$$

or

$$C = \Delta S - B$$

It turns out we can apply yet some more algebra and convert this expression into the rather simple Formula C.1 for the value of a call option. You ready? Refer back to the symbol key, take it slowly, and this might not seem so bad at all.

$$C = \Delta S - B$$
$$C = (C_u - C_d)/[(u - d)] - (dC_u - uC_d)/[e^{rt}(u - d)]$$
$$C = (C_u - C_d)e^{rt}(u - d)/(u - d)e^{rt}(u - d)$$
$$\quad - (dC_u - uC_d)(u - d)/(u - d)e^{rt}(u - d)$$
$$C = [(C_u - C_d)e^{rt}(u - d) - (dC_u - uC_d)(u - d)]/(u - d)e^{rt}(u - d)$$
$$C = [(C_u - C_d)e^{rt} - (dC_u - uC_d)]/e^{rt}(u - d)$$
$$C = [e^{rt}C_u - e^{rt}C_d + uC_d - dC_u]/e^{rt}(u - d)$$
$$C = [e^{rt}C_u - dC_u + uC_d - e^{rt}C_d]/e^{rt}(u - d)$$
$$C = [(e^{rt} - d)C_u]/[e^{rt}(u - d)] + [(u - e^{rt})C_d]/[e^{rt}(u - d)]$$
$$C = e^{-rt}[(e^{rt} - d)/(u - d)]C_u + e^{-rt}[(u - e^{rt})/(u - d)]C_d$$
$$C = e^{-rt}pC_u + e^{-rt}(1-p)C_d$$
$$C = e^{-rt}[pC_u + (1-p)C_d]$$

Call Value from 1-Step Binomial Tree
$$C = e^{-rt}[pC_u + (1-p)C_d]$$ (C.1)

The Formula C.2 for puts is darnly near identical.

P : Put option value to the long party

P_u : Put value after an up move
$$P_u = MAX(0, K - S_u)$$

P_d : Put value after a down move
$$P_d = MAX(0, K - S_d)$$

$$P = e^{-rt}[pP_u + (1-p)P_d]$$ (C.2)

For a two-step tree we have another end node (which you can reach by two different paths, recall) to consider. Take a look at Figure C-4.

To price each of C_u and C_d we re-express the formula using the appropriate node names

$$C_u = e^{-rt}[pC_{uu} + (1-p)C_{ud}]$$
$$C_d = e^{-rt}[pC_{ud} + (1-p)C_{dd}]$$

And we already know that

$$C = e^{-rt}[pC_u + (1-p)C_d]$$

FIGURE C-4

Generic Two-Step Binomial Tree

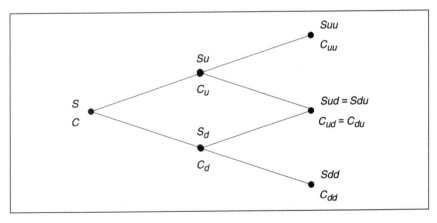

By merging these three formula together, that is, by replacing C_u and C_d in the one-step formula with their respective formulas, we arrive at a single formula C.3 for the price of a call using a two-step binomial tree:

$$C = e^{-rt}[pC_u + (1-p)C_d]$$
$$C = e^{-rt}[pe^{-rt}(pC_{uu} + (1-p)C_{ud}) + (1-p)e^{-rt}(pC_{ud} + (1-p)C_{dd})]$$
$$C = e^{-rt}[pe^{-rt}pC_{uu} + pe^{-rt}(1-p)C_{ud} + (1-p)e^{-rt}pC_{ud}$$
$$+ (1-p)e^{-rt}(1-p)C_{dd}]$$
$$C = e^{-rt}[e^{-rt}(ppC_{uu} + p(1-p)C_{ud} + (1-p)pC_{ud} + (1-p)(1-p)C_{dd})]$$
$$C = e^{-rt}[e^{-rt}(p^2C_{uu} + 2p(1-p)C_{ud} + (1-p)^2C_{dd})]$$
$$C = e^{-2rt}(p^2C_{uu} + 2p(1-p)C_{ud} + (1-p)^2C_{dd})$$

Call Value from 2-Step Binomial Tree

$$C = e^{-2rt}(p^2C_{uu} + 2p(1-p)C_{ud} + (1-p)^2C_{dd}) \qquad \text{(C.3)}$$

So what is the call option formula using an n-step tree where n is any positive integer? We'll not derive the formula (i.e., show you how we get it), but we will take a look at it, once we introduce more symbols:

n : Number of steps to a node

j : Number of up moves to a node

$n-j$: Number of down moves to a node

a : Minimum number of up moves before option is in-the-money

And here are some math functions we'll use along the way:

$n!$ n-factorial

$$n! = n(n-1)(n-2)\ldots(2)(1)$$

Example

$$5! = 5 * 4 * 3 * 2 * 1 = 120$$

$\displaystyle\sum_{i=1}^{n} x_i$ Summation of $x_1, x_2, x_3, \ldots x_n$

Example

$$\sum_{i=1}^{3} 5^i = 5^1 + 5^2 + 5^3 = 5 + 25 + 125 = 155$$

Now the number of paths from the starting node to some node $C_{u^j d^{(n-j)}}$, that is, a node n-steps away where you went up j times and down n-j times, is this:

$$\frac{n!}{j!(n-j)!}$$

And the value of a call option, from an n-step binomial tree, is given by formula C.4.

Call Value from N-Step Binomial Tree   (C.4)

$$C = e^{-rT} \sum_{j=a}^{n} \left(\frac{n!}{j!(n-j)!} \right) p^j (1-p)^{n-j} \left[u^j d^{(n-j)} S \right]$$

$$- e^{-rT} \sum_{j=a}^{n} \left(\frac{n!}{j!(n-j)!} \right) p^j (1-p)^{n-j} K$$

THE RISK NEUTRALITY THING

The appearance of the "pseudoprobability of an uptick" factor in our valuation formulas illustrates one of the basic ideas behind how we price derivatives, and it's a very very important one: The value of an option is its expected payoff in a risk-neutral world, discounted at the risk-free rate. This is true for all derivatives, by the way, not just options. A *risk-neutral* world is one in which investors are neither risk-adverse nor risk-inclined. Unlike investors in the real world, investors here require no compensation for risk. An *expected value* is just a future value times the probability of it occurring. Say you put a $100 wager on red at a roulette wheel for the chance to win double your bet if the wheel stops on a red number. Say half the numbers are red, so there's a 50 percent chance of your winning $200. The expected future value of your "investment" is $100. Yipee.[1]

The risk-neutrality thing applies to both binomial options pricing and to Black-Scholes. If this risk-neutrality thing is correct, we should be able to (1) use the risk-free rate to calculate a future value of the underlying stock in a risk-neutral world, (2) deduce a probability factor from that future stock value, (3) use this probability to

---

[1]Like most wagers in Las Vegas the expected value is actually a bit less. I only go for the shows.

FIGURE C-5

One-Step Binomial Tree, Price at Origin Unknown

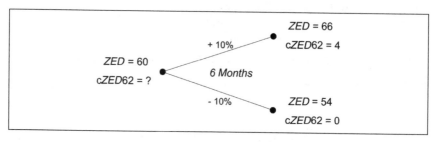

calculate an expected value of the option given its strike price, and (4) discount this option value using the risk-free rate—to get the same option value we got in a world *not* risk-neutral using no-arbitrage arguments. Let's see if we can do that with the binomial tree.

Recall the setup from the one-step binomial tree example, depicted in Figure C-5. The stock *ZED* trades for 60 and will go up or down by 10 percent in 6 months, to 66 or 54. A 62-strike call option will be worth 4 if it goes up and 0 if it goes down.

What's the value of the option? The expected value of the stock is its future value using the risk-rate of 6 percent. From that we can back out a probability like so:

$$66p + 54(1 - p) = 60\, e^{(.06)(.5)}$$
$$12p = 61.8273 - 54$$
$$p = 0.6523$$

We can assert now the call option will be worth 4 in 6 months with a probability of 0.6523, and a 0.3477 probability of being worth zero. We know enough now to calculate the expected value of the option:

$$(0.6523 * 4) + (0.3477 * 0) = \$2.6091$$

Discounting using the risk-free rate we get:

$$2.6091e^{-(.06)(.5)} = 2.5320$$

The value of the call option using risk-neutral valuation is $2.53, the same result we got using no-arbitrage arguments.

BIBLIOGRAPHY

Baird, Allen Jan. 1993. *Option Market Making: Trading and Risk Analysis for the Financial and Commodity Option Markets.* Wiley.

Bernstein, Peter L. 1992. *Capital Ideas: The Improbable Origins of Modern Wall Street.* Macmillan: The Free Press.

Bodie, Zvi., Alex Kane and Alan J. Marcus. 1996. *Investments.* Third Edition. Irwin.

Boyle, Phelim and Fiedhlim Boyle. 2001. *Derivatives: The Tools That Changed Finance.* Risk Waters Group.

Caouette, John B., Edward I. Altman, and Paul Narayanan. 1998. *Managing Credit Risk: The Next Great Financial Challenge.* Wiley.

Clewlow, Les and Chris Strickland. 1998. *Implementing Derivatives Models.* Wiley.

Cox, John C. and Mark Rubenstein. 1985. *Options Markets.* Prentice-Hall.

Culp, Christopher L. and Merton H. Miller. 1995. "Metallgesellschaft and the Economics of Synthetic Storage." *Journal of Applied Corporate Finance* (Winter).

Gonick, Larry and Woollcott Smith. 1993. *The Cartoon Guide to Statistics.* HarperCollins.

Hull, John C. 1997. *Options, Futures and Other Derivatives.* Third Edition. Prentice Hall.

Hull, John and Alan White. 2000. "Valuing Credit Default Swaps I: No Counterparty Default Risk." University of Toronto.

Jarrow, Robert and Stuart Turnbull. 1999. *Derivative Securities: The Complete Investor's Guide.* Thomson Learning.

Jorion, Philippe. 2001. *Financial Risk Manager Handbook: 2001–2002.* Wiley.

Kolb, Robert W. and James A. Overdahl. 2003. *Financial Derivatives.* Third Edition. Wiley Finance.

Kuprianov, Anatoli. 1995. "Derivatives Debacles: Case Studies of Large Losses in Derivatives Markets." Federal Reserve Bank of Richmond *Economic Quarterly* Volume 81/4 (Fall).

Lynagh, Stephen and Sanjiv R. Das. 1997. "Enron Corp. Credit Sensitive Notes." Harvard Business School. Case Study 9-297-099.

McDonald, Robert L. 2003. *Derivatives Markets.* Addison Wesley: Pearson Education.

Natenberg, Sheldon. 1994. *Option Volatility & Pricing: Advanced Trading Strategies and Techniques*. McGraw-Hill.

Neftci, Salih N. 1996. *An Introduction to the Mathematics of Financial Derivatives*. Academic Press.

Newbold, Paul. 1995. *Statistics for Business & Economics*. Fourth Edition. Prentice-Hall.

Schwartz, Robert J. and Clifford W. Smith, Jr., eds. 1997. *Derivatives Handbook: Risk Management and Control*. Wiley.

Steinherr, Alfred. 1998. *Derivatives: The Wild Beast of Finance*. Wiley.

INDEX

Note: Boldface numbers indicate illustrations and tables.

ABOUT THE AUTHOR

Michael Durbin has spent the better part of a decade contributing to the development of large-scale derivative pricing systems as an IT project manager, business systems analyst, and technical writer, primarily for Bank of America Global Derivative Products and Bank One Capital Markets in Chicago. He earned his B.S. in Communication at Northwestern University, his M.S. in Information Systems at DePaul University, and his M.B.A. in Finance at the University of Chicago. His e-mail address is michael.durbin@comcast.net.